Business, Banking
and Urban History

S. G. Checkland

Business, Banking and Urban History

Essays in honour of
S. G. CHECKLAND
Professor of Economic History
University of Glasgow 1957-1982

Edited by
ANTHONY SLAVEN
and
DEREK H. ALDCROFT

Foreword by
Sir ALEC K. CAIRNCROSS

JOHN DONALD PUBLISHERS LTD
EDINBURGH

© The Contributors, 1982

ISBN 0 85976 083 9

Exclusive distribution in the United States of
America and Canada by Humanities Press Inc,
Atlantic Highlands, NJ 07716, USA

Filmset by Burns & Harris Limited, Dundee
Printed in Great Britain by Bell & Bain Ltd, Glasgow

Preface

A. Slaven and D. H. Aldcroft

NO single collection of essays can hope to do justice to the scope of Sydney Checkland's work in economic and social history. As Sir Alec Cairncross makes plain in his foreword, the themes explored here concentrate on Sydney's later interests, those which have been most fully developed during his twenty-five years in Glasgow.

The studies in Part One explore important issues in business history. The problems confronting the early entrepreneurs in the industrial revolution form the backcloth to Professor Payne's study of the Halbeath Colliery and Salt-works. The links between organisational structure, business strategy and managerial action are explored by Professor Slaven. The problems inherent in the use of financial records, and the lessons to be drawn, are reviewed by Professor Campbell, while Mr. Robertson focuses on the impact of a powerful business personality on established organisational and bureaucratic procedures in government and industry in his study of aircraft production.

In Part Two, the studies in banking history focus on the relationship between banking systems and practices and economic change. Professor Cameron argues that banking structure is a key variable in inducing or retarding economic growth. Dr. Munn explores this linkage in the response of the Scottish banking system to the demands made upon it in a period of vigorous industrial and commercial expansion, while Dr. Cottrell looks at the links between structure and function in a different way, examining the influence of international bullion flows on central bank structure and practice.

The studies in Part Three focus on some of the urban consequences of, and urban responses to, industrial growth. The sensitive issue of the social cost, and social accountancy, of the industrial and demographic growth of Victorian cities is drawn out by Dr. Kellett. Mr. Forsyth analyses the changing economic morphology of Victorian Glasgow to illustrate general urban characteristics deriving from the competition between people and industry for the use of urban land. Mr. Hart sets out the challenges to municipal govern-ment and the response in municipal enterprise, comparing Glasgow with other cities. The comparative theme is extended by Professor Aldcroft, who identifies the nature and continuity of urban transport problems generated in the nineteenth century on a significant scale, but confronting twentieth-century cities in new ways.

These studies, taken together, echo and develop main lines of investigation and interest in British business, banking and urban history; as is evident in the list of publications compiled by Olive Checkland, they represent themes which have been enriched by Sydney Checkland in his many contributions to the study of economic and social history.

Foreword

Sir Alec K. Cairncross

THE studies in this volume are intended as a collective tribute to the work of Sydney Checkland on his retirement from the Chair of Economic History at the University of Glasgow after twenty-five years. The tripartite division of the contributions into business, banking and urban history corresponds to the three main fields of interest of his later work.

Nine of the papers included are by colleagues or former colleagues at Glasgow and, indeed, four of the nine are former pupils. Of the nine, two are friends who share Sydney's special interest in banking and finance: Rondo Cameron spent a year at Glasgow in the early sixties, and Philip Cottrell was examined by Sydney for his doctorate.

I am glad of this opportunity to join in doing honour to an old friend. For his first five years at Glasgow we were colleagues, joined almost immediately after his arrival by Tom Wilson and Alec Nove and profiting also from the company of Donald Robertson. Such a group could not fail to be highly stimulating and entertaining or to form one of the most active centres of growth in the University. The economists, then and afterwards, collaborated across departmental boundaries and Sydney played his full share in their activities, especially in the creation of a separate faculty of Social Sciences in 1976.

He was always the best of company and an ideal colleague, enlivening our discussion with his gentle good-humour, ready with suggestions but never overbearing. He had a memorable gift for puncturing an extravagant thesis by going one better so as to dissolve it in absurdity. 'You don't mean,' he would begin, and present a caricature of what had been said so compelling that it had to be unsaid at once.

My own obligations extend beyond what I owe to him as a colleague, scholar and friend. It was Sydney who in 1971 proposed to me that I should offer myself for election by the General Council to the Chancellorship of Glasgow University and who took on the responsibility, if one may so describe it, of campaign manager. At first it seemed to me so wildly improbable that I was disposed to dismiss it as a joke, though the fact that a namesake had held the office three hundred years ago kept me from dismissing the suggestion out of hand. In the end Sydney persuaded me to have a go and his judgment turned out, on Burns Night 1972, to be well-founded. So I can testify to his decisive intervention on at least one memorable occasion.

There seemed little chance when he left school in Ottawa at the bottom of the depression in 1933 that he would ever be able to pursue an academic career. He started as a ledger clerk in the Bank of Nova Scotia, continuing to study at night school in preparation for the examination that made him in 1937 an associate of the Canadian Bankers Association. After three and a half years he decided that he needed a higher-paid job if he was to save enough to go to a University and left the Bank to take employment as an accountant with the Ottawa Sanitary Laundry Company. The Company was as unorthodox in its business practices as the Bank had been orthodox. It had been taken out of liquidation by owners who had no funds of their own but contrived to acquire and install new machinery and then had to find ways of delaying payment (including the payment of wages to their staff). They looked to their new accountant to accomplish this transformation of illiquidity into liquidity by ingenious devices such as sending cheques in the wrong envelopes. No doubt this experience of 'leads and lags' deepened Sydney's understanding of banking functions. It also had the more immediate advantage of adding to his own liquid resources enough to allow him to set off for Birmingham Unversity in 1938 with £250 in his pocket.

At Birmingham he embarked on the B. Comm. course under Philip Sargent Florence and J. G. Smith, graduating in 1941 with First Class Honours. He had added to his savings by working in vacations for the Unemployment Assistance Board and as a labourer as well as by winning an exhibition for £30 at the end of his first year. He had also managed to go on a long cycling tour on the Continent before the outbreak of war, covering about 3,000 miles.

In his first year after graduation he served as President of the National Union of Students and was elected President of the International Union of Students for the following year. But by 1942 he was in the Army, spending six months in training at Sandhurst as a member of the Royal Armoured Corps and winning the belt of honour as the best cadet of his year. 1942 was also the year in which he and Olive (who took her degree in Geography at Birmingham in 1941) were married in Ottawa.

He served first with the 5th Battalion of the Manchester Regiment. It had been Tawney's Regiment and he greatly enjoyed this part of his war service. Later he was transferred to the Armoured Brigade of the Canadian Army and in the fighting after the Normandy landings in 1944 was severely wounded at Falaise, suffering nerve damage which left him with a slight limp when he came out of hospital six months later. At the end of the war he stood unsuccessfully as a Commonwealth Party candidate for Eccleshall in the General Election in July.

While in hospital, wounded and immobile, his mind had turned again to economics, and he began the study of Ricardo's ideas which continued to occupy him when he returned to Birmingham to take his M. Comm. under W. H. B. Court. The theme on which he concentrated was one that still absorbs him: the relation between economic ideas (in this case the ideas prevalent at the time of the Napoleonic War) and public policy (in particular the policies of Canning and Huskisson).

In 1946, having taken his M. Comm. in a year, Sydney Checkland was given his first academic appointment as assistant lecturer in Economic Science at Liverpool where he remained for the next seven years, rising rapidly to a lectureship in 1948 and a senior lectureship the following year. Although his appointment was in economic science under Barrett Whale (and later under George Allen), not in economic history, his main interest at that time lay in the development of economic thought. Before he left Liverpool for Cambridge in 1953 he had published eight articles on various aspects of classical economics and had been awarded the PhD of the University for this work. The articles attracted much attention and brought him into touch at an early stage in his career with two other scholars for whom he had a particular admiration — Michael Postan and Jacob Viner. They also made a deep impression on Alec Macfie who was never in doubt, when the Chair of Economic History was created at Glasgow, that Sydney Checkland was the outstanding candidate.

In the meantime Postan had pressed him to move to Cambridge and accept a lectureship in economic history. For an economist to be offered such an appointment, although common enough nowadays, was very rare in those days. Curiously enough, 1953/54 marked not only Sydney's formal trans-formation into an economic historian, but also the emergence of his interests in business and urban history. The articles he published in these years included one on 'An English Merchant House in China', one on 'English Provincial Cities' and another on John Gladstone. So the foundation was laid for much of his later work including the biography of Sir John Gladstone which appeared in 1971. But all this represented the fruit of his years at Liverpool, not Cambridge. His published work while at Cambridge was mainly on the West Indies, apart from a short contribution on Marshall in the *Economic Journal* and a longer study on 'The mind of the City, 1870-1914' in *Oxford Economic Papers*.

But it was in Glasgow that he blossomed as an economic historian and it was in Glasgow that he made his mark in many other ways. The atmosphere was congenial. The various departments of social and economic studies in the University (including the Departments of Economic History, Political Economy, Town Planning, Social and Economic Research and Soviet Studies) worked together harmoniously and in close propinquity. They shared a common interest in urban development and in the problems of modern business in an urban setting. The changes at work in Glasgow in the sixties and seventies were themselves a challenge to the social scientist to adopt an his-torical perspective and view the transformation in progress in the light of the rise and decline of the city over the past two centuries. There was the prospect of learning by doing: acting in association with Scottish businesses (including the banks) and with public bodies in the area (for example, as a Governor of the old Scottish College of Commerce and as a member of the East Kilbride

Development Corporation). The influence of the environment in which he worked is evident in Sydney's writings and activities over the past twenty-five years.

He has been a prolific writer, publishing six full-length books since he came to Glasgow, beginning with *The Rise of Industrial Society in England 1815-1885* in 1964 and ending with *British Public Policy 1776-1939*, which is due to appear this year. In addition, he edited with Olive *The Poor Law Report of 1834*, for which he wrote a long introduction. He also produced a steady stream of articles and reviews. It is characteristic that all his books span at least seventy years: he has a liking for a long perspective. It is interesting also to see the transition from 'England' in the first to 'British' in the latest of his books and the growing emphasis on Scottish subjects. *Tharsis* is a Glasgow company even if it operates in Spain, and the Gladstones were a Scottish family even if William was born in Liverpool. *Scottish Banking*, which occupied him for many years, is his major achievement although it may yet turn out to be more a requiem than a fanfare for its subject.

It would be impossible to do justice to so large an output in a brief foreword. All one can do is to draw attention to the wide range of subjects and treatment. First there is a volume in the tradition of covering the economic history of a country period by period. Then comes what is essentially a company history with some remarkable human figures like Sir Charles Tennant in an exotic historical landscape. Next, a full-scale biography of Gladstone's father with a picture of the great man's family background. Then back to business history but of a different and much more complex kind since the role of banking in the industrial growth of Scotland is a theme developed alongside a more straightforward account of the growth of the Scottish banks themselves. After this comes a study in urban history, *The Upas Tree*, with its intriguing title symbolising the conflicting elements in the rise and decline of Glasgow as an industrial centre. Finally, an historical examination of social and economic policy in Britain from Adam Smith to Keynes.

As if all this were not enough, Sydney has contributed in one way or another to a dozen books listed in the bibliography at the back of this volume and no less than half of these are due to appear this year. One gets the impression from his work over the past decade that he is steadily accelerating his output and that retirement may be his way of increasing the flow still further.

When he arrived in Glasgow in January 1957 there was no Economic History Department — only a single lecturer who had held the fort since the 1920s. At his retirement the Department includes two professors, a reader, a senior lecturer, seven lecturers and three research staff. Where economic history used to be taught to honours students in Economic Science in one paper in the final honours examination, now there is a flourishing first-year class and an honours degree in Economic History combined with a variety of other subjects. The Department also has accumulated an expanding archive of business records, chiefly from local companies, and this forms a rich source for the training of advanced students. The building up of this archive was accelerated by the creation of the second chair, in Business History, referred to above.

Apart from building up his Department, he has also made many important contributions to the work of the University. He was the first chairman of the sub-Faculty of Social Sciences when a separate faculty had not yet been born from the parent Faculty of Arts; chairman, in the turbulent years from 1970-72, of a Joint Council of Staff and Students; and a key figure on the University Court, as one of the four Senate representatives, in 1970-73. He was never content, in such assignments, to administer the *status quo* but was for ever seeking improvement and reform and putting forward his own ideas for change.

He has been increasingly active in professional activities elsewhere: with the Economic History Society, of which he was President from 1977 to 1980 — 1977 was also the year in which he was elected a Fellow of the British Academy — as Chairman of the National Register of Archives (Scotland) since 1971; on the Economic and Social History Panel of the S.S.R.C. between 1969 and 1973; as Vice-President of the Scottish Business Archives Committee and of the Scottish Labour History Committee; and in many other capacities.

All this adds up to a formidable total of academic and other activities. But it is essentially as a scholar that we seek to honour him in this volume through the bringing together of contributions on topics to which he himself has already made outstanding contributions.

No sketch of Sydney's career would be complete without recognising Olive's part in it. One cannot rear five children successfully and pursue the life of a scholar without a wife who has some claim to distinction in her own right and who is entitled to take some credit for the husband's achievements. Olive has a personality quite as colourful as Sydney's and with perhaps a little extra thrust. She has made her own contributions to social history but a still larger one is concealed in what flows from Sydney's pen. In paying tribute to him we should all wish to include her as well.

Contents

Contributors

Derek H. Aldcroft
Professor of Economic History, University of Leicester

Sir Alec K. Cairncross
Chancellor of the University of Glasgow

Rondo E. Cameron
William Rand Kenan Professor, Emory University, Atlanta, Georgia

R. H. Campbell
Professor of Economic History, University of Stirling

Olive Checkland
Research Fellow, Department of Scottish History, University of Glasgow

P. L. Cottrell
Lecturer in Economic History, University of Leicester

W. Forsyth
Lecturer in Economic History, University of Aberdeen

Tom Hart
Lecturer in Economic History, University of Glasgow

John R. Kellett
Reader in Economic History, University of Glasgow

C. W. Munn
Lecturer in Economic History, University of Glasgow

Peter L. Payne
Professor of Economic History, University of Aberdeen

A. J. Robertson
Lecturer in Economic History, University of Manchester

Anthony Slaven
Professor of Business History, University of Glasgow

PART ONE

Studies in Business History

1. The Halbeath Colliery and Saltworks, 1785-1791

Peter L. Payne

WITHIN a few months of hís appointment in 1957 to the new Chair of Economic History at the University of Glasgow, Professor S. G. Checkland conceived the idea of establishing within his Department a Lectureship in Business History. A successful appeal having been made to the business community of Glasgow and the West of Scotland, the Colquhoun Lectureship came into being in 1959. Foremost of the lecturer's duties was to 'collect and collate the surviving records of local business houses that are of historical value', thereby instigating a search that seems to have gained rather than lost momentum with the passage of time. It soon became apparent that the majority of the records that came to light in the early nineteen-sixties represented random fragments of what must at one time have been continuous series of account books, letter books, and incoming correspondence. Only rarely was there discovered a collection of records that even approached the comprehensiveness required to permit both a systematic reconstruction of a company's history and a detailed analysis of economic behaviour in the past. Nevertheless, even single items possessed some interest and their potential value as source material tended to grow with the discovery of additional fragments that had survived in similar firms or fields of activity, or in other regions of the British Isles. Sometimes, small, incomplete collections provided specific illustrations of the findings of existing industrial histories, or suggested the possibility that the accepted general picture required modification or refinement.

One small cache of records presented to the University of Glasgow on permanent loan[1] in the early 'sixties consisted of four bound volumes and two bundles of accounts and letters relating to the Halbeath Colliery and Salt Works at the close of the eighteenth century. They provide a remarkable insight into the manifold problems confronting those who sought to make or expand their fortunes by venturing into this most hazardous of industries.

I

During the period covered by the surviving records, the Halbeath Colliery became one of the largest and most important undertakings exploiting the Dunfermline coalfield. The collieries in this district were of great antiquity, perhaps 'the most ancient in Scotland',[2] but not until the mid-eighteenth century was their output of any great significance. The ministers responsible for the contribution on the Parish of Dunfermline to the *Old Statistical Account* were disarmingly precise in dating the acceleration in the area's prosperity. 'Even so late as 1763, the annual value of exported coal was only £200; and in 1771, it did not exceed £500 Sterling. The coal-mines, since 1771, have been sources of great wealth to many of the proprietors'.[3]

Be that as it may, between 1770 and 1782 Cornelius Lloyd, Junior, and Sampson Coysgarne Lloyd, merchants of Rotterdam, had either purchased the freehold or had been granted tacks to all the coal-bearing lands of the estate of Halbeath. This estate, of some 500 acres, was known to possess at least ten seams of coal. These had been discovered 'partly by Boring, and partly by some ancient workings near their Outbursts and there [was] great reason to believe that there [were] other seams beyond these'.[4] These seams dipped regularly to the North East, but the entire Dunfermline coalfield was fissured by 'dykes, faults, troubles, slips and hitches'. Whatever problems they may have caused the pitmen, these dykes were regarded as being of great benefit in colliery operations, since they rendered 'the coal more accessible in consequence of heaving it up'; they also helped to prevent 'floodings, and [the] spread of accidental fire'. In discussing these matters, the Rev. Peter Chalmers, Minister of Dunfermline, felt it 'worthy of remark, as the evident indication of a wise and kind Providence, that the greatest upheaving . . . is at Hallbeath [sic], and the northern division of the Elgin Colliery where the surface raises the highest'.[5]

However much this may have eased the getting of coal by outcrop working, and the later construction of adits, it exacerbated the difficulties of land carriage. The Halbeath Colliery was some four miles north of the Firth of Forth and its full development necessitated the building of a waggonway to Inverkeithing. Apparently put down by the Lloyds in 1781-2, the single-track waggonway utilised rails made of fir laid on fir sleepers set at 14-inch intervals. Resting on ballast and carefully graded by means of cuts, banks and bridges, the waggonway had numerous byestands to permit easy passing, and was worked by fourteen waggons. 'They go twice a day from the pits to the harbour in Winter and thrice in Summer . . ., [each carrying] betwixt 41 and 42 cwt of Coals'.[6] Valued at £1,050, the waggonway represented no less than half the total capital stock of the Colliery in 1784, or four times the amount of the next most important single item in the inventory of moveable stock and buildings, the fire engine.

In 1785, the Lloyds claimed that the sea sale was 'about 5000 waggons of Great Coal, 2000 waggons of Chews and 2000 waggons of Small, which go entirely to the North Country', but this was apparently a gross exaggeration, John Wright's report being annotated 'misrepresentation . . . the vend is not above 9000 tons'. Equally misleading was the Lloyds' belief that if 'double the quantity of great coal was wrought, it could be sold to those [North Country]

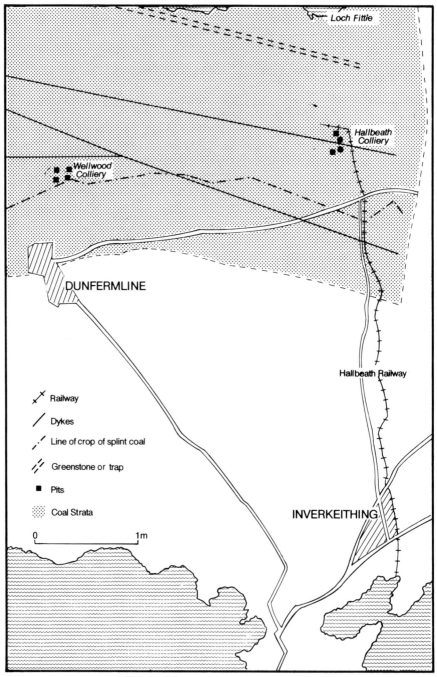

Figure 1. Location of Halbeath Colliery, redrawn from the map illustrating the Rev. Peter Chalmers' contribution to *Prize Essays and Transactions of the Highland and Agricultural Society of Scotland,* New Series, VII (1841). The contemporary spelling of Hallbeath has been retained.

markets without having recourse to London or other English Markets'. Evidently many potential adventurers were sceptical of the colliery's potential and shared John Wright's opinion that substantial additional capital expenditure on a 'new winning [was] necessary before any considerable quantity of coals [could] be wrought to profit'. Some of them may have been equally aware that the sea sale was incapable of significant expansion without the deepening of Inverkeithing Harbour or the construction of a new quay. Certainly, when the Lloyds exposed Halbeath Colliery for sale as a going concern at an auction held at the Exchange Coffee House in Edinburgh on 14th February 1785, 'no persons appeared to offer . . . the upset price of £5000'. Nor were potential purchasers attracted by a reduced upset price of £3000 when the

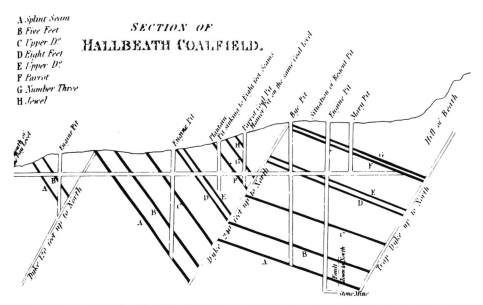

Figure 2. Section of Halbeath Colliery, c. 1841, reproduced from the essay by the Rev. Peter Chalmers.

roup was adjourned to 22nd March. A month later, even a reserve of £2000 failed to bring forth a single bidder. Not until May was William Scott, the Edinburgh banker who acted for the Lloyds, able to sell the Colliery, when John Morrison of Whitehouse, County Durham, Richard Fishwick, white lead maker of Newcastle upon Tyne, and John Campbell, Writer to the Signet, of Edinburgh came forward with an offer of £1800.

II

The motives of the new proprietors can only be conjectured. Subsequent correspondence indicates that only John Morrison possessed any detailed knowledge of the coal trade. John Campbell, who was to become the leading spirit in the enterprise, was later to confess his complete ignorance of coal-getting and vending, and the experience of the other partner seems to have been limited to the use of coal as a fuel in his other business enterprises. It is apparent that they saw the Halbeath Colliery and Salt Works as a promising speculation. Although their confidence was boosted by John Wright's calculations that with the expenditure of an additional £1500 over the next two years, their gain on an annual vend of 1000 tons would be £3258, it is inconceivable that they failed to ask themselves why the Lloyds were prepared to sell the concern — they had poured at least £3000 into fixed assets in the previous five years — for such a relatively meagre sum. Perhaps some unexpected reversal of fortune in the Lloyds' trading ventures had left them financially embarrassed?

Sweeping any doubts aside, the new partners formulated their plans. The colliery workings were to be thoroughly inspected by two men (one of whom was John Wright) thoroughly conversant with coal-mining, with a view to ascertaining exactly what capital improvements were required in both the immediate future and in the long-term. Meanwhile, the existing contractors, managerial staff, and workmen at both colliery and salt works were to be retained and efforts made to recruit additional pitmen. 'Particular enquiry [was] to be made respecting the vend of the Coal and Salt and the mode of payment with the name of the places where the above Articles are sent to.' Four new keels and two additional waggons were to be purchased immediately, and 'a ship or two . . . taken up on Freight . . . and sent to load Coals for London' and Newcastle.[7] Additional salt pans were to be constructed on the shore near Inverkeithing and the necessary extensions made to the waggonway. Plans for the improvement of the Harbour at Inverkeithing were drawn up, and provision was made for a raised incline to be constructed at the end of the pier so that the waggons could be emptied directly into the holds of the vessels.

The character of the coal itself was the subject of detailed investigation. The partners had been assured that the current output was roughly half great coal, and the rest equally divided into the categories of chews and small coals. It was believed that no difficulty would be encountered in selling the great coals and that much of the small could be used in the saltworks. How the chews could be disposed of remained unresolved. Similar uncertainties arose over the product of the various seams: coal, however similar its appearance, is not a homogeneous commodity. A certain deception might be required. '[Concerning] the Five feet coal . . . I think it will make a very good mixture with the Splint Coal if shipt when new wrought . . . [As] it will not bear the Weather so well . . . lead and vend them with the Splint . . . and I dare say the consumer will not know the difference.'[8] Nevertheless, it was imperative to discover the marketability of the various grades and sizes in order to determine future sinkings.

The partners had also to gather information on a whole host of questions that were critical to the future profitability of their enterprise. An extract from the reply of one correspondent in Aberdeen to a series of enquiries made by John Campbell illustrates their nature:

> English Coals are preferred here to Scots by the generality of Inhabitants but indeed a good deal of Scots Coals are also sold here principally to the Brewers, Manufacturers, etc. They are very seldom sold under 3/8 per Boll and not often above 4/- and 4/4. Three bolls and a half will be about a Ton weight. A stranger vessel of 50 or 60 Tons will cost about 1/- per Ton of Harbour Dues and Pillotage. Barrowstoness and St. Davids are preferred to the other Pitts on the Firth by the Consumers of that Article here — English Coal generally sells for /4d or /6d per Boll more than Scots . . . The duty on Coals will be about 3/6 or 3/8 per Ton — a little more or less depending upon Circumstances with which the practitioners in that branch are only properly acquainted.[9]

With the multiplication of technical, legal and financial questions, it became apparent that communications between the partners had to be formalised, a proper managerial structure evolved, and a number of important functions let out to contractors. All this took time, and the partners proceeded by trial and error. Initially, they had little alternative but to make do with both the men employed and the arrangements devised by the Lloyds, though within a few weeks of taking over the concern Morrison sent several experienced waggon-way drivers and keelmen up from Newcastle.[10] Their task was to eradicate the inefficiency discovered by John Morrison's son when he took up his post as colliery manager. To advise and assist his son, Morrison sent a highly skilled engineer, John Blenkinshop, apparently an expert on both fire engines and waggonway construction, who was to be paid 10/6 a day 'over and above your keeping him free of expense while with you'.[11]

By February 1786, John Morrison Jnr. was able to report considerable progress. The Old Engine was 'now in a pretty good state and will in about a fortnight lay all the Splint Coal dry south of the Main dyke'; the 'new winning', whereby further coal measures would be exploited, was well under way; the waggonway was functioning smoothly; the additional pitmen's houses had been completed, making forty in all; the two salt pans were not only in good repair but working to profit, and there was 'a very great Demand for . . . coals and salt, the quality of both being deemed preferable to any in the Firth of Forth'. Furthermore, John Blenkinshop, favourably impressed by Halbeath's prospects, had gone into partnership with an experienced mine manager, R. Thomson, also from Newcastle, and had accepted a contract from the Company to 'lay 20,000 Tons of Coal into the Ships at Inverkeithing paying all Expenses whatsoever except Rent and Salaries [at the following rates]':[12]

	s	d	
Great Coal	3	9	per Ton
Chew Coal	3	0	,,
Small or Panwood	2	6	,,

At a selling price of '6/- per Ton for the Great and 3/6 per ton for chews and panwood', John Morrison's estimate[13] of the future profits were summarised thus:

15,000 Tons of Great 2/3		£1687"10s
5,000 Tons of Chew and Small ...... /9d		187"10s
Besides the profits on 4 Salt pans per year		500"00s
		£2375"00s
Deduct for Rents, say,	£70	
Salaries	£200	
Contingencies	£138	
Premium to Undertakers over and above stipulated prices	£50	£458
Net Profits per year on 20,000 Tons		£1917

Alas for the partners, now four in number following the transfer by Richard Fishwick of half of his one-third share in the concern to John Boyes, merchant of Kingston upon Hull,[14] these calculations were based on erroneous premises. They assumed, first, that 'no Material Accident' would occur at the mines; second, that the proportion of great coal would constitute approximately 75 per cent of their total product; and third, that available markets would easily absorb an ever-growing output without any material change in the selling price (that is, the demand for Halbeath Coals was inelastic).

It was also implicit in the younger John Morrison's optimistic report that little additional capital expenditure beyond that initially contemplated for the new winning would be required to raise the Colliery's output to 20,000 or even to 30,000 tons. This belief too was mistaken. The purchase price paid by the partners in May 1795 was £1,800. Even John Wright had envisaged the need for a further investment of £1,500 spread over two years (in the second of which the Colliery was expected to be producing a handsome profit). But, by early October 1785, the total investment was declared to be £3,000, and by April 1786, the capital stock had grown to £4,050 (see Table 1). This would not perhaps have caused too much anxiety or tension had each partner been able to contribute additional capital in proportion to his original share in the company, but from the very beginning, John Morrison Senr. had been unable to put in much more than his original contribution of £600. Thereafter, to maintain his one-third interest in the firm, he was forced to borrow from his partners. In effect, this meant that Morrison was given advances by John Campbell, the only partner with command of sufficient resources to permit such an arrangement, Campbell himself having been granted credit facilities at the Royal Bank of Scotland for a sum of up to £1,500.[15] Furthermore, the relative magnitude of Campbell's stake in the firm of Campbell, Morrison & Co. — the title agreed upon in October 1785 — steadily increased with each advance of working capital made by the Edinburgh lawyer to the company. Thus, the formal record of shareholding made in the Minutes and accounts of Campbell, Morrison & Co. consistently understates John Campbell's ever-increasing influence on the conduct of the firm, a power that was particularly resented by the Morrisons.

In retrospect, the genesis of many of the problems making for the eventual

TABLE 1

The Formal Division of Shares in the Capital Stock of Campbell, Morrison & Co., 1785-1790, and of John Campbell & Co., 1790

	Oct. 1785	Share of Total	April 1786	Share of Total	May 1787	Share of Total	May 1788	Share of Total	March 1789	Share of Total	May 1790	Share of Total	Nov. 1790	Share of Total
	£		£		£		£		£		£		£	
John Campbell	1000	$\frac{1}{3}$	1350	$\frac{1}{3}$	2667	$\frac{4}{12}$	3678	$\frac{4}{12}$	4242	$\frac{4}{12}$	4741	$\frac{4}{12}$	9027	$\frac{8}{12}$
John Morrison, Sr.	1000	$\frac{1}{3}$	1350	$\frac{1}{3}$	2000	$\frac{3}{12}$	2758	$\frac{3}{12}$	3182	$\frac{3}{12}$	3556	$\frac{3}{12}$	—	—
John Morrison, Jr.	—	—	—	—	667	$\frac{1}{12}$	919	$\frac{1}{12}$	1061	$\frac{1}{12}$	1185	$\frac{1}{12}$	—	—
Richard Fishwick	1000	$\frac{1}{3}$	675	$\frac{1}{6}$	667	$\frac{1}{12}$	919	$\frac{1}{12}$	1061	$\frac{1}{12}$	3556	$\frac{3}{12}$	3385	$\frac{3}{12}$
Thomas Fishwick	—	—	—	—	667	$\frac{1}{12}$	919	$\frac{1}{12}$	1061	$\frac{1}{12}$	1185	$\frac{1}{12}$	1128	$\frac{1}{12}$
John Boyes	—	—	675	$\frac{1}{6}$	1333	$\frac{2}{12}$	1839	$\frac{2}{12}$	2121	$\frac{2}{12}$	—	—	—	—
Total Stock £	3000		4050		8000		10033		12726		14222		13541	

Source: Halbeath Colliery and Saltworks: Accounts and Letter Books.

FIGURE 3

Campbell, Morrison & Co.: Organisational Structure, 1786

Senior Partners:
- John Campbell (Edinburgh) (Cashier and Managing Partner)
- John Morrison (Chester le Street) (Technical advice and recruitment of skilled personnel)
- Richard Fishwick (Newcastle)
- John Boyes (Hull) (Sales in North of England)

Salaried Managers and, later, Junior Partners, at Halbeath:
- John Morrison Jnr. (Colliery and Saltworks)
- Thomas Fishwick (General Administration, Bookkeeping and Sales)

Principal long-term Contractors:
- R. Thomson & R. Blenkinshop (Colliery and Fire Engines)
- Wilson & Ditchburn (Leading the Coals and Care of Waggonway)
- Foulis (Saltworks)

Approximate Labour Force:
- 40–50
- 14
- 10

Sub-Contractors:
- George Topling & John Paterson (Pit sinkers)
- John Ditchburn (Smith work for engines, waggonway, horse-shoeing and maintenance of salt pans)
- Robert Shadforth (Carpentry work for engines and pitmen's houses)
- John Munro & Henry Burell (Mason work for engine house and pitmen's houses)

dissolution of the original co-partnery can be discerned within a year of its establishment. At the time, most of them could be dismissed as being the teething troubles inevitably associated with taking over and developing what was a very substantial enterprise. Certainly, the partners soon acknowledged the heavy burden being shouldered by John Morrison Jnr. in superintending the 'new winning', when they dispatched Thomas Fishwick, Richard's son, to Halbeath with the responsibility for keeping the accounts and making regular reports to the partners on every aspect of the activities of the colliery and salt works.[16] With the advice of the partners, particularly John Morrison, who sent various specialists up from Newcastle, contractors had been appointed for all the major tasks at Halbeath by the summer of 1786, by which time what appears to have been a rational division of functions had been adopted by the proprietors (see Figure 3).

Every two weeks Thomas Fishwick compiled a statistical return which tabulated the tonnage of coals (by grades) raised by Thomson & Blenkinshop, the colliery contractors; the quantity 'led' by Ditchburn & Wilson to the Harbour at Inverkeithing; the amount of coal consumed by the fire engines; and, less systematically, the amount of salt produced and shipped by Foulis, contractor to the salt works. These abstracts were sent to John Campbell who, in turn, sent copies to the other partners. Every other fortnight, Fishwick would also submit detailed observations on the amount and nature of the firm's capital expenditure, the progress of the various major projects, the state of both the coal and salt trade, the behaviour of the contractors, and suggestions for future developments. Bills drawn on the masters of the sloops and brigs who had loaded cargoes at Inverkeithing were also sent to John Campbell at regular intervals.[17]

It is these abstracts and 'public letters', as Fishwick's monthly reports were called, and the copies of well over 1,200 pieces of correspondence contained in John Campbell's private letter book, that permit a reconstruction of the activities of Campbell, Morrison & Co. at Halbeath and Inverkeithing.

III

In addition to pushing on with the vital new winning, an early task was to price the work let to the contractors (see Appendix I) and 'clear the way of all the lazy fellows' currently employed.[18] Only then could John Campbell draw up legal contracts which John Morrison Jnr. could enforce. Furthermore, it was believed that, by fixing the prices of the major jobs, an accurate assessment could be made of both future costs and profits, the latter sum providing some guide to the advisability of further capital investment. Encouraged both by calculations that indicated a highly favourable future gain on stock and by strong upward trends in both the vend of coal and the manufacture and sale of salt, they confidently believed that 'barring unforseen accidents, there cannot be a doubt of [Halbeath] answering [our] most sanguine Expectations'.[19]

By 17 July, 1786, Fishwick reported that the 'little Engine was completed . . . and has continued so effectively at work ever since that Topling is now sinking the Pit very fast to the Splint Coal — The Great Engine Pit is also going on very well, as they have passed the 3ft Coal, and are full 26 fathoms deep — In short all the operations are now carrying on with Spirit, and though the pit-men have lately been extremely disorderly and quarrelsome they are daily growing more peaceable and industrious, and will I hope ere long be perfectly reconciled to their new Taskmasters Thomson & Blenkinshop'.[20]

Labour was always to constitute a problem. As soon as the new pitmen's houses were built, Thomson was to 'go up to Newcastle and Engage 10 or 12 sober Coaliers with Families'.[21] It was believed that when the new Engine Pit reached the Splint and Five Foot Coal, and Thomson & Blenkinshop had 'A fine field of coal to work in', about sixty hewers would be required.[22] To recruit and retain such a labour force proved to be difficult. Although Robert Thomson was successful in bringing 'some English pitmen to settle at Halbeath', his 'Journey to England [had] not altogether proved successful'. Nevertheless, the contractors did 'not despair of performing their agreement [to win 20,000 tons annually]', for they had 'adopted a quite different mode of working the coals' from that employed by the previous owners. On the advice of John Morrison Snr., they had constructed stables underground and were using 'horses to put the Coals'. This meant that the contractors 'would not require so many Bearers as formerly'. Believing that 'Pitmen without Bearers are always obtainable in this country',[23] they placed advertisements in 'the public papers of Edinburgh'.[24] A number of pitmen came forward but they could not be got to raise more than an average of five tons per week, 'when those in England work more than four times that quantity'.[25] Although a more careful calculation subsequently revealed that this comparison was unfair to the Halbeath workmen,[26] the partners made great efforts to induce Thomson & Blenkinshop's men to increase their productivity. One way was to engage more men, thereby increasing the contractors' bargaining power, but this scheme was rendered largely abortive by the 'agreement among the Gentlemen of the Coal Trade . . . engaging not to employ one another's Servants without a Testimonial from the Master he has last served'.[27] Although willingly sub-scribed to by the Halbeath partners[28] who, perhaps hypocritically, believed it to be 'an advantage to the workmen as it will prevent the many unlawful com-binations they foolishly enter into and leaving their Masters service strolling through the country like Vagrants while they may be working for their familys bread at home',[29] this agreement severely circumscribed Thomson & Blenkinshop's ability to recruit workers from neighbouring pits. There was nothing for it but for the 'Gentlemen on the spot [Morrison and Fishwick] to examine narrowly into the causes of so small a quantity of coal being raised, to look into the Statements of the raisings and to find out the Individual pitmen who were deficient at one time while they bring up a larger quantity at another'. Such an examination might, it was felt, suggest some technical explanation for Halbeath's alleged low labour productivity that might be remedied, such as 'want of room' at the coalface. Meanwhile, Thomson & Blenkinshop were recommended to institute a system of rewards, such as premiums for high individual outputs, to encourage the pitmen. Furthermore, the contractors themselves were threatened with the termination of their contract if they failed to meet their annual target figure of 20,000 tons.[30]

By the Spring of 1787, 'upwards of fifty pitmen were quietly and briskly at work', many of them earning a premium of 2/6 for raising over 30 tons during each fortnightly pay period,[31] and Halbeath was producing 'at the rate of 24 thousand Tons per annum'.[32] Still the search for colliers went on but, 'notwithstanding all our advertisements', the managers reported, they 'come in very tardily and we feel it will require both time and patience before we obtain as many good men as might be employed with advantage . . .'[33] Neighbouring coalmasters, meanwhile, tried to prevent their men from defecting to Halbeath by the gift of such domestic articles as bedsteads 'in order to *encourage* them to *stay*'.[34]

Not the least important factor in creating an industrious labour force was the availability of regular employment. In the first two years of the Campbell, Morrison partnership, the periodic breakdown of engines and pumps, causing 'the colliers to be laid off', constituted the most serious threat to the stability so fervently strived for. When normal work was disrupted by flooding, the pitmen were offered alternative employment in ballasting the waggonway, exploratory sinkings, and even at the saltworks. It was imperative not to lose hewers, for once lost, the recruitment of replacements was a painfully slow and expensive business. Not until late in 1789 did the partners feel confident enough to raise the figure (from 30 to 35 tons per pay) at which premiums were payable. Three years later further refinements were considered. It was said that

> The premiums paid to the Colliers . . . have had no good effect, in the way they have been dealt out for some years past as it is only a young and strong man who can put out the weekly quantity that entitles him to 2/6 premium:— The others who are the great bulk, are discouraged. The idle days taken by Colliers are generally in the beginning of the week — to check this a premium or bounty of 6d is given at some places, on a moderate output the 3 first days of the week, and this 6d is to be reached by any person who is industrious, the old as well as the young, and when the work is fairly started early in the week it generally insures a good weeks work. The use of the 6d is not confined to this alone — it is not given except to those who bind for a year — Strangers are paid the common hewing price but no premium or bounty.[35]

Allied to, and an important corollary of, this greater sophistication in wage policy was the establishment, in 1791, of a suttlery, 'both with a view to the accommodation of the morals of the workpeople and also for profit'.[36] Within a year of its successful founding, the partners were considering the following recommendations:

On the subject of regular working, I must . . . observe that the Suttlery which has lately been established at Halbeath will one way or the other have considerable effect. A Suttlery has generally two delivery days in the week: Tuesday and Friday or sometimes Wednesday and Saturday. When a collier does not intend to work in the beginning of the week very bare or no allowance of provisions is made to him from the Suttlery on the first delivery day, neither should he on the last receive more provisions than he has wrought for without some special reason — The Suttlery in this way will have the effect of bringing about regular working but if on the other hand the work people are credited at random they will be assisted to lay idle and the Suttlery will derange the Colliery. The oversman is the best Judge of the question of Credit to be given to each Collier, each delivery day, and the Keeper of the Suttlery will do well to have the Oversman's Sanction to all the Credit he gives.[37]

IV

Whatever their initial difficulties, by the early 1790s the proprietors appear to have achieved notable success in their vital task of creating a labour force at Halbeath. Certainly, the surviving records reveal greater harmony between the colliers and the local managers and contractors than among the increasingly fractious partners. Perhaps the most significant guide to the degree of success attained by the company's labour policy was the growth in annual outputs (see Table 2). This expansion was believed to be essential for the well-being of the colliery, but it was accompanied by increasingly difficult problems in marketing.

These problems would not have been so serious had it not been for the fact that for every ton of great coal raised there was almost an equal quantity of chews and small coals brought to the surface. Great Coals enjoyed a ready market at almost every port along the East coast of Britain, from Aberdeen in the North to London in the South, as well as in Northern Europe. A large quantity of small coal could profitably be consumed at the saltworks and by the engines. It was the intermediate grade that constituted the greatest difficulty: the company's inability to sell chew coal threatened the future of the entire enterprise.

The minutes of the very first formal 'meeting of the proprietors held at Mr. Fishwick's Whitelead Factory' on 1 July, 1785 record the almost despairing cry, 'What is to be done with the Chews?'[38] Despite John Morrison Jnr. 'taking a ride . . . along the Coast, to see if the Trade could be extended'[39] and repeated 'advertisements in the public papers',[40] the problem remained. In desperation, John Campbell asked John Morrison to let it be known, particularly in Sunderland, 'that when English vessels want coals of the Forth they would get good chews at Inverkeithing', adding, 'they were not liked at London . . . but [my informant] said the prejudice was against the Country not against the Coal'.[41] Sample cargoes, at the firm's expense, were sent to Boston, Lynn, Wisbech, Peterborough, Bedford, Yarmouth, Norwich and Ipswich, and attempts were made 'to get them introduced to the public offices' in Edinburgh. It was hoped

TABLE 2

Halbeath Colliery & Saltworks: Output and Sales, 1786-1791, 1797-1802

Period	COALS			SALT		
	Raised (Tons)	Sold (Tons)	Revenue from Sales (£)	Made (Bushels)	Sold (Bushels)	Revenue from Sales (£)
11 May 1786—10 May 1787	n.d.	11,643	3,346	n.d.	n.d.	917
11 May 1787—24 May 1788	21,584	20,740	5,381	20,532	17,118	1,223
25 May 1788—22 May 1789	20,258	20,782	5,274	19,490	17,264	1,281
23 May 1789—17 May 1790	26,174	24,092	n.d.	18,246	8,927	n.d.
20 Nov. 1790—19 Nov. 1791	n.d.	28,361	6,869	n.d.	22,077	1,488
24 Nov. 1797—23 Nov. 1798	46,320	n.d.	n.d.	n.d.	n.d.	n.d.
24 Nov. 1798—23 Nov. 1799	35,193	29,775	9,404	12,167	15,316	1,198
21 Nov. 1801—20 Nov. 1802	32,519	27,499	9,305	15,873	15,386	4,630[1]

Note 1: Inclusive of duty.

Source: Halbeath Colliery and Saltworks: Letter Books and Miscellaneous Accounts.

that if the relative cheapness of chews compared with great coals was emphasised, 'private families [would] be the first to appreciate their advantages', but until that market could be opened up, it was imperative to sell them to the bottlehouses, breweries and sugar boilers of Leith and Edinburgh, and to the limeworks along the Firth of Forth. To send speculative cargoes to more distant places down the East coast was inhibited by 'extravagantly high' freight charges;[42] and detailed investigations of the prospects in Ireland revealed so small a margin between the company's minimum potential costs (calculated at 14s 6d per ton) and the expected selling price in Belfast and Londonderry (about '17/- per ton in Summer') that it 'left too little hope of success for an attempt in that quarter'.[43]

By Summer 1789, 'the unlucky Chews still hang on hand' and the managers at Halbeath began 'to fear that there [was] no alternative left except that of a landsale'.[44] So many 'inconveniences attended' such a step that further attempts were made to break into the London market. Small cargoes were consigned to Messrs William Ward & Sons 'at the Company's own account and risk . . . but 10/- is a high freight, and if they are not more successful than the former adventures to the same port, it will soon make the Company sick of these Speculations'.[45] This particular 'Chew Coal Adventure . . . left us exactly 4/7¾ per Ton'[46] and the company was encouraged to maintain its efforts. One of their fundamental difficulties was that neither the managers nor the partners fully understood the mechanism of the London coal trade. Not until Mr. Thomas Gillespie, one of the London Coal Factors, explained the nature of the business[47] did the firm enjoy any significant or sustained success in this voracious market, and even that was largely because John Campbell induced several of his many connections in London to order 'Scottish Coal from Inverkeithing'.[48]

Nevertheless, this London market was believed to be too volatile to depend upon; furthermore, Halbeath could never overcome Newcastle's advantage over Scotland in obtaining 'back freights', and so the search for markets continued. A number of cargoes were sent to Denmark and Holland,[49] but as nearly all of them resulted in a net loss this 'Trade could not be prosecuted'.[50] Enquiries were made of various brewers to discover if Halbeath Coals 'were fit for cinders' [coke] and, if so, what price they would 'fetch in proportion to the Coal itself'.[51] The idea of leaving some chews 'underground to be brought up if the Markets opened' was considered,[52] but this proved impracticable. There was nothing for it but 'to push the London Trade' by every possible means,[53] though it was not expected that any permanent success would be achieved until the Harbour of Inverkeithing was deepened: 'nothing but a Shallow Harbour', it was believed, 'keeps large ships away'.[54] Until the harbour facilities were improved — as improved they were in 1791 — it was essential to exploit every opportunity created by temporary, usually seasonal, upward movements in the price of 'The Inland Coals'.[55]

V

It is only when the magnitude of the problem of disposing of the chews is appreciated that the role of the Halbeath saltworks can be properly understood. The saltworks were not merely a profitable adjunct to the colliery; by consuming vast quantities of small coal — sometimes referred to as panwood — they constituted a vital part of the economy of the entire enterprise.[56] The almost insatiable demands of the salt pans converted what was an almost unsaleable waste product into a commodity which enjoyed a ready market throughout Scotland.[57] Not surprisingly, the proprietors of the salt pans — who were almost invariably coal masters — jealously clung to the maintenance of the duties without which the sea-salt industry could not have survived and the abolition of which, so often discussed in the late eighteenth century, threatened to cause serious damage to their integrated undertakings.[58]

Whatever other miscalculations the members of the co-partnery may have made, they never underestimated the importance of the saltworks. One of their very first decisions was 'To Extend the Coal waggonway to the Salt pan Coal Fold, so soon as the place can be determined upon, [and] to erect 4, 6 or 8 pans more',[59] for their calculations had revealed that 'Salt will not cost above 9½d per Bushel rating the Coals at 2/- per Ton — We therefore are of the opinion that 8 or 10 pans would make 1,000 Bushels of Salt per Week and would clear £25, or £1,000 or £1,200 a Year, and consume all our small Coals'.[60]

Within a year two new salt pans and a large granary had been constructed, and it was expected that the weekly output of the four pans would be between 300-400 bushels. Sales were averaging about 1,000 bushels a month even in the Summer when the stock already on hand was being run down.[61] Soon after the company's new equipment began contributing to the output, James Pinkerton, the manager of Sir John Henderson's Coal and Salt Works at St. David's, began to put pressure on Thomas Fishwick to join the Salt Society. His arguments were summarised by Thomas Fishwick in an open letter:

> Formerly Salt used to be sold in this neighbourhood for 10d or 1/- per Bushel but the Salt Makers along the Forth thinking this by far too low a price and consequently a hardship upon them — they in general (tho' not wholly) Entered upon a Combination to advance the price and so far succeeded that it is now selling at 1/6 per Bushel out of which from 2d to 3d per Bushel goes to the support and upholding of the said Society, and this is what he wishes us to become Members of, shrewdly alleging that it is unfair for us to enjoy the benefit of their Association without contributing to its support — We however declined giving him any positive Answer until we could be favoured with the Sentiments at large thereupon — but as Monopolizing is neither justifiable or lawful, we are jointly of opinion you ought not to give your Consent to any such thing, for to confine or shackle your Trade with a set of Men you know nothing of may be attended with very bad Consequences — rather determine to stand upon your own bottom as before, and we think you may safely let us advance the price of . . . the Salt to 1/6 . . . while the above Society can obtain 1/4 per Bushel clear for their Salt they will hardly be so mad as to reduce it to 10d again in opposition to us.[62]

Despite continuous efforts by Pinkerton to induce the proprietors of Halbeath to join the Association of Salt Proprietors, Campbell, Morrison & Co. stubbornly refused to participate. It is charitable to believe that this was because John Campbell, as a Writer to the Signet, felt he could not subscribe to a combination, but it is not impossible that the more cynical motives mentioned by Fishwick were predominant in arriving at this decision.

Be that as it may, the partners soon discovered that their earlier estimates concerning the salt trade were over-sanguine. The surviving statistics reveal that although sales of salt made a useful contribution to the company's revenue, the trade was subject to violent fluctuations, and burdened by infuriating, time-consuming and costly customs procedures.[63] Furthermore, the entire sea-salt trade was perpetually haunted by the fear that the legislation protecting the industry would be amended, and infinitely cheaper rock salt shipped from Liverpool freely admitted into Scotland.[64]

As long as the 'Rock Salt Importation Scheme' could be destroyed, and 'while the Salt Association holds together',[65] Fishwick felt all would be well. Certainly the saltworks appear to have been maintained at a high level of efficiency but little could be done to combat the occasional stagnation to which the trade was subject. In November 1798, for example, one of the periodic slumps in Halbeath's sales was attributed to 'underhand dealings amongst a part of the Saltmakers in the Association who are either supposed to smuggle or give premiums to the Dealers secretly and hence [enjoy] a constant demand, while the Fair Trader can scarce obtain a single order'.[66] 'Matters [did] not go on again in the usual Channels' for almost a year. Despite some abatement in the price, orders failed to 'come forward' and the granaries became 'overstocked'.[67] Sales revived again towards the end of 1791, but the manager was pessimistic about the long-term prospects: 'I heartily wish you may succeed in a cheaper method of making Salt, as in probability it will soon be required on the Firth there being a report that the Liverpool Rock Salt is to be allowed to come into Manufacture upon the common Duty, which if it should be the case it will overcome all the Saltworks in Scotland and the north of England'.[68]

Although Thomas Cockburn's gloomy prediction was perfectly accurate, no alterations in the Salt Laws took place until 1798, and 'so catastrophic [were they] in effect' that a further Act of 1799 restored some degree of protection for the Scottish salt industry.[69] The Salt Acts were finally repealed in 1822, and until that time the Halbeath Saltworks apparently continued to make a useful contribution to the firm's revenue, just over 22,000 bushels being sold in the year ending 19 November, 1791 for a sum approaching £1,500.[70]

VI

The tensions between the partners, apparent within a year of the establishment of the company, were in no way alleviated by the outward manifestations of success. Although the vend of both coal and salt approached and even exceeded the more realistic early projections, the expected profits remained curiously elusive. It was the failure of the concern to make profits that exacerbated the growing differences between the partners. While no one apparently doubted that 'ultimately this Adventure [would] prove beneficial to us all',[71] each new injection of cash seemed to bring this day no nearer. Meanwhile, John Campbell became increasingly restive. The inability, or unwillingness, of the other partners to bear the heavy capital outlays meant that by December 1786, Campbell had himself advanced £3,255 to the company, for only a third of which he was personally liable. Not surprisingly, he could not 'conceal [his] uneasiness'.

Although he expressed 'the highest regard for each of the partners and the greatest confidence in them', and acknowledged that 'in business of this sort many unforeseen Accidents must happen which create Expense', Campbell clearly entertained the suspicion that advantage 'was being taken of his lack of knowledge in the matters of coal'.[72] If, for example, John Morrison believed that the installation of new equipment was vital to the long-run success of the enterprise, Campbell could only acquiesce, but the fact that he alone among the partners paid for the improvements grew increasingly irksome.

Had the partners' original estimates of cost proved accurate, such problems might never have arisen. At the outset, Campbell, and indeed the other partners, had willingly agreed to sink the new engine pit. It was to cost £700. By the end of 1786, it was 'well over schedule' and had already cost at least twice as much. There were to be many unforeseen difficulties. In the winter of 1787, the colliery was plagued by a series of misfortunes:

> The new pit . . . is sunk to about 10 fathoms . . . but an unforeseen accident has unluckily happened to the new Engine owing to the repeated failure of the clacks, which there is hardly any chance of remedying but by drawing the Pumps, and this we fear will prove both difficult and troublesome.[73]

> The Bye pit is getting down fast, and the Great Engine continues to manage the Water . . . but by some unaccountable neglect of the Plumbers, the soldering of the Boiler top fails and will prove an Everlasting Plague to the People who attend her.[74]

> The late Innundation . . . has again been unfortunate to the Colly, as the Surface Water has unluckily found its way into all the Engine pits, but . . . we hope it will not be attended with any other disagreeable consequences Except that of laying off the greater part of the workmen for a few days.[75]

So the problems mounted. At the close of 1787 parts of the pit were flooded, the engines were completely unable to cope, and water was pouring in both from the surface and from old workings. It was imperative to install a more powerful engine and a new set of pumps, and the partners were advised that *'no other method will save the Colliery and establish her Reputation'.*[76] Increasingly desperate calls for immediate action — 'the water at the Colly is

c

now above the Five Foot Coal and there is but little hopes of the present Engine getting it lower'[77] — met with no positive response from the demoralised partners. Thomas Fishwick, grappling with one crisis after another, was obliged to emphasise, 'you will perceive how our Coal Trade begins to dwindle and fall off but . . . *the matter now rests with yourselves*'. It was apparent that the partners were at complete loggerheads. John Campbell refused to subscribe to the solution proposed by the two Morrisons, preferring instead to take the advice of an independent expert he had consulted.[79] Meanwhile, Fishwick reported from Halbeath, 'The Water at the colliery continues above the 5 ft Coal'.[80] Campbell had his way — after all, he was providing the necessary funds — but this crisis marks the beginning of the end of the original partnership. A new engine of greater capacity was to be erected together with yet another set of pumps, and civil engineering work was to be carried out to divert both surface and underground feeders into alternative channels. The expense was crushing, but Campbell agreed with Thomas Fishwick and the overseers that there was no alternative if all was not to be lost.

Work went on throughout the Summer and Autumn of 1788. 'The major part of the great Engine materials' and the pumps were sent up from Newcastle; the boiler plates from Rotherham; 'the Cylinder and everything belonging to it from Carron Co.' Skilled workmen (carpenters, plumbers and enginemen), too, came up from Newcastle on short contracts.[81] Not until November was everything in place and the 'dangerous open cutters . . . effectively stopped'.[82] After the almost inevitable teething troubles, by the end of the year the new equipment had 'complete command of the water'. The exhausted managers at Halbeath could not refrain from observing that 'our neighbours at Fordel [Sir John Henderson's mine] have been almost completely flooded'.[83] The last pay of 1788 (20 December 1788-3 January 1789) recorded that the raisings totalled 1,170 tons; an annual rate of output of 30,000 tons had been achieved.

VII

Success had come too late to save the partnership. The Morrisons, whose advice had been disregarded, could put in no more funds to meet the costs involved in the recovery of the mine and the establishment of its long-term viability; their plans, much cheaper to implement than Campbell's scheme, were designed simply to meet the immediate crisis posed by the inundation of the workings. Campbell had had his way because he alone was able to make the necessary advances, yet as the expense of the recovery operation mounted, he expected the Morrisons to contribute their share. The essence of the complex difficulties which ensued is revealed in a passage of one of the manager's public letters:

. . . as the Erecting of [the new engine] has turned out such an expensive Job altogether you will find by the Abst. that the receipts from our J.C. have exceeded the Remittances above £1500 since 24th May last . . . as these press so heavy upon [him] he naturally grows more and more impatient that the *principal articles* in the *two last Minutes* [concerning the payment by 'the several partners [of] their respective Deficiencies'] are apparently disregarded, and till they are fully complied with he seems determined to make no further Advances than what are absolutely necessary to pay the Workmen — we shall therefore be in a very unpleasant situation . . .[84]

In the event, John Campbell paid the outstanding bills but he would go no further. The other partners must pay their deficiencies 'without delay', except for John Morrison who at 'his own earnest request' was given three months' grace.[85] When it became apparent that the delinquent partners were incapable of meeting their obligations, a meeting took place at Newcastle at which John Morrison and Richard Fishwick agreed 'to convey to Campbell one-third of their respective shares of Halbeath Coalliery, being two twelfth parts of the whole Coalliery for the sum of £2,400 with the Profit or Loss consequent upon it'.[86] Although other resolutions obliged John Campbell to offer the two twelfth shares to two experienced colliery managers and, 'in the case of their refusal', to give Richard Fishwick and John Morrison the power to reclaim their shares 'on paying up their respective deficiencies', neither alternative seemed capable of realisation.[87] John Campbell, by accident or design, now owned half the Company, the capital Stock of which stood in March 1789 at no less than £12,726.

The next six months were characterised by bitter arguments between the partners. Letters from the Morrisons, father and son, to John Campbell became increasingly abusive, reflecting their resentment of Campbell's predominance in the Company when they had carried so much of the responsibility for, and the physical burden of, the practical working of the mine. But when the younger Fishwick, obviously shocked at the increasing acrimony of the exchanges, threw his support behind John Campbell, the Morrisons were powerless; they could always be outvoted. Meanwhile, John Boyes, whose active interest in the conduct of the affairs of the Company had never extended beyond pushing sales in the North of England, resigned from the partnership, his one-twelfth share being conveyed to Richard Fishwick.[88]

The immediate consequence of Thomas Fishwick's support of John Campbell was that it became impossible for the former to continue to share the management of the colliery and saltworks with the younger Morrison. Fishwick, who had brought considerable administrative and commercial ability to the running of Halbeath, could not be placed in sole charge because of his ignorance of the technical side of coal getting, and John Campbell would not countenance putting John Morrison in control, if for no other reason than that he believed the younger Morrison was largely responsible for the fact that 'our expenditure [has] exceeded all bounds and successive Calculations'.[89] There was no alternative but to bring in an outsider.

During the crisis of 1787, Campbell had frequently expressed his profound regret that the company had not taken the 'advice of an able *Scotch Viewer* accustomed to the quantity of Water . . . to be expected in this Country. [Had we done so we] would have saved the company an immense expense'. Campbell clearly believed that the Morrisons had miscalculated both the power of the engines and the size of the pumps required at Halbeath. They had, he implied, been misled by their experience of the Great Northern coal-field. They could hardly be blamed too severely for this, but it did show the necessity for an informed second opinion.[90]

To avoid similar costly mistakes in the future, it had been resolved 'that there be constantly upon the Spot a Viewer of some Abilities'.[91] After a search locally proved unsuccessful, Thomas Bateman had been appointed.[92] Not only was he said to be a man of considerable ability but, even more important, he was the brother of John Bateman, manager of Lord Lowther's Colliery at Whitehaven, perhaps the most extensive in Britain.[93] It was expected that John Bateman would interest himself in Halbeath's affairs.

The increasing differences between the partners, the growing incompatibility of the two managers at Halbeath, the assumption of many of John Morrison's duties by Thomas Bateman, and John Campbell's financial control of the enterprise, gave him the opportunity to push through a radical reorganisation of the company. In October 1789, it was agreed to appoint Thomas Cockburn of Limekilns — a 'highly experienced Scotch manager' — General Agent and Bookkeeper, 'he to be in the place of Mr. Thomas Fishwick and Mr. John Morrison Jnr.'[94]

Intended to reduce 'the disagreeable animosities that have subsisted amongst some of the partners', this new 'arrangement' served only to exacerbate the differences between them. By the winter of 1789, the situation had become intolerable: the Morrisons refused even to attend meetings of the Company, the necessity for which were becoming ever more urgent.[95] In March 1790, John Campbell, goaded beyond endurance by a series of insulting letters from the younger Morrison, abandoned his usual judicious and conciliatory style to fire off one final corrosive reply: 'All of [your letters are] further proof of your consumate modesty and discretion. You seem in fair train to enter the lists for the prizes of Bilingsgate — When you shall shew even those discretions which even the lowest pitmen may be supposed possessed of and shall cease to be the squirt of your father and your own ill-humour you shall then hear from me . . . Till then I refer you to the public letters'.[96] Not until the following month did tempers cool sufficiently to permit — with the aid of legal intermediaries — any rational discussion of the firm's future form and organisation. The Morrisons — still heavily indebted to the company — decided to sell out; they had had enough. But what was their third share really worth? The finances of the concern were now so muddled that further bitter disagreement ensued.[97] Campbell, despairing of ever recovering the advances he had made to the company on behalf of the Morrisons, instructed Heron and Wilkinson, attorneys of Newcastle, to 'prepare matters for every legal measure against father and son short of imprisonment. They have only themselves to blame . . .'[98]

The threat of legal action proved decisive. It was decided to appoint two experienced colliery viewers (John Grieve of Muirkirk and William Stobbart of Fatfield, County Durham) to ascertain precisely what the Morrisons' share was worth and, if they could not agree, James Pinkerton, a merchant of Leith, was appointed Umpire, with power to make a final valuation. In the event, the two arbitrators failed to reach complete agreement, leaving the last word to Pinkerton. The entire proceedings were drawn out and of considerable complexity but essentially what they were designed to elicit were (a) the capital stock of the enterprise as at November 1790; (b) the amount of the Morrisons' debt to the company; and (c) the value of the company's 'excessive dependence' upon Campbell's previous advances. Once these magnitudes had been determined it was a comparatively easy calculation to discover how much John Campbell should pay the Morrisons to buy them out completely. The value of the Halbeath Colliery and Saltworks in November 1790 was agreed to be £13,540; the Morrisons' $\frac{4}{12}$ share being worth £4,514. But when allowances had been made for Campbell's advances to the company on behalf of the Morrisons (and the amount he had foregone in interest payments by doing so), it was agreed that he be entitled to buy the Morrisons' share for a total of £1,710.[99] From 20 November, 1789, John Campbell owned eight of the twelve shares, Richard Fishwick, three, and his son, Thomas, one; the firm became known as John Campbell & Co., 'the management of the whole Concern to remain with T. Cockburn'.[100]

VIII

In January 1791 John Campbell wrote to his late partner, John Boyes, 'Notwithstanding all our disasters, Halbeath is now doing well';[101] and to John Bateman, 'Manager of Lord Lowther's Coal', he offered one of Richard Fishwick's one-twelfth shares: 'both of us will be happy that you become a partner'. He had no wish to dispose of either his original one-third share or that which he had purchased for the Morrisons, as 'matters appear so prosperous . . . the raisings average 1400 Tons per fortnight'.[102]

The ever-optimistic Campbell was not the first to discover that increasing output was not incompatible with stagnant profits or even losses.[103] So rapidly were the existing seams being wrought out that it soon became necessary to sink new pits and add new branches to the waggonway.[104] These necessary developments and the expense of the company's contribution to the improvement of Inverkeithing Harbour, without which the growth of the colliery would have been brought almost to a standstill, involved further capital expenditure.[105] Despite borrowing £3,070 on the company's bond in May

1791,[106] and the retention of all the profits of both the salt and coal trade, Campbell continued to have to make advances to the company. To his long-suffering partner, Richard Fishwick, he had to confess in January 1792, 'I really expected that a part of our profits might be divided [this year] . . . we have been deceiving ourselves'.[107]

This was apparently to be a continuing theme throughout Halbeath's existence. In the year ending 19 November, 1791, the 'gain on sales' of over 28,000 tons of coal and 22,100 bushels of salt amounted to only £735. The explanation of this disappointing result is prefaced by the following statement, 'But in said Year there are many Extra Expenses which are not again likely to occur'.[108] It is a statement which seems to have been often repeated throughout the long life of this remarkable enterprise.[109]

NOTES

1. By Thomson, Dickson and Shaw, W.S., and J. A. Campbell and Lamond, C.S., Edinburgh.

2. Sir John Sinclair (ed.), *The Statistical Account of Scotland*, Vol. XIII (1974), p. 469.

3. *Ibid.*, p. 470.

4. John Wright, 'A View of Halbeath Colliery', 29 March, 1785, Halbeath Colliery and Salt Works: Letter Book I, p. 15. (Hereafter cited L.B.)

5. The Rev. Peter Chalmers, 'Mineralogical and Geological Report on the Dunfermline Coal-Field', *Prize-Essays and Transactions of the Highland and Agricultural Society of Scotland*, New Series, Vol. VII (1841), p. 301.

6. John Wright, *op. cit.*, p. 18.

7. Minute of a meeting of the partners, Bykerhouse, 6 May, 1785. L.B. I, pp. 25, 27.

8. John Morrison Senr. to John Morrison Jnr., 2 August, 1785. L.B. I, p. 31.

9. Extract of a Letter from Aberdeen regarding Coals, 11 June, 1785. L.B. I, p. 29.

10. It will become apparent that much of the expert advice and skilled labour called upon by the new proprietors of the Halbeath Colliery was of English origin. For the general context, see Baron F. Duckham, 'English Influences in the Scottish Coal Industry, 1700-1815', in John Butt and J. T. Ward (eds.), *Scottish Themes: Essays in Honour of Professor S. G. E. Lythe* (Edinburgh: Scottish Academic Press, 1976), pp. 28-45.

11. John Morrison Senr. to John Morrison Jnr., 2 August, 1785. L.B. I, p. 34.

12. Within a few months these rates had been scaled sharply downwards. See Appendix I.

13. John Morrison Jnr. to John Morrison Senr., 28 February, 1786. L.B. I, p. 51.

14. Minute of a meeting of the partners, 18 October, 1785. L.B. I, p. 36.

15. This arrangement was doubtless facilitated by the fact that Campbell was the eldest son of John Campbell, first cashier of the Royal Bank. See *A History of the Society of Writers to Her Majesty's Signet* (Edinburgh, 1890), p. 32.

16. Minutes, 22 April, 1786. L.B. I, p. 56.

17. Halbeath Colliery and Salt Works: Miscellaneous Accounts and Papers, and Bill Book.

18. J. Morrison Senr. to J. Morrison Jnr., c. 10 July, 1786.

19. Letter from Mr. Thomas Fishwick to the Company, 8 July, 1786. L.B. I, p. 58.

20. Letter from Thomas Fishwick to the Company, 1 August, 1786. L.B. I, p. 68.

21. John Morrison Senr. to J. Campbell, 15 August, 1786. L.B. I, p. 69.

22. T. Fishwick to the Company, 21 August, 1786. L.B. I, p. 71.

23. T. Fishwick to the Company, 2 November, 1786. L.B. I, pp. 77-78.

24. T. Fishwick to the Company, 2 February, 1787. L.B. I, p. 109.

25. Minutes of a meeting of the Proprietors held at the Queens Head, Newcastle, 17 January, 1787. L.B. I, p. 90.

26. See Appendix II.

27. Minutes of a meeting of the Proprietors, 9 March, 1787. L.B. I, p. 129. Five years later, Campbell had second thoughts about the operation of the testimonial, sometimes referred to as a 'Line of Leave'. In a lengthy correspondence with Sir John Henderson, proprietor of Fordel Colliery, over a bankman employed at Halbeath, Campbell questioned the legality of the 'Line of Leave'. 'I am now of opinion that . . . the resolution entered into at Kirkcaldy is not only illegal and contrary to the act of 1775 giving freedom to Colliers but adverse to sound policy and tending either to drive the Colliers and others out of the Country or to retain them against their will. It is our resolution therefore not to be governed by this rule but to receive pitmen and servants of every description who are *not under engagement* to other Collieries . . . [although] we will discourage every attempt in our people to entice them away . . .' J. Campbell to Sir John Henderson of Fordel, 23 June, 1792. John Campbell's Letter Book, pp. 405-6. (Hereafter cited J.C.L.B.)

28. Indeed, John Campbell played a leading role in attempting 'to bring about a General Concert over all Scotland not to take Coaliers of other Coalieries, which will give us more the Command of them'. There are many references to this matter in the Halbeath papers; the quotation is from a letter John Campbell to John Boyes, 4 June, 1787. J.C.L.B., p. 19.

29. Letter from James Fishwick to the Company, 20 February, 1787.

30. Minutes of a meeting of the Proprietors at Halbeath Colliery, 9 March, 1787. L.B. I, p. 128. One cannot avoid the suspicion that John Morrison's criticisms of the average output per man at Halbeath may have been sharpened by his knowledge of large-scale collieries on the Tyne and Wear.

31. T. Fishwick and J. Morrison Jnr. to the Company, 2 March, 1787. L.B. I, p. 120; 'Account of Coals Raised by the Different Colliers of Halbeath from 27 April to and with 25 May'. L.B. I, p. 148; 'The reward of Half a Crown to each man who raises 3 Tons per day (5 days in the week) and at each pay has had a wonderful effect ——— On the first trial only 3 or 4 had it, last pay we gave it to 19 men. This partly accounts for our great raisings of late. We are doing more than 2,000 Tons per month . . .' J. Campbell to John Boyes Jnr., 4 June, 1787. J.C.L.B., p. 18.

32. T.F. and J.M. Jnr. to the Company, 4 April, 1787. L.B. I, p. 134.

33. T.F. and J.M. Jnr. to the Company, 3 May, 1787. L.B. I, pp. 140-1.

34. J. Campbell to Jamieson, Stein and Co., Kilbegie, Alloa, 27 April, 1787. J.C.L.B., p. 12.

35. Report on Halbeath Colliery, 23 January, 1792. L.B. 2, pp. 207-8.

36. J. Campbell to Pat. Campbell, 29 April, 1791. J.C.L.B., p. 330.

37. Report on Halbeath Colliery, 23 January, 1792. L.B. 2, p. 208.

38. Minutes of a meeting of the Proprietors, 1 July, 1785. L.B. I, p. 31.

39. John Morrison Senr. to J. Morrison Jnr., 2 August, 1785. L.B. I, p. 33.

40. Thos. Fishwick and J. Morrison Jnr. to the Company, 1 June, 1787. L.B. I, p. 146.

41. J. Campbell to J.M. Senr., 2 June, 1787. J.C.L.B., p. 18.

42. The foregoing sentences are based on John Campbell's correspondence [the quotations are from his letters in J.C.L.B. dated 22 September, 1788 (p. 122), 26 November, 1788 (p. 130), 28 November, 1786 (p. 131)] and the Company's first Letter Book (L.B. I), 4 October, 1788 (p. 283), 17 October, 1788 (p. 285), 26 December, 1788 (p. 300), 22 January, 1789 (p. 306).

43. Thos. Fishwick and John Morrison Jnr. to the Company, 26 June, 1789. L.B. I, p. 354.

44. R. Fishwick and John Morrison Jnr. to the Company, 24 July, 1789. L.B. 2, p. 4.

45. R. Fishwick and J. Morrison Jnr. to the Company, 27 August, 1789. L.B. 2, p. 14.

46. Thos. Fishwick to the Company, 1 October, 1789. L.B. 2, p. 29.

47. Thomas Gillespie to Thomas Cockburn, 8 March, 1791, L.B. 2, pp. 152-5. Part of this letter is reproduced in Appendix III. For Thomas Gillespie (or Gillespy) see the numerous references in Raymond Smith, *Sea-Coal for London: A History of the Coal Factors in the London Market* (London: Longmans, 1961), esp. pp. 78, 92, 144-5, 173-6.

48. For example, John Campbell to Pat. Campbell, 29 April, 1791. J.C.L.B., pp. 330-31: '. . . we are now introducing our Coal into London and from their superior quality have every reason to

think they require only to be known — We however look to Scotch friends to help on the Sale . . . These [Halbeath] Coals are allowed to be superior to St. Davids [the harbour in Inverkeithing Bay owned by Sir John Henderson of Fordell] and . . . their introduction into London is an object to us of great importance'.

49. John Campbell to Richard Fishwick, 20 May, 1791. J.C.L.B., p. 334; John Campbell to Lord Kinnaird, 4 June, 1791. J.C.L.B., p. 338.

50. T. Cockburn to the Company, 19 April, 1790, L.B. 2, p. 119; John Campbell to David Dale, 24 January, 1791, J.C.L.B., p. 308.

51. John Campbell to Hugh Bell, Brewer, 23 July, 1791, J.C.L.B., p. 346. Bell's answer is interesting. It reads, in part, 'Good Cynders will command a certain Sale — Newcastle cost 8/- per Chaldron, besides 8/- freight, 5/- duty, fees, mettage, Carriage, Pilferage, etc. You see there is a large field — As to process from Coals to Cynders I am ignorant — an experiment upon a small scale seems proper and you may send me a few Bags'. Copy letter from Hugh Bell, Brewer, to John Campbell, 29 July, 1791, L.B. 2, p. 200.

52. John Campbell to Thomas Cockburn, 11 June, 1791, J.C.L.B., p. 339, and John Campbell to T. Fishwick, 5 July, 1791, J.C.L.B., p. 344.

53. This was done principally by letters to well-connected Scotsmen, usually in Government circles, who spent at least part of the year resident in London. One such was sent to Sir John Sinclair, an extract from which provides the general flavour: '. . . if you use Scotch Coal in London and find ours suit [please] order your people to get Inverkeithing Scotch Coal — They should be mixed with English to make a good and thrifty fire — Mr. Thos. Gillespie, Broker or any of the 12 Brokers who deal in Scotch Coals will supply those by whom you are served with Coal . . . I long to see the Coal duty to the north abolished — I trust you will then have all good fires in yr . . . Country — So great was the want of firing last winter in parts of the highlands that they were actually burning their miserable household furniture to keep them from perishing with Cold . . .' John Campbell to Sir John Sinclair, 21 June, 1791, J.C.L.B., p. 341.

54. Thomas Cockburn to the Company, 6 April, 1790. L.B. 2, p. 106.

55. For example, '. . . my friend Mr. Boyes of Hull writes as follows — "[I am informed] that the present time is favourable [for] your Chews. At this port the Inland Coals are higher by 3/- per Chaldn. than is usual and likely to continue scarce and dear — you must obtain your freight low. There is no doubt of a ready sale"'. John Campbell to Thomas Cockburn, 10 November, 1791, J.C.L.B., p. 361.

56. For example, during the year ending 24 May, 1788, 64 per cent of the coal raised at Halbeath was 'consumed by the Salt pans'. See also Appendix V.

57. A substantial quantity of the salt produced at Inverkeithing and elsewhere on the Forth was shipped to England (see Appendix IV), where it had long enjoyed a good reputation. Attention has most recently been drawn to this point by Dr. Joyce Ellis, 'The Decline and Fall of the Tyneside Salt Industry, 1660-1790: A Re-examination', *Economic History Review*, 2nd Series, XXXIII (1980), p. 51.

58. See the very clear statement of the position of the Scottish salt-makers made by Dr. John Roebuck in 1785, National Library of Scotland, Ms 640, f. 166, quoted by Archibald and Nan. L. Clow, *The Chemical Revolution* (London: Batchworth, 1952), pp. 60-61.

59. Minute of the Proprietors, meeting at Newcastle, 6 May, 1785. Letter Book 1, p. 27.

60. John Morrison Senr. to John Wright, 6 May, 1785. L.B. I, p. 28.

61. T. Fishwick to the Company, 1 September, 1786. L.B. I, pp. 73-4. The dimensions of the two new salt pans were 21 feet x 12 feet x 15 inches in depth; the older salt pans purchased from the Lloyds were approximately 19 feet x 10 feet x 20 inches in depth. Thomas Cockburn to Richard Fishwick, 17 January, 1792. L.B. 2, p. 204. Cf. A. & N. Clow, *op. cit.*, pp. 55-6; and see J. Butt, *Industrial Archaeology of Scotland* (Newton Abbot, David & Charles, 1967), pp. 132-4.

62. Thomas Fishwick to the Company, 9 December, 1786. L.B. I, pp. 80-81. In this letter Fishwick was reporting a conversation he had had with Pinkerton. Pinkerton later wrote two letters to the company on the subject: these are reproduced in Appendix IV.

63. For example, '. . . as the Customhouse officers continue to weigh this article as *Misers would*

their gold it must not only alarm but discourage the salt merchants from future speculations and we fear we shall be under the necessity of making our customers some trifling abatement by way of compensation [for the delay imposed on their vessels].' Thomas Fishwick and John Morrison Jnr. to the Company, 30 April, 1789. L.B. I, p. 344.

64. In 1799 the proprietors of the Halbeath Saltworks calculated the loss that they would sustain if Liverpool Salt were to be admitted into Scotland at the Scots Duty at £3,625. The details are reproduced in Appendix V.

65. The phrases are from the open letter from John Morrison Jnr. and Thomas Fishwick to the Company, 3 April, 1789. L.B. I, p. 338.

66. Thomas Fishwick to the Company, 16 November, 1789. L.B. 2, p. 44.

67. Thomas Cockburn to the Company, 20 March, 1790. LB. 2, p. 94; John Campbell to John Ogilvie, 20 November, 1790. J.C.L.B., p. 295.

68. Thomas Cockburn to Richard Fishwick, 17 January, 1792. L.B. 2, p. 204.

69. For the details, see A. & N. Clow, *op. cit.*, pp. 60-63.

70. Anonymous report on the Halbeath Colliery and Saltworks, 23 January, 1792. L.B. 2, p. 206. For the same period sales of coal brought in nearly £7,000.

71. The words of John Campbell in a letter to Messrs Fishwick, Morrison and Boyes, 22 December, 1786. L.B. I, pp. 83-7.

72. *Ibid.*

73. Thomas Fishwick to John Morrison, 4 September, 1787. L.B. I, p. 155.

74. *Ibid.*, 31 October, 1787. L.B. I, p. 169.

75. *Ibid.*, 12 December, 1787. L.B. I, 178.

76. *Ibid.*, 28 December, 1787, based on a long report on the state of the colliery by all the overseers. L.B. I, pp. 180-182.

77. Thomas Fishwick to the Company, 5 March, 1788. L.B. I, p. 219.

78. *Ibid.*

79. John Morrison Jnr. to Thomas Fishwick, 6 March, 1788; Thomas Fishwick to the Company, 10 March, 1788; John Campbell to the Company, 11 March, 1788. L.B. I, pp. 221-3.

80. T. Fishwick to the Company, 20 March, 1788. L.B. I, p. 204.

81. The principal references are all from the open letters to the Company by Thomas Fishwick, 27 June, 1788; 22 July, 1788; 11 August, 1788; 21 August, 1788. L.B. I, pp. 214, 249, 262, 264.

82. *Ibid.*, 17 October, 1788. Cutters were apparently the surface streams which had to be diverted from the colliery workings.

83. *Ibid.*, 6 February, 1789. L.B. I, p. 309.

84. Thomas Fishwick and John Morrison Jnr., 10 February, 1789. L.B. I, p. 302. The quotation in square brackets is taken from the Minutes of a Meeting of the Proprietors, 19 and 20 March, 1788. L.B. I, p. 230.

85. J. Campbell to Messrs Fishwick and Morrison, 17 February, 1780. J.C.L.B., p. 155.

86. 'Minutes of a Meeting [at the Turkshead, Newcastle] respecting Halbeath Affairs', 12 March, 1789. L.B. I, p. 332.

87. *Ibid.*, paragraphs 2-5. Johnson and John Bateman, to whom the shares were offered, were prepared to pay only £1,600 for them; this offer was refused as being 'far too low and in every way inadequate to the real value of the Colly'. Thomas Fishwick and John Morrison Jnr. to the Company, 26 June, 1789. L.B. I, p. 354.

88. John Campbell to J. Boyes Jnr., 3 November, 1789. J.C.L.B., p. 201; John Campbell to R. Trotter, W.S., 2 November, 1789. J.C.L.B., p. 199.

89. J. Campbell to Robert Rankine, 13 November, 1789. J.C.L.B., pp. 204-5.

90. J. Campbell to Richard Fishwick, 29 December, 1787; John Campbell to J. Boyes, 1 December, 1787 and 1 January, 1788. J.C.L.B., pp. 65, 72-73.

91. Minute of a Meeting of the Proprietors, 19-20 March, 1788. L.B. I, p. 232.

92. John Campbell to Thomas Bateman, 13 December, 1788. J.C.L.B., p. 134.

93. See Oliver Wood, 'A Cumberland Colliery During the Napoleonic War', *Economica*, XXI (1954), p. 54.

94. Minutes of a Meeting held at Inverkeithing, 29 October, 1789. L.B. 2, p. 37.

95. John Campbell to Robert Rankine, 13 November, 1789. J.C.L.B., p. 204.

96. J. Campbell to J. Morrison Jnr., 29 March, 1790; at the same time Campbell informed Thomas Cockburn that 'my correspondence with Messrs Morrison shall now be at an end'. J. Campbell to Thomas Cockburn, 21 March, 1790. J.C.L.B., pp. 249-51.

97. John Campbell to John Morrison Senr., 23 March, 1790. J.C.L.B., p. 254, in which Campbell informed Morrison that if something was not done soon, he would 'be obliged to proceed in a legal enforcement of my just demands . . . This, Sir, I shall do with reluctance'. The fundamental question to be determined was 'how much are [the shares] worth at present — Not what they cost'.

98. Series of letters from John Campbell to Ralph Heron and William Wilkinson, 17-21 April, 1790. J.C.L.B., pp. 262-5.

99. Decreet Arbitral by James Pinkerton, 28 February, 1791. L.B. 2, pp. 180-191; 'Memorandum respecting the settlement with Messrs Morrison for their Share in Halbeath Company purchased by Mr. Campbell', dated 31 December, 1798. Halbeath Accounts and Papers.

100. 'Memorandum inserted at the Opening of the Company's Books of the date 20 November, 1790'. L.B. 2, p. 149.

101. John Campbell to J. Boyes, 5 January, 1791. J.C.L.B., p. 302.

102. John Campbell to John Bateman, Whitehaven, 21 January, 1791. J.C.L.B., p. 304.

103. Although a substantial 'gain' on the Halbeath Colliery was made in 1798, when an output of no less than 46,320 tons of coal was recorded (see Table 2), it was followed by at least four years of losses (see note 109), when the annual output probably averaged well over 30,000 tons, substantially more than in the latter half of the 'eighties. A detailed examination by the proprietors to ascertain why a 20 per cent fall in output between 1798 and 1799 produced a fall in costs of only 8 per cent (and hence contributed to turning a 'gain' of £1,639 into a loss of £1,285) concluded that 'a number of the articles of charge are stationary whatever the produce may be, such as most of the salaries, etc.' Halbeath Colliery and Salt Works: Accounts and Papers, 'Comparative View of the Produce and the Cost of Halbeath Coals for the Years 1798 and 1799'.

104. Thomas Bateman to the Company, 12 January, 1790. L.B. 2, p. 64. Thomas Cockburn to the Company, 20 March, 1790. L.B. 2, p. 94.

105. There is a considerable correspondence on the improvement of Inverkeithing Harbour. Originally to be surveyed by Whitworth, the engineer of the Great Canal, the matter was eventually left in the care of his 'substitute', Charles Abercrombie. The final cost of cutting a deeper channel and making extensive improvements to the pier was estimated to be well over £600 of which approximately half was met by the Town. The relevant letters are contained in John Campbell's Letter Book and the second of the Halbeath Letter Books. See also Bruce Lenman, *From Esk to Tweed* (Glasgow, 1975), pp. 32-3, 60-1.

106. Minutes of the Proprietors of Halbeath Colliery, 7 May, 1791. L.B. 2, p. 196.

107. John Campbell to Richard Fishwick, 17 January, 1792. J.C.L.B., pp. 372-3.

108. Anonymous, partially damaged, report on the affairs of Halbeath Colliery, dated 23 January, 1792. L.B. 2, pp. 206-9.

109. The miscellaneous papers of the Halbeath Colliery and Saltworks make it possible to reconstruct the following series at the turn of the century, when the enterprise was owned by John Campbell, who held seven-twelfths of the capital stock, John Gibson four-twelfths and Andrew Young one-twelfth:

Year ending	Capital Stock	Gain (+) or Loss (—) on Stock
24 November, 1798	£11,608	+£1639
23 November, 1799	11,962	— 1285
22 November, 1800	13,015	— 1347
21 November, 1801	13,565	— 3176
20 November, 1802	n.d.	— 248
19 November, 1803	20,914	n.d.

John Gibson, besides being a member of the Tyne Ironworks, appears to have been concerned in several other companies on both sides of the Border. At the end of the second decade of the nineteenth century he held six-seventeenths of Halbeath's capital stock of approximately £18,000 'from which, he claimed, he . . . received but £150 per annum to support his wife and eight children'. Baron F. Duckham, *A History of the Scottish Coal Industry, 1700-1815* (Newton Abbot: David & Charles, 1970), p. 192.

APPENDIX I

Examples of Contracts entered into by Campbell, Morrison & Co., July 1786

Robert Thomson & John Blenkinshop have Agreed to Win Work, draw to the bank and fill into the Waggons 20,000 Tons great, chew and small Coals annually or any increased quantity that shall be required and in such proportions as the Mine will produce for the term of 5, 7 or 9 Years at the following rates:

	s.	d.
For Hewing, drawing or bearing & laying on bank great Coal, finding labour and Materials at per Ton of 21 Cwt	1 "	8
Filling ditto into Waggons		$1\frac{1}{4}$
Upholding Gins, Ropes & Tubs		1
Grieves, Labourers, Extra Smith & Wrights		$-\frac{3}{4}$
Surface Damages on Halbeath Estate		$-\frac{1}{4}$
Propt Timber Deals etc.		$-\frac{1}{2}$
Binding Pitmen		$-\frac{1}{2}$
Miscellaneous		$-\frac{1}{4}$
Total for great Coal per Ton, of 21 Cwt	2 /	$0\frac{1}{2}$
Chews ditto	1 /	9
Small ditto		$11\frac{1}{2}$

George Topling has Agreed to sink the little Engine Pit for £3 " 10s per fathom and to inspect the sinking of the other Engine Pit.

John Shadforth has Agreed for the Carpentry Work of the great Engine:

The Regulator Beam	£4 " 0 " 0
Cylinder	2 " 10 " 0
Timber to lay under ditto	10 " 0
Sheer Legs and Capstans	1 " 10 " 0
Laying high Loft and flooring Beamholes	2 " 3 " 0
Heaving up Beams, Cylinder & Boilers	2 " 5 " 0
Making Spears	1 " 1 " 0
Plug frame	16 " 0
Roofing etc.	1 " 0 " 0
Tackhead Cistern	3 " 5 " 0
Making Pumps for Tackhead Cistern and Fixing ditto	2 " 0 " 0
Flooring Doors, Windows, Stairs etc.	2 " 0 " 0
Miscellaneous	3 " 15 " 0
	£26 " 15 " 0

The Company finding Materials
Also to keep said Engine after the pit is sunk at
    8 hours finding materials, per week   £— " 13 " 0
    16   ditto   ditto   1 " 2 " 0
    Constant going   ditto   1 " 8 " 0

Source: Halbeath Colliery and Saltworks, Letter Book I, pp. 64-6.

APPENDIX II

Mem^{dm} of what one Coalier can work in England and in Scotland

An English Collier on an average for a days work, hews one Score of Twenty peck Corves each Corf weighing better than $5\frac{1}{2}$ Cwt for which he has generally from 2/- to 2/6 per Score, varying according to the hardness or softness of the Coal, whereas the Scotch Colliers in general do not work above $2\frac{1}{2}$ Tons Great Chews and small, tho' the greatest number of them are able to work even in the splint Seam near 4 Tons per day — At Halbeath we give our men 2/10 for hewing a Board of 4 feet Wide, 4 feet high and 1 yard deep which will produce about 2 Tons of Great and 2 Tons of Chews and Small, and these men are capable of hewing one day with another between $\frac{3}{4}$ and 1 Yard so that a man that chooses to work will make between 2/- and 2/6 each day which is good wages.

Source: Halbeath Colliery and Saltworks: Letter Book I, p. 118. Undated, but c. February 1787.

APPENDIX III

Extract from letter from Thomas Gillespie, Coal Factor, London, to Thomas Cockburn, 8 March, 1791

I am much obliged to you for the application respecting Halbeath chews, but apprehend you do not rightly understand the nature of my business or the general manner in which the Coal Trade is carried on here. All the Coals that come here are sold thro' the medium of about 12 Coal factors or Brokers (of which I am one) whose duty it is to enter the Coals at the Custom house, give Bond for payment of the Duties, find out Buyers for the Coals, get the best prices the mkt will afford, receive the money and guarantee the Debts. All which is done for a Commision of $2\frac{1}{2}$ per cent. In a Coal new to our mkt. this is attended with an Extra degree of Trouble but at the same Commission, under an Expectation of a continuance of the Connection as long as the factor does to the best of his power. No person here will engage to take any certain quantity of Coals annually (however much they may be known) because the Coals differ both in quality, size etc. at different times and the mkts vary accordingly. In order to bring Coals to the London mkt you have taken the first proper step that of having a safe harbour and convenient depth of water at all times. The next step is to induce Ships to load them, but as none will take the risk of a mkt for a Coal new in its name, Quality etc., this can be done only by your freighting a few Ships at first on your own account — . . . freighting Ships with Coals has never been profitable to the freighters nor is it likely so to be or even pay for itself . . . [Nevertheless] the owners of a new Coal are obliged to freight them untill the value of them is known at mkt and Ships will then load them as readily as any other. The Expenses on Coals at this mkt are high, the Duties to Government and the Corporation of London are 10/- per London Chaldron an allowance of one chaldron out of 21 and two pounds per cent discount are allowed the Buyer. These with the Brokers Commission are charges on the freighter . . . It will be advisable that you freight only one ship first, that the Coals may be of a greater size and freeness from Slates, Stones, etc. and in general such as you can send them in future, not sending them better or worse than you may probably be able to continue. A Vessel of about five or six score London chaldrons (say 105 to 126 Chaldrons) will be enough for a first Cargo (the London Chaldron is about 27 Cwt. or 4 Tons to 3 chaldrons) and the days of Delivery here should be about ten in order to give an opportunity of two or 3 mkt days (of which we have three in a week) for the Sale. The Expense here on such a Cargo will be a much better guide to you than any account I can write you, but this is our general opinion that the prime cost of St. Davids Coals & Expenses usually paid by the freighter stand him 19/6 to 20/- per Chaldron . . . I will endeavour to do all in my power here for your interest and will give you as nearly as I can learn the Buyers Sentiments.

Source: Halbeath Colliery and Saltworks: Letter Book II, pp. 152-56.

APPENDIX IV

Letter from W. James Pinkerton, Otterston, 18th December, 1786

Dear Sir

In compliance with my promise to you this morning I now sit down to give you some account of the Society of Salt proprietors in Scotland.

About 20 years ago when the Salt Trade was reduced to nothing by the Competition and Rival-ship of the different Proprietors (Salt selling then often as low as /8d and never so high as 1/- per Bushel) several Meetings of the Trade were called together and at last after much conversation a Society was formed.

It is found now from a great many Years Experience that the quantity of Scots Salt annually consumed in the Coasting and Inland Trade from the Firth of Forth is nearly about 200,000 Bushels. Therefore if more Salt is made than this quantity the Market must be overstock'd or means must be fallen upon to export it out of the Country. The proprietors finding that they had more Salt pans than were necessary to make this quantity wisely agreed to limited these quantities to 3,000 Bushels for each pan and they have found from Experience that after allowing for the time lost in repairing their pans this quantity of 3,000 Bushels is nearly as much as a pan can make one year with another. It would perhaps be the interest of the proprietors to limit their quantities still further so as to prevent the necessity of Exporting Salt at a low price altogether, as Exporting Salt is always attended with a great loss to the Society the price which they get being seldom more than 8d per Bushel and frequently not so much. But as this restriction would bear hard upon some works in which the Owners are obliged to bring all their small Coal above ground to prevent it from taking fire which it would do if left below the Society think it better to Export a small part annually at the common Expence and allow every Proprietor to make a greater quantity than he otherways could do.

And in order to raise a fund for Exporting this Surplus Salt, the Society have agreed to tax them-selves with a penny three half pence and sometimes it has been known to rise to two pence per bushel on all the Salt sold to Land sale and shipped Coastwise. This is paid quarterly on the Sales of each work into the hands of the Society's Banker. For sometime past the Society have sold their Surplus Salt to the Fisheries at 10d and for Exportation at 8d per Bushel. When therefore any work ships a Cargo of Salt for the fisheries at 10d per Bushel that work settles with the Mercht. for the 10d and the Society's Clerk sends them an order on their Banker for 6d or 6½ a Bushel more which makes up the price to 16d or 16½d. The same that he would have got for his Salt had he sold it Coastwise at 1/6 the present price after paying the 1½d or 2d of Tax to the fund and so on for Salt exported at 8d. And by this plan of limiting the quantity in a certain degree and Exporting the Surplus or selling it to the fisheries the price has been kept up to 18d per Bushel of which each proprietor neats 16d or 17d according as the Tax happens to be either 2d, 1½d or 1d per Bushel.

The Society is founded upon principles of the nicest Equality and every thing goes on wich great Harmony. When one work has more Salt on hand than it ought to have according to the proportion of its making, the Society order it immediate relief by taking away a Cargo of Salt from it.

I hope Sir, that you and the proprietors of Halbeath Coaliery will see the propriety of joining the Society. Here you have a well regulated branch of Trade ready to your hand without any trouble on your part and I dare say that you would give a great deal to have the Coal Trade of this Country equally well regulated and adjusted. And if so I have no doubt but you will readily join in supporting a Society under whose wings you are at present enjoying so good a price for your Salt, for should the Society dissolve, which must be the consequence should your work and others rise and take advantage of the Institution without contributing their share of Expence towards supporting it, the Society will undoubtedly dissolve and leave every proprietor to shift for himself and whenever this shall happen Salt will fall to Ten pence & Eleven pence per Bushel, the price at which it sold before the Society existed. Every proprietor can calculate the loss he would sustain by this reduction in the price of Salt.

Thus, Sir, I have given you in a loose and hurried scrawl a short state of the Salt Business as managed by the Society of Salt proprietors on the Forth. I wish I may have expressed myself so that you may understand it. I hope I have, and it will give me very great pleasure to introduce you or any other Gentlemen connnected with Halbeath Coaliery to that Society. And if you can think of becoming a member I have no doubt of being able to prevail with the Gentlemen of that Society to second our views with regard to raising the price of Coal in the Forth. I wish you a pleasant journey South and shall be very happy to have the pleasure of seeing you at Otterston when you return to these Northern Regions. In the meantime I remain

Letter from Mr J. Pinkerton to Mr. Morrison, Otterston 27 January, 1787

I have yours of this date. In answer thereto you have below the Salt works in the Association of Salt Proprietors vizt

Col. Wemyss for Wemyss work quantity	45000	Bushels
Dr. Roebuck for Barrowstoness	45000	Do
Messrs Caddels for Grange	14000	Do
John Caddell for Cockenzie	30000	Do
Mr Veitch for Dysert	17000	Do
Newark Co. for Newark	30000	Do
Mr. Oswald for Kirkcaldie but this work is now given up was	13000	Do
Sir Jn. Henderson for St. Davids	6000	Do
Mr. Erskine for Drumochy but this work is now given up was	6000	Do
	206000	
Deduct Kirkcaldy and Drumochy	19000	
Total Salt made by the present Society	187,000	Bushels

This quantity may vary a few thousand Bushels more or less as circumstances occur.

About 3500 Bushels serve the Land sale at all the works. 115000 to 120000 is carried Coastwise. 25000 to 40000 Bushels are sold for fishcuring and Exported annually to relieve such works as may have too much on hand. The Salt sold to Land & Coastwise pays the Tax of 1d and 1½d per Bushel to defray the loss of what is sold for Fish curing and for Exportation at a low price.

The proprietors are allowed to make 3000 Bushels of Salt for each pan they have. After a work is fixed upon its number of pans, the Society is not fond of allowing a greater number afterwards, because this is throwing so much more Salt into the Market and increasing ye Tax upon the Salt sold to the Land & Coastwise. But when any particular work gives up, & more Salt is wanted to answer the demand than the remaining works can make, then each work is allowed to make an additional quantity to supply the Market.

The great Secret is to make only such a quantity of Salt as the Consumption of the Country requires and to sell that at a good price. Whereas were every person to make as much as they could without any Rule as was the Case before the present Society was formed — the Competition in the market brings down the price so low that only those works which pay little Carriage on the Coal used in making Salt can carry on in the business. Whereas such works as yours and ours where the Carriage is distant & Expensive must give up making Salt altogether.

If you wish to be informed of any other particulars relating to this business you can always command.

Source: Halbeath Colliery & Saltworks: Letter Book I, pp. 103-108.

APPENDIX V

View of the Loss Halbeath Company will Sustain In the Event of Parliament Permitting the Importation of Liverpool Salt into Scotland at the Scots Duty — By such a Measure Not only their Salt Works at Inverkeithing but also the other Salt Works in the Forth will be Annihilated, As Liverpool Salt may be Sold after being Imported at a lower price than the Manufacture of Marine Salt Costs:

The Capital Sunk in this Concern amounts to	£1415 " 8 " 6 Stg. & consists of		
Agents House & Garden	Value at	£100	
Four Salt Pans, with Pan & Salters Houses	ditto	900	
Three Salt Granarys	ditto	300	
Pan Pond with Pumps valued at £95 & utensils at £20 " 8 " 6		115 " 8 " 6	
		£1415 " 8 " 6	

1 The Annual Profits on an Average of the last five years amounts per the Co.'s Books to   £443 " 15 " 8
But as the Coals Consumed in Making the Salt (309 Tons Chews & 3424 Tons Small) is charged at 4¼d per ton less than what they are sold to Strangers for, it falls to be deducted to ascertain the Net Gain — viz 3733 Tons @ /4¼d per ton   66 " 2 " 1
And as no Salary for Management is Charged a reasonable proportion of those paid by the Co. also falls to be deducted, say   60 " 0 " 0   126 " 2 " 1

     Net Ann Gain of the Salt Works   317 " 13 " 7

2 The Annual Profits the Colliery derives from the Consumption of the above 3424 Tons Small Coals, which is at the rate of ./6d per ton, and which must in future remain Underground as a Market cannot be had for them   say   85 " 12 " 0
And by leaving these Small Coal Underground which are naturally produced from the Great and the Chews without any extra trouble to the Colliers He will be deprived of a part of his Earning, of course will insist for an equivalent (which cannot justly be denied) by increasing the price paid for Hewing the Great & Chews equal to the present price paid for Small, which is threepence half penny per ton, will on 3424 Tons amount to   49 " 18 " 8

     Colliery   135 " 10 " 8

     Total Annual Loss to be Sustained   £453 " 4 " 3

Now if the Company shall be deprived of this Annual Sum In Consequence of the above measures their eventual Loss (Capital Included) may be fairly estimated at Eight years purchase, making the Sum requisite at a Compensation therefore Three Thousand, Six Hundred & twenty five pounds, fourteen Shillings Sterling, say £3625 " 14 " 0 Stg.

Source: Halbeath Colliery and Saltworks: Miscellaneous Accounts, January 1799.

2. Management and Shipbuilding, 1890-1938: Structure and Strategy in the Shipbuilding Firm on the Clyde

Anthony Slaven

WHEN Sydney Checkland was instrumental in founding the Colquhoun Lectureship in Business History in the University of Glasgow in 1959, shipbuilding records were among the first to be listed and acquired by Peter Payne, the first holder of the lectureship. Throughout his tenure of the chair in Glasgow, Sydney Checkland has encouraged the Colquhoun Lecturers, first Peter Payne, and secondly myself, to seek to draw general lessons from the bewildering riches of the detailed company papers. This chapter is an attempt to provide some general statements on the structure of shipbuilding firms, and on the strategy of management, particularly in the market place.

I Industry Profile

It is relatively easy to establish an outline picture of the shipbuilding industry. Commenting on the pre-first world war situation, the 'Survey of the Metal Industries' described shipbuilding as '. . . a large number of firms varying greatly in size and mostly independent, of which only a few were public joint stock companies. Some were shipbuilders only, but some combined shipbuilding with either repairing, or marine engineering, or both . . . There was very little community of ownership between shipowners and shipbuilders'.[1] In general terms this remains an acceptable statement of the organisation of the industry throughout the period to 1938.

Between 1919 and 1938 no fewer than 108 companies were at some time operating as shipbuilders in Scotland.[2] In 1938 about 49 were in operation, and only 39 companies were in continuous existence throughout the period. Of these 39, only nine appear to have been public companies, six seem to have remained as proprietorship or partnership concerns, and the remaining 24 were apparently private limited companies. On the Clyde itself in 1938 there were 32 shipbuilding and marine engineering firms; six were public companies, four were proprietorships, and the remainder, 22, private limited companies.[3]

The mixture of business activities referred to in the Survey is also clear in 1938. Of the 32 establishments in the Clyde district, nine were marine engineers only, 11 shipbuilders, and 12 combined both functions.[4] The characteristic size differential among firms is also easy to establish. In the decade 1891-1900, some 38 firms on the Clyde delivered 3.8 million tons of shipping:

seven firms produced half of this while only three companies, Russell & Co, Connell & Co and Denny Bros, delivered over a quarter of the total. In 1938 the Clyde launched 443,615 tons, ranging from the 14 vessels totalling 2,500 tons delivered by Ferguson Bros to the four vessels contributing 100,080 tons from John Brown & Co at Clydebank. Three firms, John Brown's, Lithgows and Harland and Wolff, delivered half the tonnage in that year.

The variety in the industry is also reflected in the range of ship types produced and market areas served. The Shipbuilders Association recognised 73 distinct vessel categories by detailed specification, though for most purposes these can be grouped into the six broad market areas indicated in Table 1. It is clear that complete specialisation of production was rare. On the Clyde only Charles Connell & Co built exclusively in one category, though most firms had one or two areas of specialisation. Thus Lithgow was predominantly a cargo builder; John Brown's were mainly passenger liner and naval builders, and the Blythswood Co mainly tanker and general cargo builders.

These features combined to produce an industry of great variety and complexity. The mix of firms gives every shade of combination in vessel-type construction. The scale of enterprise represents a spectrum of gradations from the very large to the very small. In ownership terms, some few small companies remained independent proprietorships like William Fife and Sons of Fairlie. Some remained in family control but took on the protective cloak of private company status like Stephens of Linthouse and Lobnitz of Renfrew. Some others operated as full-blooded public companies like Fairfield Shipbuilding and Engineering Co.

The degree of independence of operation also presents complex variations. Most firms appear to have been quite independent in their operation. Some, at one stage or another, or for specific purposes, joined in informal and formal associations with other concerns. Thus John Brown's and Fairfields were linked with Cammell Laird in the Coventry Syndicate to co-ordinate foreign naval work. As another example the Stephens joined with four other Clyde builders to take control of the Steel Company of Scotland in 1920. Some few, like John Brown's at Clydebank and Beardmore's at Dalmuir were, strictly speaking, simply the shipbuilding section of much larger vertically integrated industrial empires.

Given such a kaleidoscope of circumstances, one has to recognise that an attempt to generalise on the nature of the shipbuilding firm, on the task and function of management, on the response of firms to changing conditions, may be doomed to failure. It may be that such variety reflects uniqueness, and it may be that comment on the above may have to be highly contingent, focusing on the structure, function, problem and response relationships in each firm as a highly specific and individual case. On the other hand it is arguable that, in spite of the rich variety outlined above, there are significant regularities running through the firms and the industry, regularities which

TABLE 1

Percent total of tonnage delivered by category by major firms on the Clyde 1919-1938

Firm	Total Tonnage	Cargo	Passenger	Pass/Cargo	Naval	Tankers	Special
Lithgows Ltd	1,027,867	68.4	2.6	5.8	0.0	22.4	8.3
Harland & Wolff'	731,594	39.3	9.6	27.2	0.03	21.0	2.3
John Brown & Co	723,525	11.0	55.1	11.0	17.0	3.7	2.2
Barclay Curle & Co	617,122	49.7	8.0	30.6	0.0	11.1	0.5
Alex Stephen & Son	406,928	40.2	36.7	13.1	2.4	5.6	2.0
Fairfield S. & E. Co	384,400	12.7	39.1	26.7	15.7	3.8	2.0
Scotts S. & E. Co	357,472	37.5	9.5	31.3	10.6	9.7	1.5
Wm. Hamilton & Co	333,325	61.5	3.1	9.2	0.8	25.4	0.2
R. Duncan & Co	307,960	62.8	0.0	0.2	0.0	34.9	2.0
Blythswood Co	273,309	22.9	0.0	15.6	0.0	58.7	2.7
Beardmore & Co	267,365	10.4	36.8	25.5	10.1	12.9	4.2
D. & W. Henderson	265,512	92.8	3.1	1.0	0.0	2.6	0.5
Greenock Dockyard Co	252,223	72.2	0.0	0.7	0.0	24.6	2.5
Charles Connell & Co	232,508	100.0					
Yarrow & Co	41,690	14.7	0.0	1.2	62.8	6.8	14.5

Prepared from material abstracted from the *Glasgow Herald Annual Trade Reviews 1919-1938* by Miss J. M. Verth and reproduced with her permission.

make it possible to characterise a typical or model establishment. This may be approached in terms of three sets of features:

(1) the typical relationships of the firm with the external world;
(2) the typical organisational relationships within the firm;
(3) the typical strategic horizons available to the firm.

The next section will attempt to elaborate these 'typical' features.

II The Firm in Profile

II.1 *The external linkage*

A feature of manufacturing firms is that they must seek to establish a production base in which they are secure, and from which they can compete in the market place.[5] A corollary of this is that the production base selected or developed establishes the product, or product line, manufactured by the company, and in turn this indicates clearly the area of the market in which the company has chosen to work, and in which it can most effectively employ its 'core skills'.[6] From Table 1, it can be seen that in building ships each major Clyde firm concentrated its effort in one or a few specialised areas of the market, reflecting the particular 'production base' of the firm. In general terms it seems clear that shipbuilding and marine engineering firms may be described as being typically 'Single Product' or 'Dominant Product' firms, that is firms locating themselves primarily in one line of business or being diversified only to a very small degree.[7]

In shipbuilding, this single or dominant product characteristic has encouraged the evolution of a highly specific process, a single distribution channel, through which the ship reaches its market. Ships are large capital goods, they take a considerable time to build and represent a substantial investment. The level of demand for ships is a derivative of many factors, not least the expectation of shipowners in relation to the ebb and flow of world trade and the course of freight rates. In these circumstances, while ships were occasionally built 'on spec', the normal procedure was to build in response to a specific order. The external linkage, or distribution channel, by which the order from the market place was fed into the firm, was the competitive tender. Yards were usually invited by shipping lines to tender for specific contracts, though most managements employed a system of agents to solicit orders without, if possible, entering into competition with rivals. This point of contact with the external world of the market place, and the device of competitive tendering, represent, as we shall see, one of a few key areas in which shipbuilding management was required to exercise its skills. The typical shipbuilding firm was therefore identified in the market place by a characteristic, specialised, product line, and its linkage to the market place was dependent on the skill with which its management manipulated the tendering system to obtain orders.

II.2 *The internal organisation of the firm*

(a) *Production transactions*

The task of building a ship is basically an assembly operation, the assembly of thousands of parts either purchased from suppliers or manufactured *in situ*. The large number of tasks involved, and the logical sequence of stages in construction, point to a specialisation by function as the basic work-organisation formula in a shipyard. In the period we are concerned with even the smallest yard had three major departments. The *Estimating Department* prepared the tenders on the basis of information provided by the *Costing Department* which costed each item and task separately; the third department would be the *Shipyard* itself. In larger establishments specialisation beyond the Estimating and Costing Departments was frequently grouped under the heading 'Works Department' comprising Shipyard, Engine Works, Boiler Works, Dock and Fitting Out Basin etc. Each of these major departments was itself composed of a large number of specialised sub-units. In John Brown's at Clydebank the Shipyard was functionally divided into 19 separate departments, one of which, the Ironworks, was then subdivided into six specialised categories. The Engine Works comprised 16 separate departments, and so on.[8]

Given this arrangement, the central task of management is plain. It is to co-ordinate the flow of work, to keep the progress of work in many different sub-units in balance, to allocate resources to each section to ensure that the work advances steadily to produce within given costs and within stated times the desired product. An integrated effort must therefore be produced from a large number of functionally specialised and essentially separate tasks. In a large yard with half-a-dozen or more vessels in progress, all at different stages of construction, the complexity of the management problem can be appreciated. The typical shipbuilding firm, in organising its production, elected for a system that may conveniently be described as an integrated and sequential work pattern of transactions built up from functionally specialised sub-units.

(b) *Measurement, reward, control*

To describe the managerial task and the work organisation in the above terms is one thing; to determine how such a linked and balanced production process is implemented and made to work is the next matter of concern. The implementation of this policy of production clearly requires the establishment of guidelines, incentives and sanctions. In other words the effective operation of the shipbuilding company requires a control system, broadly taken as synonymous with managerial structure implementing managerial policy. It further requires a system of reward for effort and achievement, which in turn implies some form of performance measurement of both management and workforce.

Measurement of performance

It is quite clear from the business papers of the Clyde shipbuilders that the crucial test of work performance was related primarily to cost, though in the engineering section cost criteria were rivalled by technical and quality factors. Cost and quality control dominated management at all levels within the shipbuilding firm. There could indeed be no other test of work performance at the sub-unit and department level. None of these units was in direct touch with the market place, hence measurement in relation to a desired market share, or rate of return on capital, was inappropriate. The test of the market applied only to the finished ship and hence to the firm as an entity. This formulation may be modified to take account of departmental production for direct sale. Thus shipyard engine works could and did produce equipment for sale in addition to production for installation in vessels under construction in the yard. The same may be said of boilers and much other equipment. Such transactions could be allocated to individual departments, and many yards did compile profit and loss data by department. These, however, are mainly internal accountancy procedures, and the final measurement of performance still may be said to rest with the firm as a whole, rather than with the individual departments.

Shipbuilders were clearly aware of this and sought to apply complex cost-work controls at every level in the production hierarchy; they were also constantly seeking to improve the costing procedures. Hence in 1883, James and George Thomson sent an agent, Robert Carswell, 'to the offices of the Barrow Shipbuilding Co. in order to enquire into their Commercial system, with a view to the adoption of anything . . . therein which would be an improvement on our own system'.[9] Carswell reported in some detail, concluding that 'with regard to the Barrow System generally, I think it is in many respects admirable, but it is much too costly and somewhat complicated in the process of obtaining results'. Again in 1890, the same firm, ever anxious over costs — with good reason — dispatched Messrs. Crawford & Bremner to report on the organisation and work of Harland and Wolff at Belfast. Each department was described and compared with the equivalent at Clydebank. The remarks reveal the perpetual cost-consciousness of management: 'Mr Carlyle . . . controls the place pretty much from the office and lays great stress on judging departments by the information obtained here [the Counting House], and he stated that their first consideration was to lay out their work to deliver as promised to their customers, and as the heads of departments know that whenever the costs were completed they would require to appear and explain any excess cost, the Foremen were consequently compelled never to overlook that only economical production would pass unchallenged'.[10] In their general remarks the reporters commented, 'considering the somewhat extravagant expenditure in many of the departments, compared with what it is here [Clydebank] it does appear somewhat curious how they can work so cheaply as to procure an enormous amount of freight carrying tonnage'.[11] The same considerations are evident in the very detailed documents on accounting in the works issued at Clydebank in 1935 which, under the name of the general manager, concluded with the instruction, 'The foregoing instructions relating to the system of costs, accounts etc. are to be strictly adhered to'.[12]

Rewards

The rewards offered for achievement, and as incentives in the containment of costs, are less clearly specified. It is not clear how far down the work hierarchy rewards penetrated in any systematic way. By and large the workman-craftsman, apprentice or labourer, appears to have been held to have been sufficiently rewarded by the rate for the job and the period of employment. Good workmanship was, however, clearly appreciated and could bring a personal dividend in at least two ways: either in mobility and ready acceptance by other employers and/or in advancement and promotion within the firm. While foremen took men on, employers regularly asked past employers for references. Denny Bros at Dumbarton kept volumes specifically entitled 'Certificates of Character', whose content gives considerable insight into the nature and attitudes of both workers and managers.

The other positive reward for good workmanship was upward movement in the firm. It was common practice in all yards to recruit under-foremen from the ranks of the men. In giving evidence in 1916 before the Board of Trade Committee on Shipping and Shipbuilding, Thomas Bell, managing director of John Brown & Co at Clydebank, emphasised the policy that 'our foremen are recruited from the men themselves, solely by selection'.[13] He also made it plain that an apprentice 'has very little likelihood of becoming an under-foreman or foreman if he has not attended the classes [night-classes] and we note those who have not'.[14]

The whole thrust of the policy of incentive and reward appears to place emphasis on values like 'loyalty', 'stability' and 'long service'. Most of the major shipbuilding firms considered here, Denny, Thomson, John Brown, Fairfield, Stephen, appear to have stressed these characteristics in relation to their assessment of the worth of a workman. 'Regular' workmen were approved of, and most companies had a stock of tenement property which was normally available only to men in this category.

Stability in service was encouraged also by broader means. For example, John Brown & Co advanced £2,000 at 4 per cent to Mr John Russell, 'a local Purveying Contractor, for the erection of a large Workmen's Restaurant adjacent to the Shipyard gate'.[15] At Linthouse, the Stephens employed similar devices. In 1919 they opened a boys' club with gymnasium, reading room, games room, baths etc.[16] The following year Stephens acquired ten acres of ground at Shieldhall, west of the yard, for the purpose of forming a recreation ground. They also opened a new canteen, which 'has been greatly taken advantage of and appreciated by the workmen'.[17]

Above the level of general workman the rewards became more direct, but again placed emphasis on loyalty, service and stability. Foremen and under-foremen could frequently aspire to company cottages at cheap rents. In good times foremen could expect to share in annual bonuses. The Clydebank organisation regularly voted sums for this purpose, for example 'Bonuses to foremen etc £1,000 approved',[18] and again 'bonuses of £2,450 to be paid on 7th July'.[19] In bad times the foremen had by far the best chance of being retained on the payroll when other workers were readily paid off. Thus in the depth of depression in 1932 the Clydebank Board papers in referring to maintenance on the giant Cunarder, No 534 (*Queen Mary*) reported, 'our Head Foremen, who are the only ones retained by us, are willingly working as labourers cleaning up the vessel etc'.[20] Similarly: '. . . In the Engine Works our Foremen continue to be working at men's pay, overhauling some of our principal machines, several of which were badly in need of truing-up'.[21]

The rewards to senior management were mainly financial, good service being rewarded by steady if slow advancement through the respective department to the coveted position of a major departmental head. The conditions of service of the most senior personnel like the chief draughtsman, chief naval architect, head of engine works, head of shipyard etc were normally negotiated individually and renewable at intervals, frequently every three or five years. This appears to have been the common practice in the firms on the Clyde. The most successful among these departmental heads could aspire to become directors of the company, whereupon they were usually entitled to a commission, normally from 1-1½ per cent of net profits each year. Thus in 1890 J. & G. Thomson offered a Mr Crawford the post of yard manager 'at £800 + 2½ per cent commission giving a salary of not less than £1,000 per annum'.[22] In the same company the Naval Architect and Chief Draughtsman were engaged for three years at £500 each per year, while the Estimating Naval Architect received £350 for three years.[23] Similarly at Linthouse, 'Mr Shirley B. Ralston and Mr Thomas M. Ilmoil having today been elected Directors, the emoluments of each shall be determined as follows — in addition to the fixed present salary, each shall receive an annual bonus of 1 per cent on the net profits earned at Linthouse as shown in each years balance sheet'.[24] An even more favourable arrangement was agreed with the newly appointed joint managers of the Engine Department at Clydebank in 1920. The senior of the two was to receive £2,000 per annum in monthly instalments plus commission of 1 per cent on net profits on the whole Clydebank works, with the provision that in a year when the commission was less than £1,000 it would be made up to that figure. The second appointee was to receive £1,600 in monthly instalments plus 1 per cent commission, 'and in any year when the salary plus commission are less than the equivalent of what £2,000 per annum meant in 1914, the sum payable on commission shall be increased to such total'.[25]

The rewards for senior management were clearly substantial. The carrot was there for every aspiring boy who entered the yard, for as Thomas Bell commented, 'it appears to be a very general conclusion arrived at by many employers that a manager who is well grounded in scientific studies and who has spent a number of years amongst the men, knows their feelings, habits and prejudices and can manage and govern them much better than many others who have spent a far greater time in deeply studying abstract science'.[26] Application and experience combined with faithful service were clearly the keys to advancement.

Success and good workmanship clearly attracted rewards; failure and carelessness equally clearly carried penalties. For the men this meant dismissal. In theory this sanction also applied to management, though it seems to have been exercised but rarely. Perhaps the testing of top management proved too difficult in a system in which all the measures of performance were designed as cost control limits for each detailed sub-stage in production. If there was a failure it could readily be attributed to the mistakes in some sub-unit not directly the responsibility of senior management. Certainly in the period and companies reviewed here, dismissal of senior managers appears only to have occurred on four occasions, though the researching of the company papers is by no means complete. Three of these cases involved the yard managers at the Fairfield Co: two for incurring losses on contracts in 1893 and 1914 respectively, the third in 1919 for overstepping of authority in ordering equipment.[27] The other dismissal involved the manager of the Repair Works at Linthouse following a succession of heavy losses: '. . . the position of the Repair Department has been a source of anxious consideration by the Directors as it has been recognised that the conduct of the department was not satisfactory. Since the close of the year . . . the manager of the Department has been forced to resign and it is intended to close the premises and in future conduct the business from Linthouse'.[28]

Control system

The remaining feature to consider is how the whole production process was controlled, that is to outline the general control system established by the senior management. Enough has been said to indicate that the typical shipbuilding firm was strongly hierarchical in its organisation. The cardinal feature appears to have been the maintenance and exercise of *personal* control over major policy decisions, the strategic policies. Operating or tactical decisions required to implement policy were clearly delegated to departmental heads and then increasingly subdivided and delegated downward in the functional ladder through supervisors, foremen, under-foremen etc to the shop floor. At the lower levels the guidelines controlling action (decision rules) were so detailed and precise that decision taking and action fused together to create the impression that the decision was almost automatic and unthinking.[29] The *personal* characteristic refers here to the individual or group exercising control at the top, normally the small management board. Thomas Bell was in no doubt about the necessity of this system: 'Personally I may say I am very much against developing individual works too much. It is impossible to manage them if you do. It is the personal factor, and I do not care how splendid the works are; the personal factor cannot spread itself out too much'.[30]

The evidence from the Boards of other Clyde firms reinforces this view. All important powers lay exclusively in the hands of a few individuals comprising the Board. At J. & G. Thomson's all tenders had to be brought before the Board, but if the Board could not be conveniently convened the managers and resident directors could 'act at best discretion, provided that no guarantee of importance or other conditions of grave responsibility . . . shall form part of this undertaking'.[31]

The overall management system of the Clyde shipyards can clearly be described in Burns and Stalker's terms as a 'Mechanistic System', in which authority is concentrated at the top of the organisation, work is functionally specialised and organised in sub-units, and inter-action between members of the concern is vertical, between superior and subordinate.[32]

II.3   *Strategic horizons or policy options*

We have so far concentrated on two typical sets of characteristics of ship-building companies, their single or dominant product line status and their mechanistic managerial organisation. The two are not unrelated. Given the nature of the product, the choice of a hierarchical control system, to monitor production based on the co-ordination of specialised functions in a linked sequence, represents a rational use of resources and skills. Such a structure does, however, build in certain other characteristics.

We have seen that the fundamental managerial task within the firms is to balance the allocation of resources among the needs of the various specialised departments that comprise each firm. Each sub-unit has to be considered in relation to all the others, and both bottlenecks and surplus capacity have to be avoided. The interdependence of these sub-units, the way in which resources are allocated among them, and the fact that successful completion of the ship depends on a maintenance of the balanced work flow, significantly limits the policy options open to the firm at any point in time. This may be better understood by considering the production system of the typical shipbuilding firm as a substantially 'closed system' of interdependent parts, open to the outside influences mainly at the point of market contact.

In these circumstances the major policy horizons open to management are limited to three areas: first to decisions affecting market shares; second to decisions affecting the improvement of the product; third to decisions affecting the process of production, in particular the degree of interconnection or sequence of work among the parts of the production line. Typical management perspectives therefore may be said to encompass the market share of the company, the product policy, the production process, and the balance or degree of integration among the units in the production line.

A further consequence is that these parameters may be held to strongly influence the research interest of the typical shipbuilding firm. It is clear from the company papers that detailed and systematic company-based research and development was rare. In terms of the characteristics delineated above, research would only be entertained by a company in an unassailable position in a highly specialised market. In general, company interest in research was dictated by the specific needs of particular contracts. This more modest responsibility clearly falls within a policy horizon as outlined above. Longer-term research, which did not meet an immediate contract need, or hold a quick promise of contributing to an extension of the market-share, or to improving on or economising on production, fell outwith typical management strategy and was felt to be best handled by outside bodies. When the benefits of such longer-term research were proved, the requisite technology could be secured by purchase or by licence arrangements. Thomas Bell is again specific on this issue in his evidence to the Board of Trade committee: '. . . Undoubtedly central national laboratories or testing shops must be of immense use to the country, as it appears to me that only those firms which are engaged in specialities can afford to indulge in properly organised research work'.[33]

One further feature of these shipbuilding firms should be introduced here. The mechanistic management system concentrating authority in a few hands encouraged the maintenance of a strongly paternalistic aspect to relationships in the firms. This was, of course, particularly evident in management-work-force relations and was a striking feature of firms, big and small, throughout this period.

III   The Model, or Typical Firm

It is now appropriate to summarise the firms' profile in a schematic way to establish clearly the characteristics and relationships which have been sketched out in the preceding section. The approach taken in attempting to delineate the characteristic features of the firm has been adapted and developed from the work of Bruce Scott on the stages of corporate development.[34] The outline developed here for the shipbuilding firm is depicted in Table 2.

The assumptions underlying the model are that we can generalise about company growth and managerial action because there are 'significant regu-larities in the way in which companies are organised', and that 'these regu-larities stem from the managerial requirements of a similar set of activities more than from "size" or "age" per se'.[35] The model emphasises what Scott calls 'a cluster of internal managerial characteristics',[36] which at this level of abstraction permits general statements to be made about any firm with reference to the 'ideal-type characteristic' in relation to product type and policy, market posture, management-company structure and so on. The model clearly also facilitates comparison between firms in similar general terms.[37]

The model of the shipbuilding firm, as set out in Table 2, may also be taken as a base against which it is possible to make some assessment of the condition and working arrangements of individual companies. Scott's work suggests that

TABLE 2

Ideal Type, Shipbuilding and Marine Engineering Firms

Company Relationship	Company Characteristics	Ideal Type Shipbuilder
I External Links	1 Product Line	1 Single/Dominant Product Line
	2 Market Link (distribution)	2 Direct to order: one set of distribution channels
	3 Organisation Structure	3 Specialisation based on function
	4 Product-Service Transactions	4 Integrated pattern of transactions □→□→□→ Market
II Internal Organisation	5 Research and Development	5 Contract sponsored but increasingly external by purchase or institutionalised
	6 Performance and Measurement	6 Largely impersonal based on cost and technical criteria
	7 Rewards	7 Routine, based on loyalty and service
	8 Control System	8 Personal control of strategic or policy decisions. Substantial delegation of operating decisions policed by detailed guidelines
III Strategy Horizons	9 Policy Choices	9 Focus on market shares, product and process improvement, degree of integration of sub-units.

such assessments might be possible in four ways.[38] As developed here the model permits us to address four questions concerning the product-market link, the internal work sequence; the general company structure, and the control system of the company.

First, given the model characterisitcs, we can ask if the product choice and product-market linkage developed by any company is reasonable in the context of the company resources and the prevailing industry opportunities.

Second, given the product-market relationship, is the firm's internal organisation appropriate, that is, has the firm organised its own work processes and sequence effectively in relation to its chosen market area and product-market linkage?

Third, given the existing patterns of transactions, that is the sequence and type of work within the firm, is the company organised in such a way as to permit the transactions to be undertaken effectively?

Fourth, is the control system appropriate to the best working of the company, that is are the measures, rewards and controls chosen by management appropriate to or congruent with the way in which the company has been subdivided?

In each of these areas, the model outlined in Table 2 suggests the typical arrangements. Consequently, if addressed systematically, these questions in relation to the model characteristics should offer points of reference against which individual and general company policy may be discerned and evaluated, company adjustments may be perceived, and company successes and failures may be more readily understood. As an example of how such points of reference may be employed, the marketing policy adopted by John Brown & Co at Clydebank in the inter-war period may be set against the model characteristics.

IV John Brown's and the Market

The model we have built up suggests that the market share is one of only three main areas of strategic choice open to the management of the closed system type of firm typical of the shipbuilding industry. In this situation this should be an area in which the management would be expected to be active. This is certainly the case as far as the Clydebank firm was concerned. Even as the first world war was in progress, Brown's management was seeking to stabilise the firm's market position by entering into alliances with buyers and associations with suppliers. Five such arrangements had been concluded by 1919. The first was in 1916 in which Brown's joined with Fairfields and Harland and Wolff in a ten-year arrangement to build steamers for the Canadian Pacific Railway Co.[39] In 1918 berth allocation agreements were reached with Lord Pirrie, the Orient Steam Navigation Co[40] and the Cunard Steamship Co.[41] A year later existing links in the Coventry Syndicate[42] were extended with the agreement of Fairfield and Cammel Laird.

Given the highly volatile nature of the shipping industry, this cultivation of 'builders friends' was a favoured device of shipbuilders. The prosecution of the policy and the negotiation of the links was placed in the hands of the managing director. Only heads of firms in shipbuilding and shipping appear to have been involved in setting up these relationships. It seems certain that no approach by an aggressive sales team would have been tolerated by the heads of the great shipping companies. The 'personal' approach is again highlighted.

All the links mentioned above were formally drawn up and signed by both parties, but it is significant that few penalties were involved if the shipowner did not fulfil his obligation to take up a berth. No builder could afford to offend his regular customers: the highly structured and controlled model of the shipbuilding firm as a producing unit contrasts strongly with the evident weakness of the company as a sales unit in the market place. These arrangements were an advantage in buoyant conditions permitting shipyards to plan work allocation over the length of contracts in hand, but it is apparent that shipbuilders had no power to effectively manipulate the market to maintain their share in a downswing.

In Clydebank's case such agreements provided the firm with full order books at the end of the war. But by early 1920 the signs of impending trouble began to appear. Sensing their misjudgement in rapidly expanding their liner fleet, Cunard were suggesting that the berthage reservation be cancelled 'in view of the extraordinary high costs of shipbuilding and disappointingly slow deliveries of ships'.[43] Brown's had then two Cunard liners on the stocks, and this suggestion by Cunard is indicative of how the Clydebank yard was organised, particularly in terms of the first two questions set out above. A large order book meant security of work, but it is clear that shipbuilders took on contracts and only then thought about meeting the terms. Clydebank had bulging order books in 1920, but the critical flow of work necessary to deliver the vessels was disrupted by scarcities of steel, shortfalls in labour supply, and disruptions through disagreement over wages and conditions. Looked at in terms of the model, market commitments in excess of the smooth working capacity of the internal transactions of the firm had been entered into. The question of balance had been pushed to one side and serious bottlenecks had resulted. Information from the papers of other Clyde yards suggests that this was a typical feature and a recurrent failing of management in times of boom.

In this instance, with internal work arrangements badly out of balance with product-market requirements, suspension of work was the compromise agreed by anxious owners and perplexed builders. At Clydebank work on the two Cunarders ceased early in 1921; construction was stopped on two vessels for Lord Pirrie and was carried on at half-pace on two others. Work proceeded normally on only one contract.[44] This was the beginning of two decades of generally depressed demand. Brown's fat order book gave some protection to the company until 1923, by which time the berths were emptying.

The firm's marketing strategy was then placed under a type of stress which was well known from previous recessions, but which now became the normal market environment for much of the period between the wars. The first strategy was to try to keep alive the slender threads binding the company to its 'friends' in the shipping industry. Lord Pirrie had placed seven orders with Clydebank between 1918-20, but in 1923, when asked for an order 'at whatever prices are obtainable', Pirrie could only reply to Bell that 'you can rely on me to bear you in mind if anything turns up'.[45] Pirrie died in 1924, severing the already tenuous relationship; the Cunard and Canadian Pacific agreements were terminated in 1926; Brown's now found themselves plunged into an environment of scarce orders and fierce competition. Where the previous over-ordering had placed the internal production system under stress, the now empty berths and under-utilised capacity within the firm drove the marketing strategy to a compulsion to obtain orders at almost any price.

In common with other builders, Brown's now adopted a second type of market strategy, that of varying their tender prices in direct relation to the need to secure an order. While the strategy of over-ordering marked a departure from the rational use of the production system of the firm, this latter tactic of taking orders at almost any price marked an even more absurd departure in severing the cost consequences from the capital structure requirements of the concern. Under stress to preserve their market share (defined here in yard capacity terms), Brown's management appear to have indulged in almost indiscriminate tendering in the 1920s. In the decade 1919-28, Clydebank tendered for merchant vessels on 221 occasions: 26 tenders were accepted, 23 of these being gained between 1922-28, a success rate of less than 12 per cent.

The concessions made to obtain even this order book are clear. In contrast to the position before 1921, all these contracts were taken at fixed prices; only six included any element of charges in the contract price. Without exception the vessels were to be paid for by bills over lengthy periods requiring Clydebank to secure extensive overdraft facilities from its bankers. Previously contracts had regularly been financed directly by cash instalments from the ship owners. In contracts taken before 1921 Brown's added from 7½-10 per cent on cost for profit. Of the 23 contracts taken from 1922-28, eight were delivered at a loss, twelve earned less than 3 per cent profit, and three attracted profits between 5-12 per cent. The net loss on the contracts in this period was in excess of £211,000.

It would be easy to explain this experience as due largely to the very difficult circumstances in the market place, but the relationships established in the model suggest that we should focus more closely on the marketing strategy itself and on the consequences of this strategy for the internal transactions of the firm. The two parts of the firm, the product-market relationship and the internal work organisation, were clearly not in harmony. It seems plain that in taking on work in the 1920s management ignored their own cost control

systems, entered into arrangements which could only weaken the capital structure of the establishments, and placed continuity of work as an objective
beyond any economic rationality. Continuity of work was seen as the means
of survival for the company, but work continuity on the terms undertaken at
Clydebank in the 1920s threatened rather than secured the objective of survival in the longer term.

While the 1920s were difficult years, the decade 1929-38 brought un-
precedented problems. Almost no new orders were forthcoming and competition became fiercer still. This is understandable in that between December
1930 and December 1937, 70 per cent of Britain's berth and plant capacity
remained idle.[46] At this point the old link with the Cunard Co appeared to save
Clydebank. The berths had been entirely empty for over three months in 1930
when Brown's landed the contract for the giant Cunarder, No 534, later to be
the *Queen Mary*. This represented three to four years' work when on all sides
yards were closing. In the event the relief was temporary. Work ceased on No
534 on 12 December, 1931 and was not resumed until 3 April, 1934, 28 months
later. There was no other contract to take its place, for after the losses of the
1920s the Clydebank management seem to have followed a more cautious
tendering policy in the 1930s. Bell, the managing director, was certainly convinced that contracts which covered only material and labour 'became solely a
liability instead of an asset, and the resultant losses can best be avoided by
keeping the works empty'.[47] Acordingly between 1929-38, Clydebank tendered
for merchant vessels on only 63 occasions and gained only eight merchant contracts. All included a modest addition for general charges, about 10 per cent on
average, or about half the level normal before 1921. Each contract also earned
a modest profit. The total contract price of the eight vessels was £11.8 million,
of which the two *Queens* represented £8.3 million.

Brown's marketing strategy in the 1930s delivered only eight merchant
vessels over a period of ten years to provide work for a firm with an eight-
berth capacity. How could such a large establishment survive on such a slender
workload? Partly the prestige attached to the giant Cunarders may have kept
the creditors at bay: more important, the weak thrust into the merchant
market was tolerable because of the revival of the firm's other specialism,
naval construction. Orders from the Admiralty began to revive from 1932-33.
Between 1932-38 some 17 naval orders were obtained, and those completed
before the outbreak of war earned profits of 8-12 per cent while the value of
the naval contracts represented about half the value of all construction at
Clydebank in the 1930s.

Conclusions

This brief outline has attempted to establish the main features of the market
problem confronting shipbuilders between the wars. Arrangements with ship-

owners, the sensible first line of defence, dissolved in the weak demand conditions prevailing from 1921-38. This loss of control of the link to preferential purchasers threw the shipbuilders into a situation in which the burden of large unused capacities compelled fierce and unconstructive competition for orders which were taken at prices which frequently proved ruinous to the embattled builders.

While managerial response has not been pursued in detail here, the main directions of that response have been established. In the market place the strategy was to cling to residual alliances and hope for better times, allied on occasion to indiscriminate tendering at or below cost with little thought for the cost consequences for the firm in the long run. Within the firm management strategy focused on cost cutting; a variety of means was used, including pressure on wage rates, employing more apprentices than journeymen, marginally improving working arrangements and modifying or replacing machinery. Significant rearrangements of work systems do not appear to have been considered.

The logic of the model firm suggests that the interdependence of the parts, that is functional relationships among the sub-units of the firm, is so close as to make any substantial change in the relationships unlikely. Reducing capacity would clearly have an effect on the relationships of each sub-unit, and the model-cohesion suggests that such a move would be resisted. It is certainly true that the individual firms appear to have been quite incapable of reducing their own capacity even when it was in long-term disequilibrium with the available workload. What management could not accomplish independently, the shipbuilders sought to attempt co-operatively in the interest of group survival. This was both a production and a market strategy and took the form of National Shipbuilders Security Ltd, established in 1930 to buy up and eliminate redundant capacity. Joint initiative in the market place also promoted the Shipbuilding Conference in 1928 to combat unfair contract conditions, to control tendering abuses, and to research and develop measures of assistance. The success achieved by this body was imitated in European countries, and in 1937 the International Conference was established to link the European and British Conferences in a co-operative way. A significant feature of this strategy was a preference for 'self help' in the interest of keeping the government out.

This is another story, but is briefly referred to because each of these developments can be understood as a logical ramification of the model of the shipbuilding firm outlined here. All these steps can be understood in terms of management strategy and managerial adaptation designed to preserve the integrity of the 'closed-system' company to which the managers clearly had a highly developed sense of loyalty and service. The tenacity of the mechanistic firm and its survival in spite of damaging weaknesses in management strategy is little short of astonishing, and is one further feature which may be better understood in the scheme of relationships discussed here.

E

NOTES

Note: UCS is the notation used to preface the collection of business papers of the constituent companies of the former Upper Clyde Shipbuilders.

UCS 1 represents the Clydebank (Thomson and John Brown & Co) collection.

UGD is the notation used for a University of Glasgow Deposit, as a classification of records held by the business collection in the University.

1. *Board of Trade*, 'Cttee on Industry and Trade; A Survey of the Metal Industries', 1928. Ch. IV, The Shipbuilding Industry, p. 370.

2. Totals compiled from data in the *Glasgow Herald Trade Review*, and *Directory of Shipbuilders*.

3. Compiled from *Glasgow Herald Trade Review* and *Stock Exchange Year Book*.

4. Allocation to each category compiled from *Glasgow Herald Trade Review*, 1938.

5. E. T. Penrose, *The Theory of the Growth of the Firm*, 1959, pp. 109-11.

6. See the discussion in J. C. Spender, *Programmes of Research into Business Strategy*, pp. 26-30. A Discussion Paper for the A.T.M. policy Studies Group Meeting at the City University, Gresham College, April 1976.

7. For the development of the analysis leading to this terminology see Spender, pp. 25-30.

8. UCS 1/8/47, 'Instructions to Officials relating to System of Costs, Accounts etc, J. Brown & Co. Ltd., Clydebank, 1935'.

9. UCS 1/3/1, 'James and George Thomson, Clydebank; Report on Barrow Shipbuilding Coy, 1883'.

10. UCS 1/3/5, 'Report to Messrs James & George Thomson Ltd. on the Shipbuilding and Engineering Works of Messrs Harland & Wolff Ltd., Belfast, October, 1890'.

11. *Ibid.*

12. UCS 1/8/47.

13. UCS 1/9/189, 'Draft minutes of evidence of Mr. Thomas Bell, Board of Trade Cttee on Shipping and Shipbuilding, Dec. 15th, 1916 p. 24'.

14. *Ibid.*, p. 15.

15. UCS 1/1/1, 'John Brown & Co., Clydebank. Minute Book No. 2, 29th March, 1915'.

16. UGD 4/12/2, 'Alexander Stephen & Sons Ltd; Minutes of the Ordinary General Meeting, 30th July, 1919'.

17. *Ibid.*, 19th August, 1920.

18. UCS 1/1/13, 'John Brown & Co., Clydebank; Minute Book No. 1, 17th June, 1908'.

19. UCS 1/1/1, 'John Brown & Co. Minute Book No. 2, 27th June, 1911'.

20. UCS 1/5/30, 'Clydebank Cttee of the Board, 1st April 1932'.

21. *Ibid.*, 30th September, 1932.

22. UCS 1/1/12, 'J. & G. Thomson Ltd., Minutes of Directors, 4th November, 1890'.

23. *Ibid.*, 7th January, 1896.

24. UGD 4/12/2, 'Alexander Stephen & Sons Ltd., Minutes of Directors' Meetings, 21st January, 1921'.

25. UCS 1/1/1, 'John Brown & Co; Minute Book No. 2, 29th April 1920'.

26. UCS 1/9/189, ' p 22; Bell, evidence to Cttee on Shipping and Shipbuilding, 1916'.

27. The circumstances are reported in M. S. Moss and J. R. Hume, *Workshop of the Empire*, 1977, p. 123.

28. UGD 4/12/1, 'Alexander Stephen & Sons Ltd., Minutes of Ordinary General Meeting, 6th July, 1928'.

29. See H. A. Simon, 'The Role of expectations in an adaptive or behaviouristic model', in M. J. Brown (ed.), *Expectations, Uncertainty and Business Behaviour*, 1958.

30. UCS 1/9/189, 'Bell's evidence to Cttee on Shipping and Shipbuilding, 1916, pp. 7-8.

31. UCS 1/1/12, 'J. & G. Thomson Ltd., Minutes of Directors, 17th Feb, 1891'.

32. For a clear statement of the characteristics of this management system see T. Burns & G. Stalker, 'Mechanistic and Organistic Systems of Management', in *Management of Innovation*, 1961, pp. 110-25; reprinted in M. Gilbert (ed.), *The Modern Business Enterprise*, 1972, pp. 329-46.

33. UCS 1/9/189, 'Bell's evidence to Cttee on Shipping and Shipbuilding, 1916, p. 30'.

34. Bruce R. Scott, *Stages of Corporate Development, Part I*, 1971, Harvard Business School, 4-371-294 BP998.

35. *Ibid.*, p. 1.

36. *Ibid.*, p. 5.

37. *Ibid.*, p. 6.

38. *Ibid.*, p. 21.

39. UCS 1/1/1, 'Clydebank Cttee of the Board, Minutes, 30th Nov., 1916'.

40. *Ibid.*, 1 August 1918.

41. UCS 1/21/138, 'Berth Allocation Agreement; Cunard Co. 17th April, 1918'.

42. UCS 1/9/5, 'Scheme for Syndicate Procedure, 16th May, 1919'.

43. UCS 1/5/10, 'Clydebank Cttee of the Board, 25th June, 1920'.

44. UCS 1/5/20, 'Clydebank Cttee of the Board, 4th May, 1921'.

45. UCS 1/5/22, 'Clydebank Cttee of the Board, 10th May, 1923'.

46. UCS 1/9/79, 'Memorandum on Conditions now existing in the Shipbuilding Industry. Shipbuilding Conference, December, 1938'.

47. UCS 1/5/31, 'Clydebank Cttee of the Board, 27th April, 1932'.

3. Costs and Contracts: Lessons from Clyde Shipbuilding Between the Wars

R. H. Campbell

ONE of the notable changes in the years since Sydney Checkland was appointed to his chair in Glasgow has been the massive accumulation of business records in the University Archives and elsewhere. He helped to initiate the collection through the agency of the Colquhoun lectureship in business history. Its foundation in 1959 came at a critical time, just as so many of the great business enterprises of Glasgow's past began to lose their identity in mergers or to be liquidated into an oblivion which would have been complete in many cases had their records not been rescued in time. Financial records bulk large in those which have survived and offer a special attraction to those who seek the quantitative analysis which has become increasingly popular among historians in the last twenty-five years. This study, which examines a major group of business records preserved in the west of Scotland, has two objectives. The first is a negative one: the methodological objective of showing the difficulties of using some records for quantitative investigations by examining how one series, apparently with considerable potential, is flawed by quirks in its compilation, which are evident only after detailed investigation. The second objective is positive: to show how it is still possible to use the material, faults and all, not for its most obvious direct use but indirectly to elucidate some important historical problems.

Business records provide an insight into the operation of a firm, unadulterated by the amendments or annotations of subsequent commentators, but the reliability of the records depends on the competence of their compiler and his objectives. Any source material must then be approached agnostically, perhaps quantitative and financial records particularly so. Historians can assume too readily that they have greater objectivity, though the basis of the compilation of the quantitative material can be as unreliable as any literary evidence and its quantitative exactness may merely endow the source with spurious accuracy. The reliability is always questionable because of different ways of compiling and of presenting evidence between firms and even in one firm, especially before any standard professional practices had been accepted.

The possibility of using the same financial evidence in different ways is more easily recognised through the growth of a distinction between financial and managerial accountancy. Even when the distinction was not made, when cost accountancy was hardly recognised as an independent financial exercise dependent on different techniques and principles,[1] firms kept records which were at least as useful as aids to management as indicators of overall financial success. The overall financial record shows the commercial success of a firm but the strength of the comprehensive view can also be its weakness, particularly if it includes financial returns on activities which are not in the main line of a firm's business and the success or failure of which may influence its overall performance. In addition, the time-period of one year usually covered by the accounts of a firm can be an inappropriate period in which to examine the success or otherwise of various activities. For these reasons some other form of financial record may provide a useful alternative or supplementary source of information on a firm's commercial success.

One such source of information which is available in the heavy engineering and shipbuilding industries is the financial records of the contracts for the supply of individual products, such as ships or steam locomotives. The main activities of the firms in the industries were concentrated on the production of a relatively limited number of commodities, so that the records of their contracts cover much of these specialist firms' activities. The records do not explain the estimating procedures or pricing policies of the firms. The information in the financial records of the contracts became available only long after the quotations had been made. The contracts provide an *ex post* commentary on pricing policy, which may not coincide with whatever was expected, or even planned, *ex ante*. By comparison of the total cost with the price received an indication is available of whether the contract was considered profitable or otherwise and by how much, and may cast some doubt on whether the procedure for estimating the tender price in contracts was based on satisfactory or even on consistent principles. An apparent attraction of using such material is that it enables the structure of costs to be examined in detail and the overall financial results in the main line of a company's interests to be identified and judged in isolation from whatever contribution they happened to make to the profitability of a company during a particular period of financial accounting. A converse disadvantage is that the dating of a contract, by perhaps the date of the launching of a ship or completion of the contract, is only one of several possible dates which might have been made. In one respect such a test may be even more vital to the long-term future of a firm as it provides a test of its competitive success in its main activity without the confusion caused by the introduction of other elements, a test of a firm in fields in which competitive success may have been necessary for survival.

The historian may use the details of the contracts for the purpose of testing a firm's competitiveness, but they were compiled initially with different objectives in mind. Relatively limited use was made of the information to make an assessment of the profitability and future prospects of some of the main activities of firms. The record was a working financial record, geared to the practical needs of production. In some cases the technical specification is as important as the recorded costs of implementing the technical prescription, and in others the record can be regarded as primarily a way of checking any form of financial peculation. These somewhat lowlier origins — at least in the eyes of much contemporary management — may explain why these records do not seem to have been used by higher management.

Though the financial history of the contracts provided a detailed record of costs so that at any point of time it was immediately possible to determine what costs had been attributed to it, the apparently reliable and objective nature of the record depended on the certainty with which costs could be attributed to particular contracts. In most cases that was easy. The labour and the material used could be identified and often priced with a great degree of accuracy. Difficulties arose over other costs about which the attribution to a particular contract was often a matter of guesswork. The latter were of two main types: first, the problem of the cost at which the products of one section of a firm were to be charged to another and, second, the problem of the attribution of what were considered appropriate shares of fixed or overhead charges to various sections of the enterprise.

The first problem, of inter-departmental charging, was a fertile source of dispute within firms and was of vital significance for any firm which was trying to determine the relative profitability of different lines of production, perhaps with a view to expansion or closure in particular fields, or in attempts to determine the desirability of purchasing from outside suppliers. While the attribution of costs between different departments was therefore important, its significance was usually internal and did not affect the overall costing of the contract, particularly its overall profitability. The second problem, the question of the allocation of the overheads, is very different. Detailed investigation of the contracts of different firms shows how practice varied. There can be no consistent or comprehensive practice, because overhead or fixed costs have to be covered by a firm only in the long-run. If the period being considered is long enough, or the particular contract sufficiently comprehensive of a firm's activities, the overhead costs must be covered, but many contracts did not need even to contribute to overheads, and certainly they did not need to provide whatever was regarded as a full contribution for a firm to be able to survive. The problem facing a firm was whether it had the liquid resources to meet the immediate demands to meet the cost of some extraordinary heavy expenditure rather than whether its income was adequate to cover whatever allowances were considered appropriate in a particular accounting period. The problem of ensuring adequate liquid resources at key times in a firm's history is then as important as its profit and loss on individual contracts or in some period of financial accounting, and one to which business historians should direct attention, to try to identify sources of supply of liquid funds both external and internal to the firm. It also shows the need to use the contract records, not only for what information they yield about profit and loss, but about the light they shed on a firm's cash flow. If an adequate cash flow can be ensured to cover immediate requirements, provision for other costs can be postponed, but only for a period. Contracts must be costed to permit some attribution to be made of a contribution to meeting fixed costs if the firm is to survive in the long-run and to enable its competitive performance in its main lines of production to be judged. If there is no acceptable, objectively defensible rule on how the overheads ought to be distributed, the subjective nature of the attribution will mean that the absolute costs of contracts must always be questionable, but if there is consistent practice in the attribution, which it is reasonable to expect within a firm, if hardly to be expected between firms, then the relative performance between firms would be reliable. Unfortunately there is no such consistency, certainly not between firms and not always within a firm. The earlier the records, the more the inconsistency of practice applies, because it is only in recent years that statutory requirements or more generally acceptable rules of professional practice in management as well as in financial accountancy have forced, or encouraged, the adoption of common practices.

The variety of practice is evident in the four shipbuilding firms of the Fairfield Shipbuilding and Engineering Company, John Brown Shipbuilding and Engineering Company, Alexander Stephen and Sons, and William Denny and Brothers.[2]

Fairfield's contract records included a sum for 'charges' or overheads. It was determined differently at different times but was always substantial, making any defence of the practice of one period over that of another very difficult to justify. In the later years of the nineteenth century contract records included an allowance for 'charges' of ten per cent of the direct costs of wages and of materials used in the construction of the hull and 20 per cent of the same costs of the machinery. From vessels completed in 1899 until 1925 the fixed proportion gave way to a variable but roughly similar proportion of around 11 to 12 per cent of the direct costs of both hull and machinery. For vessels completed between 1925 and 1936 the allowance was fixed once again at 12.5 per cent. In the later 1930s the allowance varied even more widely than in the earlier years of the century as attempts were made to achieve a more exact attribution of all the indirect costs to a contract. Whether the share of overhead costs attributed to a contract was accurate under any of the methods followed in Fairfield's costings is impossible to determine, but it was always substantial, and less rigid methods followed in the later 1930s did not alter the proportions greatly. An attribution was made, even when doing so converted the record of the contract from a profit to a loss.

The consequence of Stephen's practice was similar though not because it followed an automatic allocation of a fixed sum to cover overheads as with Fairfield's. The amounts were calculated individually for each contract and, described as 'establishment charges', they were then expressed in the records as a percentage of wages, including foremen's wages, which were separately stated in much of the 1920s. The proportion of wages costs was not being used

— as was the proportion of wages and material costs in Fairfield's until the mid-1930s — to determine the allowance which should be made. It was calculated after the allowance had been made and varied substantially, from below 30 per cent to over 80 per cent, but was generally about one-third. Though the method of calculating the allowance differed, when expressed as a proportion of total costs the different practices of Fairfield's and Stephen's had similar outcomes overall.

Denny's and Brown's followed practices which intended results similar to Fairfield's and Stephen's respectively, but trading conditions brought differences in practice which placed Denny's and Brown's in one group and Fairfield's and Stephen's in another. Brown's, like Stephen's, calculated contributions to overheads on an individual basis, but the contribution fluctuated almost wildy, so that apparent accuracy of the final outcome of the contract can be misleading. Sometimes no allocation was made at all and in others the amount was a round one, sometimes added after the first costing of the contract had been completed. Denny's procedure was even more rigid than Fairfield's, with a precise formula to determine the allocation. Until the end of the 1920s the costing of each contract assumed that a contribution was made to overhead charges equal to 15 per cent of the prime costs of wages and materials. From the late 1920s until the mid-1930s the proportions were slightly over 17 per cent of the hull and 15 per cent of the machinery. The intended proportions were therefore very similar to Fairfield's. Also, as in the case of Fairfield's, Denny's adopted a more elaborate system from the mid-1930s, though in Denny's case the procedure was still based on a contribution to overheads of a fixed proportion of prime costs, of 50 per cent of the direct labour costs incurred on both hull and machinery, though the proportion based on the hull was later reduced to 45 per cent. But within this apparently fixed and rigid formula for dealing with the insoluble problems of allocating overhead charges in the costing of contracts, Denny's presented the record in two ways which can give the appearance of their records of contracts being less unsuccessful than they were. First, a loss was recorded generally only when the price received was inadequate to cover even prime costs; in such cases a full allocation of overheads to the contract in accordance with the formula generally applied would have led to an even greater loss. Second, when prime costs were covered, but when the surplus still left in the contract price received was inadequate to provide the full allocation towards overheads in accordance with the general formula, a loss of whatever would have been necessary to achieve that allocation was not recorded, but merely a nil profit. Taking both points together: in most cases a recorded loss meant that even prime costs were not covered in those contracts and one of nil profits meant only some but not a full allocation to overheads according to the formula. On these principles, of the 161 contracts recorded 116 gave a profit, 34 had a nil profit and 11 a loss.

Denny's contract records can give an impression of more profitable contracts than the strict application of the firm's formula required, but they came nearer to Brown's than to that of the apparently more similar practice of Fairfield's, when they moved to still more optimistic ways of recording the costing of their contracts. In 13 contracts profits were recorded, though none had a full allocation of overhead charges as required by Denny's formula. Of the 13, ten could have met the allocation though the profits on them would have been reduced correspondingly, but three could not and should have been classified on the normal basis as having nil profit, so changing the distribution of Denny's contracts to 113 with profits, 37 with nil profits and eleven losses. These may seem only minor alterations. More significant is the change in the distribution which follows the recording of the full attribution of overheads. Then ten of the remaining 113 profitable contracts still retain a profit but at a reduced level, the 37 with nil profit join the eleven losses (on each of which the loss is increased), giving a total of 48 losses out of 161 contracts instead of the eleven so recorded. The method of presentation may be justified, even the deviations from it on the legitimate assumption that it is not necessary for every contract to contribute to the covering of overheads for the firm to be able to continue, even successfully and profitably overall, but the presentation and the deviations shows the need to use such records with care and with qualification.

The four firms examined planned to enter some contribution to overheads in the financial record of a contract, but on occasions some made no entry at all. The best price obtainable was taken so long as it covered prime costs. It is also evident that even those which provided for an attribution to overheads in the costing of their contracts did not maintain consistent practices and that the presentation could lead to a less pessimistic way of recording the information. No one method can be easily defended against another, but the implementation of all was influenced by trading conditions. A method which did not attribute overhead costs by a fixed formula would seem to be more susceptible to such pragmatic alterations, because of the ease with which a contribution from one contract could more easily be inserted or removed. But the experience of Denny's shows that even a formula did not guarantee the full attribution of overheads when trading conditions were adverse. The existence of different methods of dealing with the attribution of overheads may seem to rule out comparisons of contract costs between different firms, and inconsistencies in practice within a firm may seem to rule out much analysis of them within the company. Certainly any use of the material must be made with care but, after taking account of the peculiarities of dealing with overheads, some useful indicators, though not precise quantitative assertions, about the state of shipbuilding are possible.

It is useful to begin by comparing Fairfield's with Brown's and Denny's with Stephen's. The first pair had comparable interests with their specialisation in the building of large passenger liners and of warships, for which demand was

virtually non-existent in the 1920s and grew only slowly in the 1930s. Details
of 61 contracts can be examined for Fairfield's, of which 44 recorded a profit
and 17 a loss. Their incidence varied. From 1922 to 1924 Fairfield's recorded
the profitable completion of contracts for six ships and for six engines; from
1925 to 1934 contracts for 17 ships and one engine were profitable and those
for 14 ships were not; from 1935 to 1938, 14 ships recorded profits and three
losses. Superficially the performance of Brown's, its most comparable rival,
was similar. It is possible to use financial information on 59 contracts, on 41 of
which a profit was recorded and a loss on 18. Four of the contracts with losses
and two with a profit were for engines. As with Fairfield's, the losses were concentrated, but in two periods: the first — of eleven — was also in the late
1920s; the second — of the remaining seven — from 1936. The emergence of
losses in the late 1930s is a significant difference from the experience of Fairfield's, but the difference becomes greater and even more to Brown's detriment
when the comparison is made between the two firms in the light of knowledge
of their different practices in dealing with overheads. Fairfield's formula and
Brown's specific method are each defensible, but Brown's variable allocations
meant that many of their apparently profitable contracts were so because of
the deduction or elimination of an attribution for overheads in the costings.
Information on the attribution of overheads is available on 58 of 59 contracts
examined. Of these an attribution of over 10 per cent of the total cost was
made in 17 cases, four of which were for one engine contract and for three
ships launched by 1924, and the remaining 13 fell in launches from 1934. In the
other 41 contracts 20 had no allocation for overheads at all. The introduction
of such conditions shows the unreliability of assuming that Brown's were
building ships as profitably as Fairfield's, though the costing of the contracts at
face value might seem to indicate so.

   The other pair of shipbuilders, Stephen's and Denny's, provide a contrast in
practice. Stephen's, like Brown's, recorded sums as charges which varied
according to the ship; Denny's, like Fairfield's, worked according to a formula.
But, unlike Brown's, Stephen's continued to make substantial attributions to
overheads even when trading conditions were adverse, while Denny's, unlike
Fairfield's, did not follow the formula for attributing overheads rigidly when
conditions did not seem to warrant doing so. The consequences of these
policies are evident in their contract costs. Full details of the costings of only 42
contracts of Stephen's can be analysed between 1923 and 1935, but information on the profitability of another 17 to 1938 may be examined, giving a total
of 59. Of these, 33 were recorded as making a loss and 26 as making a profit.
By contrast, Denny's experiences seemed much more favourable. As has
already been pointed out, Denny's records enable a total of 161 contracts to be
examined, the greater number than in the other firms reflecting the smaller size
of many of the vessels covered by its contracts, not the warships and the
passenger ships of Fairfield's and Brown's or some of the major cargo ships of
Stephen's. Sixty of the Denny contracts were for the Irrawaddy Flotilla

Company, which used a small type of vessel, and another large group were passenger ferries and well-known vessels which were to ply on the Firth of Clyde such as the *Glen Sannox*, the *Duchess of Montrose*, the *Queen Mary*, the *Caledonia*, the *Wee Cumbrae* and the *Countess of Breadalbane*. Denny's recorded only eleven losses, apparently a much better performance than Stephen's, indeed apparently the best performance of all four firms. Once again the influence of the policies of costing overheads must be introduced. Stephen's always made a major attribution of overhead costs on the costing of their contracts. Of the 42 on which full information on costings is available, only ten had less than 10 per cent of total costs attributed to overheads, and of those, apart from two, which had nothing attributed, the proportion was over seven per cent. Stephen's substantial allocation was then one factor which led to an apparently less successful record. By contrast, Denny's eleven losses should be increased to 48 by also adding all those contracts on which the price earned failed to cover the standard attribution required by the firm's formula and to ensure a practice of dealing with overheads as consistent as Stephen's. Then the apparent contrast between Denny's and Stephen's is less marked. It is also interesting that of the eleven contracts recorded as losses by Denny's, only one of which (in 1929) covered its prime costs, nine were of ships launched between 1924 and 1927. Denny's experienced their least profitable contracts in the mid- to late 1920s, sharing the experience of Fairfield's and Brown's.

Because of the complexities and inconsistencies, perhaps even the un-reliability, of the accounting record, of the costing of contracts, it is easy for historians to dismiss them as unreliable, without realising that doing so involves the elimination of a large group of records used by contemporaries, some parts of which are cited by historians without adequate qualification of the weakness of the records. Historians may deplore how the peculiarities of compilation limit the use they may make of the records, but the way the records of contracts were compiled and adjusted provides an insight into the ship-builders' approach to business problems. It is necessary to approach the records, not to see what use historians may make of them for a variety of purposes, but to see what conclusions contemporaries may have drawn from them. The records, especially the ways of treating overheads, indicate difficult trading conditions, of which contemporaries were well aware before confirma-tion in the *ex post* records of contracts. They do not indicate an irretrievably difficult situation from which it was desirable to be extricated as quickly as possible. Even with a stricter interpretation of the allocation of overheads in Brown's and Denny's, many of the contracts can be regarded not merely as covering prime costs but as also making as reasonable a contribution to over-head charges as can be judged, a performance which compares favourably with the experience of the North British Locomotive Company.[3] The period of least satisfactory contracts was in the later 1920s. Thereafter, especially in the early 1930s, the problem was to gain contracts rather than the unprofitable nature of those which were obtained. If that is the conclusion, even after ensuring the comparability of contracts by recognition of the need to provide for some standardisation of allowances for overheads, it was even more certainly the conclusion reached by any contemporaries who examined the record of the contracts as they stood.

The provision, or often the lack of provision, for overheads in the accounts provides confirmation of that conclusion and, even more interesting, gives an insight into how contemporaries regarded the problems they faced. It was hoped that the contracts could be seen to make some contribution to covering overhead or fixed costs. Such problems could have been ignored in the costing of contracts, regarding the meeting of fixed charges as a separate issue, the incurring of which, or not, would be determined independently. Whether it was possible to do so or not would be determined by the revenue generated on the contracts. That was not the approach of the four firms being examined. While they were ready, even anxious, to make an attribution towards overheads, the variations in the provisions made in the costing of the contracts, especially in those of Brown's and Denny's, show that even those firms which recorded a contribution to overheads, if that was possible, were still willing to classify a contract as profitable even when it made little or no contribution to overheads. The overriding objective was to ensure that prime costs of labour and materials were covered. Denny's shows that objective most clearly. With one exception their presentation recorded a loss only when prime costs were not covered and no contribution to fixed costs as they calculated them was made. Only ten contracts out of a total of 161 failed to make such a contribution, and they fell in the mid-1920s. In Fairfield's, of the 17 losses in the period only three, completed in 1929 and 1930, failed to make some contribution to cover prime costs of production out of 61 contracts in total. If all the contracts recording losses are examined, it is evident that most made a major contribution to covering overhead costs, and the three which did not do so did not cause any alarm. In Stephen's, only eight out of the 25 losses on the 42 contracts on which full costings are available were sufficiently large that they did not contribute to cover prime costs fully. In the case of Brown's, 18 losses are recorded, and in ten even prime costs were not covered. One of these was in 1936 but the others were in the mid-1920s.

It is easy to designate, even to castigate, the approach as short-term, as provision for meeting fixed charges in the future had to be made if the firm was to continue to operate efficiently. Failure to do so could be interpreted as an example of running down the firm without regard to the long-term requirements of providing the resources for internal renewal or external development. These are the long-term criticisms of the historian, possessed of the retrospective knowledge of half-a-century — and indeed only too painfully aware that the firms concerned are no more — that the industry failed to maintain its international ability to compete. Contemporaries approached these problems differently. It is not reasonable to expect an immediate move to be made from a field of industrial production, even from methods of production in which the firms concerned, like many others in the west of Scotland, had built up a reputation. Their major objective was to remain in operation and to try to obtain any orders which would enable them to do so. Brown's records demonstrate this approach with clarity.[4]

The desire to remain operational may seem short-sighted to the historian, but a move from that approach is likely to have been brought about through the influence of two groups of forces. On the one hand is the gift of far-sighted perspectives of the future, which may be possessed rarely by entrepreneurs. The other, much more commonly, are factors which force the entrepreneur into alternative action. Even if the pull of the former is recognised, the absence of any push from the latter is likely to inhibit expansion into the uncertainty of new enterprises. The contract records demonstrate two ways in which the push was not present. The first was that prime costs were generally covered. The desire to remain operational was not then being transferred into pressure on liquid resources. The importance of the maintenance of liquidity in perpetuating a business in difficult trading conditions is often more vital than its overall profitability. Historians should seek to explain the cash flow of firms if they want to explain their survival, and the cash flow is perhaps a more probable determinant of entrepreneurial action than the level of profits, which is, in any case, usually determined only after a considerable interval of time. Cash flows operate much more immediately on the range of options open to those who make the operational decisions. Of course an analysis of the cash flow of a firm does not reveal such further hazards to adequate liquidity as the bankruptcy or illiquidity of customers or restraints on bank lending, but they become relevant only when there is at least the formal ability to meet prime costs as in the contract records. That was the first and major hurdle to be overcome for any firm which wanted to remain operational, and it was overcome in most contracts.

The second way in which the contract records show the absence of the push to change is that the pressure on liquid resources seems to have been most acute in the late 1920s, when most of the loss-making contracts were recorded. The period of greatest pressure was not protracted because, though the contracts may have been scarce, the improvement in the 1930s is evident, especially when rearmament and the activities of National Shipbuilders Security Ltd were evident. In the 1920s the severity of trading conditions was evident in the record of the contracts, but it was not coming after a protracted period of pressure on liquid resources. Thereafter the record of the contracts indicated a diminution of such pressure and reduced the push to consider ceasing operations or to be forced out of them. It was therefore reasonable for contemporaries to conclude from the contract records that prime costs were usually being covered and that the period of most serious pressure on their liquid resources was in the 1920s and was soon removed. There was little more to do but remain operational and to await the revival of demand, which did come. The policy of seeking contracts, if not at any cost, at least so long as they covered prime costs, was defensible policy, and was in most cases achieved successfully. The records of the contracts may not give historians all the information they would like them to yield, at least not with the degree of reliability they wish, but they do illuminate some of the actions of contemporaries which historians are often too ready to criticise. Perhaps the most important general conclusion to draw from this study is the need to examine the liquidity of firms in periods of depression. That more than profit and loss may determine the range of options which they can follow should be recognised. Above all, change may come more probably when liquidity is restricted.

One postscript to the main analysis is possible. The contract records become uncertain by the attempt to include some attribution for overhead costs and by its effects on the profitability of the contracts. When the variability of overhead costs is removed, and with it its consequences for other parts of the record, such as the overall profit and loss, the evidence becomes much more reliable. The records of direct costs are then more reliable. Within them it is possible to examine the relative contribution of the costs of labour and of raw materials. Their ratio is more consistent in the construction of hulls than in the production of the more complicated machinery in which the contribution of varied skilled labour can place additional difficulties in the way of comparisons.

Few firm conclusions can be drawn from the evidence, though it can be compared with experience elsewhere. The most obvious feature of the evidence is the steady ratio of labour to materials in the construction of the hull, both within a firm and between firms, with the only noticeable difference being between naval contracts and the rest. No link is obvious between either ratio and profitability, which is hardly surprising because of the influence of the calculation of overhead costs on profitability, providing further confirmation of the extent to which the buoyancy of the market determined the number of the contracts and their profitability.

NOTES

1. S. Pollard, *The Genesis of Modern Management* (London, 1965), chapter 6.

2. The records from which this study and the Tables are derived are as follows:

Fairfield Shipbuilding and Engineering Company. In Strathclyde Regional Archives Glasgow, Vessel Cost Book, UCS 2/71/2, and Contract Cost Book, UCS 2/74/2.

John Brown Shipbuilding and Engineering Company. In University of Glasgow Archives, Comparison of Costs and Estimates Books, UCS 1/86, supplemented from Managers' Progressive Costs Books, UCS 1/77.

Alexander Stephen and Sons. In University of Glasgow Archives, Final Costs Books, UCS 3/23/4 and 5.

William Denny and Brothers. In University of Glasgow Archives, UGD 3/21/1 and 2.

3. R. H. Campbell, 'The North British Locomotive Company between the Wars', *Business History*, XX, 2, July 1978, 217.

4. R. H. Campbell, *The Rise and Fall of Scottish Industry, 1707-1939* (Edinburgh, 1980), 166; A. Slaven, 'A Shipyard in Depression: John Browns of Clydebank 1919-38', *Business History*, XIX, 2, July 1977, 197.

Costs and Contracts

TABLE 1. *Fairfield Shipbuilding and Engineering Company*
(in this and the following Tables an asterisk indicates a naval vessel)

| Ship | Date | Total Costs (% of total costs) | | | | | | | | | | Total cost | Price received | Profit | Loss | % Wages of Materials | % of Hull |
		Wages	%	Materials	%	Fixed charges	%	Machinery	%	Additional	%						
595	1922	401,348	30.6	740,830	56.5	169,058	12.9					1,311,236	1,449,839	138,603		54.2	31.0
596	1922	280,530	30.0	527,220	56.4	127,705	13.6					935,355	1,043,848	108,493		53.2	30.2
597	1920	88,963	40.5	106,287	48.4	24,417	11.1					219,667	259,019	39,352		83.7	40.4
600	1925	289,447	26.0	695,257	62.5	128,152	11.5					1,112,856	1,358,696	245,840		41.6	26.7
601	1925	179,431	26.1	429,672	62.6	77,353	11.3					686,456	812,305	125,849		41.8	26.8
602	1921	70,517	33.1	119,352	56.1	22,980	10.8					212,851	251,104	38,253		59.1	32.1
603	1925	305,064	31.1	530,383	54.1	144,131	14.8					979,578	980,432	855		57.5	31.4
605E	1920	3,915	21.3	12,272	66.8	2,184	11.9					18,371	24,250	5,879		31.9	—
606E	1920	3,915	21.3	12,272	66.8	2,183	11.9					18,370	24,250	5,880		31.9	—
609	1921	71,531	30.9	132,591	57.4	27,021	11.7					231,143	258,206	27,063		53.9	30.2
611E	1923	8,377	26.7	18,020	57.5	4,957	15.8					31,354	35,000	3,646		46.5	—
612E	1923	7,644	29.4	12,047	46.4	6,283	24.2					25,974	30,500	4,526		63.5	—
613E	1923	7,438	28.9	12,047	46.8	6,264	24.3					25,749	30,500	4,751		61.7	—
614E	1923	7,304	28.5	12,046	47.1	6,245	24.4					25,595	30,500	4,905		60.6	—
616*	1924	319,396	34.5	504,958	54.4	103,043	11.1					927,397	990,065	62,671		63.3	39.8
617	1925	109,316	34.9	168,738	54.0	34,757	11.1					312,811	283,336		29,475	64.8	35.4
618	1926	42,488	36.6	60,712	52.3	12,900	11.1					116,102	109,000		7,102	70.0	36.7
619	1926	123,184	29.8	343,660	59.1	45,857	11.1					412,701	404,093		8,608	35.8	32.0
620	1927	123,679	30.9	231,934	58.0	44,451	11.1					400,064	379,394		2,170	53.3	33.6
622	1927	106,348	34.7	166,357	54.2	34,087	11.1					306,792	305,420		1,372	63.9	37.8
623	1926	137,439	37.0	193,192	51.9	41,328	11.1					371,959	416,968	45,009		71.1	45.3
625	1928	94,433	29.7	188,481	59.2	35,365	11.1					318,279	344,611	26,332		50.1	33.5
626	1928	82,896	27.6	183,890	61.3	33,348	11.1					300,134	344,674	44,540		45.1	33.0
628	1930	322,925	34.6	506,200	54.3	103,641	11.1					932,766	1,143,492	210,726		63.8	41.8
629	1928	93,784	32.0	166,959	56.9	32,593	11.1					293,336	301,384	8,048		56.2	35.6
630	1929	134,011	31.8	240,117	57.1	46,767	11.1					420,895	409,526		11,369	55.8	34.2

Table 1 (continued)

Ship	Date	Total Costs (% of total costs)										Total cost	Price received	Profit	Loss	% Wages of	
		Wages	%	Materials	%	Fixed charges	%	Mach-inery	%	Addi-tional	%					Mat-erials	of Hull
631	1928	83,418	88.9		50.0	10,427	11.1					93,845	85,153		8,692	n/a	32.7
632	1929	53,141	38.9	68,183	50.0	15,164	11.1					136,488	122,614		23,874	77.9	39.5
633	1929	88,499	53.1	131,476	53.1	27,497	11.1					247,472	236,943		10,529	67.3	42.1
634	1930	422,075	27.7	930,967	61.2	169,130	11.1					1,522,172	1,268,647		253,525	45.3	28.1
635	1929	17,504	44.4	17,523	44.5	4,379	11.1					39,406	39,990	10.4		99.9	44.3
636	1929	11,146	36.7	15,839	52.2	3,373	11.1					30,358	29,130		1,228	70.4	33.3
637	1929	51,716	36.3	74,807	52.6	15,816	11.1					142,339	161,798	19,459		69.1	36.2
638	1930	82,384	34.8	124,756	52.6	25,892	10.9			4,000	1.7	237,032	209,540		27,492	66.0	34.6
639	1931	76,836	33.7	122,174	53.6	24,896	10.9			4,000	1.8	227,906	209,480		18,420	62.9	35.0
640	1931	127,474	31.5	232,704	57.4	45,023	11.1					405,201	426,699	21,498		54.8	34.2
641	1930	23,148	36.9	29,952	47.7	6,638	10.6			3,000	4.8	62,738	62,000		728	77.3	36.5
642	1930	20,978	35.2	29,285	49.2	6,283	10.6			3,000	5.0	59,546	62,000	2,848		71.6	36.2
643	1931	32,192	36.0	43,333	48.5	9,440	10.6			4,400	4.9	89,365	100,000	10,635		74.3	21.1
644*	1931	17,683	36.6	22,668	46.9	5,044	10.4			2,950	6.1	48,345	52,590	4,245		78.0	35.6
645* / 646*	1933	128,100	30.9	218,514	52.7	43,327	10.4			25,000	6.0	414,941	467,981	53,040		58.6	38.5
647E*	1934	39,963	27.4	83,584	57.4	15,443	10.6			6,663	4.6	145,653	162,898	17,245		47.8	—
648*	1935	160,722	31.2	250,383	48.7	51,378	10.0			52,000	10.1	514,483	586,308	71,815		64.2	32.5
649	1934	16,654	37.3	19,934	44.7	4,573	10.2			3,459	7.8	44,620	46,552	1,932		83.5	33.1
650*	1935	35,899	40.8	34,217	38.9	8,764	10.0			9,100	10.3	87,980	88,060	80		104.9	40.3
651*	1936	78,242	34.4	109,065	47.9	33,739	14.8			6,545	2.9	227,591	260,781	14.3		71.7	39.7
652*	1936	62,296	30.6	104,734	51.4	29,539	14.5			7,175	3.5	203,744	353,316	49,572		59.5	36.9
653	1935	132,082	31.6	229,573	55.0	51,845	12.4			3,960	1.0	417,460	409,455		8,005	44.1	32.2
654	1935	13,117	36.3	16,132	44.7	3,656	10.1			3,198	8.9	36,103	35,543		560	81.3	31.1
Dock gates 655	1935	1,464	35.5	2,224	53.8	441	10.7					4,129	4,902	773		65.8	35.5
656	1936	20,233	35.2	23,275	40.5	9,162	16.0			4,774	8.3	57,444	52,186		5,258	86.9	29.2
657	1936	6,194	30.5	11,411	56.1	2,609	12.8			110	0.6	20,324	22,200	1,876		54.3	38.7

F

Table 1 (continued)

| | | | | | Total Costs (% of total costs) | | | | | | | | | | | | % Wages of | |
Ship	Date	Wages	%	Materials	%	Fixed charges	%	Mach-inery	%	Addi-tional	%	Total cost	Price received	Profit	Loss	Mat-erials	of Hull
658*	1938	329,165	33.8	461,907	47.4	144,202	14.8			38,700	4.0	973,974	1,156,246	182,272		71.3	37.2
659*	1938	114,857	35.0	153,825	46.9	51,638	15.7			7,685	2.4	328,005	359,729	31,724		74.7	38.9
660*	1938	96,420	32.8	146,727	49.9	43,002	14.7			7,685	2.6	293,834	352,750	58,916		65.7	37.3
661	1937	142,673	30.7	242,280	52.2	79,296	17.1					464,254	488,344	24,090		58.9	30.7
662	1937	21,989	35.2	26,305	42.1	9,883	15.8			4,323	6.9	62,500	65,303	2,803		83.6	32.2
663	1937	17,729	31.8	25,911	46.5	7,846	14.1			4,290	7.6	55,776	63,060	7,284		68.4	30.8
664	1938	128,447	28.8	242,280	54.4	74,964	16.8					445,691	449,166	55,475		53.0	29.6
665E*	1938	189,499	28.9	368,441	56.2	94,749	14.5			3,000	0.4	655,689	689,851	34,162		51.4	—

TABLE 2. *John Brown Shipbuilding and Engineering Company*

| | | | | | Total Costs (% of total costs) | | | | | | | | | | | | % Wages of | |
Ship	Date	Wages	%	Materials	%	Fixed charges	%	Mach-inery	%	Addi-tional	%	Total cost	Price received	Profit	Loss	Mat-erials	of Hull
495	1925	244,953	30.7	496,970	62.3	56,000	7.0					797,923	903,232	105,232		49.3	30.3
496E		16,005	22.6	45,465	64.2	7,325	10.3			2,019	2.9	70,814	79,585	8,771		35.2	—
497	1923	23,435	31.6	40,751	54.9	9,433	12.7			596	0.8	74,215	76,582	2,367		57.5	31.9
498	1923	30,916	30.9	56,711	56.6	11,000	11.0			1,501	1.5	100,128	100,558	400		54.5	33.2
499	1923	32,213	33.5	55,331	57.6	7,000	7.3			1,487	1.6	96,031	100,300	4,269		58.2	35.6
500	1924	281,050	35.0	502,597	62.5	20,000	2.5					803,647	829,372	25,725		55.9	34.7
501E		39,177	41.1	56,107	58.9							95,284	71,413		23,871	69.8	—
502E		51,251	39.3	79,277	60.7							130,528	134,840	4,312		64.6	—
503	1924	21,827	32.2	36,304	53.6	9,000	13.3			605	0.9	67,736	72,173	4,437		60.1	33.8
504	1924	80,117	33.1	161,628	66.9							241,745	223,043		8,702	49.6	33.2
505	1924	80,911	33.2	162,739	66.8							243,650	223,057		20,650	49.7	33.5
506	1925	78,348	40.2	116,554	59.8							194,902	171,724		23,178	67.2	39.1

Table 2 (continued)

Ship	Date	Total Costs (% of total costs)										Total cost	Price received	Profit	Loss	% Wages of Materials	% Wages of Hull
		Wages	%	Materials	%	Fixed charges	%	Mach-inery	%	Addi-tional	%						
507	1926	67,981	39.2	104,567	60.2	61,803	11.4			1,048	0.6	173,596	160,399		13,197	65.0	37.5
508	1924	131,314	24.2	349,028	64.4					20	0.0	542,164	n/a			37.6	26.1
509	1925	41,273	33.7	81,360	66.3							122,633	123,352	719		50.7	32.6
510	1925	42,356	34.5	80,240	65.5							122,596	123,352	756		52.7	33.4
511E		12,397	31.7	26,598	67.9					160	0.4	39,155	37,250		1,905	46.6	—
512*	1927	294,464	28.6	475,478	46.1	82,000	8.0			178,505	17.3	1,030,447	1,106,953		23,494	61.9	37.7
513*	1927	305,427	32.7	467,246	50.0	11,000	1.2			150,512	16.1	934,185	1,105,464	171,279		65.4	43.2
514	1926	121,438	31.0	233,260	59.5	30,800	7.9			6,453	1.6	391,071	422,628	31,557		52.1	31.0
515	1926	120,260	31.1	233,032	60.3	26,500	6.9			6,423	1.7	386,215	427,071	40,876		51.6	30.9
516	1928	243,314	34.7	445,355	63.6					11,959	1.7	700,628	590,628		110,315	54.6	32.0
517	1929	203,607	31.2	436,471	66.9					12,225	1.9	652,303	588,615		63,688	46.6	30.7
518	1928	266,007	29.1	585,014	64.0	40,000	4.4			23,738	2.5	914,759	920,578	5,819		45.4	27.9
519	1920	125,607	35.8	165,304	47.1	40,257	11.5			19,839	5.6	351,007	n/a			76.0	38.5
520	1927	39,155	37.6	62,289	59.7	1,078	1.0			1,746	1.7	104,268	120,308	16,040		62.9	37.2
521E		9,979	25.6	25,165	64.6	3,253	8.4			546	1.4	38,943	38,400		543	39.7	—
522	1929	188,499	29.9	429,842	68.2					11,691	1.9	630,032	587,748		43,284	43.9	29.4
523	1928	240,140	26.2	601,585	65.6	58,000	6.3			17,604	1.9	917,329	924,424	7,095		39.9	26.7
524	1928	233,163	25.6	597,448	65.5	63,659	7.0			17,514	1.9	911,784	925,995	14,211		39.0	26.1
525*	1929	82,407	34.8	126,514	53.3	15,000	6.3			13,286	5.6	237,207	288,703	51,496		65.1	43.9
526*	1929	81,744	37.1	125,198	56.9	13,158	6.0					220,100	233,470	13,370		65.2	43.2
527	1929	71,596	31.4	142,948	62.7	10,000	4.4			3,350	1.5	227,894	230,300	2,406		50.1	30.0
528	1929	62,435	30.6	138,301	67.9					3,123	1.5	203,859	229,348	25,489		45.1	29.2
529	1930	60,843	30.3	137,247	68.2					3,080	1.5	201,170	223,091	21,921		44.3	29.0
530	1930	526,236	26.7	1,503,983	71.4					40,997	1.9	2,107,216					29.0
										less credit		33,283					
												2,073,933	2,128,292	54,359		37.4	24.6
531*	1930	70,203	33.3	127,016	57.8	6,000	2.8			12,931	6.1	211,150	227,414	16,264		57.5	39.5

Costs and Contracts

Table 2 (continued)

Ship	Date	Wages	%	Materials	%	Fixed charges	%	Mach-inery	%	Addi-tional	%	Total cost	Price received	Profit	Loss	% Wages of Mat-erials	of Hull
532*	1930	68,063	33.1	124,713	60.6					12,891	6.3	205,667	230,115	2,448		54.6	39.4
533	1930	45,807	38.1	72,331	60.1					2,162	1.8	120,300	137,235	16,935		63.3	37.4
536*	1933	23,161	25.6	48,840	54.0	7,664	8.5			10,863	11.9	90,528	95,116	4,588		47.4	26.3
537	1934	22,645	25.2	48,946	54.4	7,504	8.3			10,826	12.1	89,921	95,116	5,195		46.3	25.9
538*	1934	61,937	27.3	120,691	53.2	27,752	12.2			16,475	7.3	226,855	236,908	10,053		51.3	32.7
539*	1934	62,913	27.9	119,236	52.8	28,206	12.5			15,524	6.8	225,879	236,908	11,029		52.8	33.1
540*	1934	45,891	34.2	64,789	48.2	5,371	4.0			18,296	13.6	134,347	134,718	371		70.7	34.3
541	1934	86,492	31.8	155,829	57.4	29,327	10.8			94	—	271,742	283,250	11,508		55.5	31.2
542*	1936	259,718	28.7	449,716	49.7	126,121	13.9			69,788	7.7	905,343	908,317	2,974		57.8	33.2
543E*		84,603	20.8	247,855	61.0	37,173	9.1			36,838	9.1	406,469	401,477		4,992	34.1	—
544	1936	61,657	36.6	105,590	62.7					1,291	0.7	168,538	154,867		13,691	58.3	37.2
545	1936	106,379	30.9	205,294	59.6					32,543	9.5	344,216	348,369	4,053		1.8	30.9
546	1936	105,508	30.7	205,648	59.8					32,760	9.5	343,916	348,369	4,453		51.3	31.0
547*	1936	71,347	29.4	123,490	50.8	34,490	14.2			13,532	5.6	242,859	236,882		5,968	57.8	34.2
548*	1937	73,161	29.0	130,319	51.7	34,777	13.8			13,644	5.5	251,901	235,997		15,904	56.1	34.4
549*	1937	243,202	32.4	353,966	47.1	79,672	10.6			74,485	9.9	751,323	720,537		30,786	68.7	35.7
550*	1937	72,389	21.1	165,259	48.1	36,172	10.5			70,033	20.3	343,853	359,708	15,855		43.8	27.2
551*	1937	67,796	20.0	168,176	49.5	33,834	10.0			69,744	20.5	339,550	359,708	25,858		40.3	26.7
554*	1940	842,856	33.7	1,155,559	46.2	364,938	14.6			138,099	5.5	2,501,452	2,892,343	390,884		72.9	38.0
555*	1938	241,423	29.8	404,672	49.9	80,430	9.9			84,112	10.4	810,637	814,315	3,678		59.7	35.0
556*	1938	89,773	29.0	157,146	50.8	40,920	13.2			21,608	7.0	309,447	313,007	3,560		57.1	34.2
557*	1938	88,366	28.7	157,221	51.1	40,317	13.1			21,652	7.1	307,556	313,008	3,452		56.2	34.3
558*	1939	365,297	31.2	569,125	48.7	163,572	14.0			72,044	6.1	1,170,038	1,150,544		19,008	64.2	37.5
559	1939	133,784	29.4	288,322	68.5	22,985	5.1			9,213	2.0	454,304	448,420		5,341	46.4	29.8

TABLE 3. Alexander Stephen and Sons

Ship	Date	Total Costs (% of total costs)										Total cost	Price received	Profit	Loss	% Wages of	
		Wages	%	Materials	%	Fixed charges	%	Mach-inery	%	Addi-tional	%					Mat-erials	of Hull
502	1923	22,785	30.3	40,439	53.8	11,886	15.9					75,110	62,500		12,610	56.3	37.2
503	1924	20,158	33.3	31,382	51.9	8,951	14.8					60,491	51,516		8,975	64.2	37.4
504	1925	192,868	29.4	383,629	58.5	78,728	12.0					655,225	681,568	26,343		50.3	32.7
505	1924	35,875	35.7	51,986	51.7	12,602	12.6					100,463	90,828		9,635	69.0	40.2
506	1925	28,540	30.9	53,206	57.7	10,552	11.4					92,298	81,190		11,108	53.6	34.6
507	1925	89,363	30.6	169,045	57.9	33,514	11.5					291,922	307,000	15,078		52.9	35.0
508	1925	88,506	30.6	167,017	57.9	33,172	11.5					288,695	307,268	18,593		53.0	36.4
509	1925	7,881	36.3	11,330	52.2	2,500	11.5					21,711	21,159		552	69.6	41.4
510	1926	59,635	29.9	116,716	58.6	22,941	11.5					199,292	210,000	10,078		51.1	34.1
511	1926	9,202	25.4	17,620	48.5	9,475	26.1					36,297	27,546		8,751	52.2	38.6
512		4,659	30.1	6,994	45.1	3,849	24.8					15,502	12,629		2,893	71.4	41.6
513	1927	50,623	26.0	102,510	52.7	41,500	21.3					194,633	186,967		7,666	49.4	32.5
514	1927	25,697	30.6	40,030	47.6	18,285	21.8					84,012	78,000		6,012	64.2	41.3
515	1927	25,004	30.8	40,184	49.4	16,070	19.8					81,258	77,000		4,258	62.2	41.0
516	n/a																
517	1927	71,174	27.5	158,954	61.3	29,096	11.2					259,224	223,628		35,596	44.8	39.0
518	1928	84,646	32.4	141,422	54.2	34,932	13.4					261,000	224,016		36,984	59.9	37.7
519	1928	241,359	25.1	631,789	65.8	87,191	9.1					960,339	985,388	25,049		38.2	32.9
520	1928	20,294	34.3	31,334	53.0	7,511	12.7					59,139	54,207		4,932	64.8	41.2
521	1928	20,094	34.5	30,842	52.9	7,343	12.6					58,279	55,265		3,014	65.2	41.3
522	1929	43,609	33.5	72,038	55.4	14,442	11.1					130,089	121,555		8,534	60.5	43.0
523	1929	51,968	30.3	101,056	59.0	18,208	10.7					171,232	186,000	14,768		51.4	33.8
524	1930	28,441	33.0	47,073	54.6	10,708	12.4					86,222	79,040		7,182	60.4	39.4
525	1930	47,077	33.7	74,186	53.0	18,578	13.3					139,841	130,346		9,495	63.5	41.0
526	1929	7,307	35.9	10,092	49.7	2,926	14.4					20,325	21,355	30		72.4	46.0
527	1930	47,209	27.7	95,978	56.4	17,379	10.2			9,706	5.7	170,272	169,079		1,193	49.2	31.5
528	1929	50,723	28.6	106,492	60.0	20,295	11.4					177,510	187,483	9,973		47.6	33.8

Table 3 (continued)

Ship	Date	Total Costs (% of total costs)										Total cost	Price received	Profit	Loss	% Wages of	
		Wages	%	Materials	%	Fixed charges	%	Machinery	%	Additional	%					Materials	of Hull
529	1930	113,496	29.1	239,196	61.4	35,713	9.2			1,000	0.3	389,405	407,715	18,310		47.4	34.7
530	1930	111,622	29.1	236,516	61.7	34,188	8.9			1,000	0.3	383,326	401,591	18,265		47.2	34.8
531	1930	89,250	24.2	249,425	67.8	26,386	7.2			3,000	0.8	368,061	337,779		30,282	35.8	39.9
532	1931	117,087	31.9	211,135	57.4	36,378	9.7			3,000	1.0	367,600	332,667		34,933	55.5	39.4
533H	1931	5,735	37.4	7,748	50.6	1,839	12.0					15,322	19,765	4,443		74.0	41.8
534	1931	143,013	26.0	332,591	60.6	67,740	10.5			5,900	2.9	549,244	631,051	81,807		43.0	34.4
535	1931	132,354	24.8	327,328	61.3	68,474	10.9			5,900	3.0	534,056	631,537	97,481		40.4	32.9
536	1932	n/a															
537	1932	24,952	37.0	41,898	62.1					640	0.9	67,490	64,000		3,498	59.6	38.5
538	1934	20,018	34.8	36,604	63.7					958	1.5	57,580	64,110	6,530		54.7	36.4
539	1934	2,990	37.8	4,019	50.8	900	11.4					7,909	10,250	2,341		74.4	42.7
540	1934	117,802	26.8	283,901	64.5	33,250	7.6			5,133	1.1	440,086	405,330		34,756	41.5	37.4
541	1934	29,180	34.0	48,396	56.4	7,549	8.8			745	0.8	85,870	75,550		10,320	60.3	38.6
542	1934	2,747	35.3	4,127	53.0	900	11.7					7,774	11,145	3,391		66.6	40.0
543	1934	81,845	32.3	143,969	56.8	24,503	9.6			3,335	1.3	253,652	231,252		22,400	54.7	39.4
544*	1934	83,593	34.4	117,346	48.2	33,914	14.0			8,375	3.4	243,228	255,236	12,008		71.2	54.9
545*	1935											228,159	254,260	33,899			
546	1935	17,235	33.8	27,108	53.1	6,080	11.9			575	1.2	50,998	47,816		3,182	63.6	40.2
547*	1936											104,853	103,886		967		
548*	1936											98,923	102,364	3,441			
549	1936											93,986	86,791		7,195		
550	1936											85,687	74,500		11,187		
551	1936											79,896	73,120		6,776		
552*	1937	n/a															
553*	1937	n/a															
554	1937											119,584	115,859		3,725		
555	1937											16,099	18,500	2,401			

Table 3 (continued)

Ship	Date	Wages	%	Materials	%	Fixed charges	%	Mach-inery	%	Addi-tional	%	Total cost	Price received	Profit	Loss	% Wages of Mat-erials	of Hull
						Total Costs (% of total costs)										% Wages of	
556	1937											165,556	162,004		3,552		
557	1938											772,868	779,532	6,664			
558	1937											84,221	86,222	2,001			
559	1937											117,732	130,793	13,061			
560*	1939	n/a															
561	1938											194,390	187,578		6,812		
562	1938											188,751	187,578		1,173		
563	1938											99,121	100,314	1,193			
564	1938											130,253	147,092	16,839			
565	1938											126,003	145,507	19,504			

TABLE 4. *William Denny and Brothers*

Ship	Date	Wages	%	Materials	%	Fixed charges	%	Mach-inery	%	Addi-tional	%	Total cost	Price received	Profit	Loss	% Wages of Mat-erials	of Hull
						Total Costs (% of total costs)										% Wages of	
1151	1922	4,302	39.4	5,194	47.5	1,425	13.1					10,921	11,860	939		82.8	34.3
1152	1922	5,031	27.8	10,275	59.2	2,364	13.0					18,120	20,150	2,030		46.9	21.6
1153	1924	76,398	41.8	100,019	54.7	6,339	3.5					182,756	182,756	Nil		76.4	42.1
1154	1923	4,952	29.4	9,715	57.6	2,199	13.0					16,866	17,000	134		51.0	23.4
1155	1923	5,012	29.6	9,725	57.4	2,211	13.0					16,948	17,000	52		51.5	23.9
1156	1923	As 1155															
1157(H)	1924	10,904	50.2	10,799	49.8	—	—					21,703	20,366		1,337	101.0	50.2
1158	1924	24,023	41.1	34,425	58.9	—	—					58,448	47,205		11,423	69.8	58.9

Table 4 (continued)

| Ship | Date | Total Costs (% of total costs) | | | | | | | | | | Total cost | Price received | Profit | Loss | % Wages of | |
		Wages	%	Materials	%	Fixed charges	%	Machinery	%	Additional	%					Materials	of Hull
1159	1924	2,431	30.8	4,440	56.2	1,030	13.0					7,901	9,596	1,695		54.8	30.8
1160	1924	As 1159															
1161	1924	As 1159															
1162	1924	As 1159															
1163	1924	3,318	34.6	5,108	53.2	1,170	12.2					9,596	9,596	Nil		65.0	29.0
1164	1924	57,856	39.0	90,503	61.0	—	—					148,359	140,826		7,533	63.9	38.2
1165	1924	53,877	38.0	88,000	62.0	—	—					141,877	140,396		1,481	61.2	38.6
1166	1924	2,761	35.3	4,043	51.7	1,020	13.0					7,824	8,750	926		68.3	26.9
1167	1924	78,380	34.8	119,535	53.1	27,221	12.1					225,136	225,136	Nil		65.6	34.8
1168(H)	1924	3,368	20.3	11,036	66.6	2,161	13.1					16,565	19,969	3,404		30.5	20.3
1169(H)	1925	3,503	22.4	10,073	64.5	2,037	13.1					15,613	19,220	3,607		34.8	22.4
1170	1925	25,567	43.4	33,352	56.6	—	—					58,919	58,532		387	76.7	44.6
1171	1926	47,015	42.0	65,023	58.0	—	—					112,038	96,000		16,038	72.3	41.8
1172	1925	1,238		752		69		2,001				4,060	4,060	Nil			61.9
1173	1925	61,260	33.3	98,094	53.2	24,034	13.1					184,255	197,680	13,425		62.4	35.8
1174	1925	55,968	31.8	95,957	54.6	22,922	13.1					175,733	197,733	21,828		58.3	34.6
1175	1925	2,410	31.0	4,353	56.0	1,015	13.0					7,778	9,239	1,461		55.4	29.6
1176	1925	As 1175															
1177(H)	1925	1,265	28.3	2,618	58.6	583	13.1			886	0.5	4,466	4,850	384		48.3	28.3
1178	1925	As 1177															
1179	1925	As 1177															
1180	1925	2,477	34.5	3,772	52.5	938	13.0					7,187	8,250	1,063		67.7	32.0
1181	1925	As 1180															
1182	1926	18,850		21,526		272		29,000				69,648	69,648	Nil			46.4
1183	1926	4,460	29.2	8,843	57.8	1,995	13.0					15,298	17,500	2,202		50.4	26.4
1184	1926	As 1183															
1185	1926	As 1183															

Table 4 (continued)

| Ship | Date | Wages | % | Total Costs (% of total costs) | | | | | | | | Total cost | Price received | Profit | Loss | % Wages of Materials | of Hull |
				Materials	%	Fixed charges	%	Machinery	%	Additional	%						
1186	1927	2,432	32.5	4,082	54.5	977	13.0					7,491	8,840	1,309		59.6	33.9
1187	1927	As 1186															
1188	1927	2,313	31.6	4,061	55.4	956	13.0					7,330	8,840	1,510		57.0	33.9
1189	1927	As 1188															
1190	1927	5,796	35.8	9,363	57.9	1,018	6.3					16,177	16,177	Nil		61.9	36.6
1191	1927	5,796	35.7	9,428	58.1	995	6.2					16,219	16,219	Nil		61.5	36.3
1192	1927	119,761	39.3	184,770	60.7	—	—					304,531	262,823		41,708	64.8	42.0
1193	1927	88,474	40.6	129,473	59.4	—	—					217,947	216,857		1,090	68.3	43.7
1194	1928	82,855	38.2	126,259	58.2	7,762	3.6					216,876	216,876	Nil		65.6	41.8
1195	1928	80,742	37.2	124,004	57.2	12,103	5.6					216,849	216,849	Nil		65.1	40.9
1196	1927	6,290	31.8	10,931	55.2	2,582	13.0					19,803	20,391	1,588		57.5	32.1
1197	1929	As 1196												''			
1198	1929	6,326	32.2	10,773	54.8	12,564	13.0					19,663	20,322	1,659		58.7	32.6
1199	1929	As 1198												''			
1200	1927	5,512		4,312		—		3,710		284		13,818	13,254		564		56.1
1201	1927	5,768	36.6	8,627	54.8	1,348	8.6					15,743	15,743	Nil		66.9	37.3
1202	1927	5,392	35.7	7,861	52.0	1,855	12.3					15,108	15,108	Nil		68.6	83.4
1203	1928	69,252	40.2	95,866	55.6	7,269	4.2					172,387	172,387	Nil		72.2	42.7
1204	1928	5,944	31.1	10,667	55.9	2,492	13.0					19,103	20,030	927		55.7	32.1
1205	1928	6,309	32.2	10,755	54.8	2,560	13.0					19,624	20,204	580		58.7	33.7
1206	1928	85,127	37.4	115,432	50.7	27,332	11.9					227,891	227,891	Nil		73.7	38.5
1207	1928	2,568	33.6	4,078	53.4	996	13.0					7,642	8,465	823		63.0	34.8
1208	1928	As 1207												''			
1209	1928	As 1207												''			
1210	1928	As 1207												''			
1211	1928	5,281	34.1	8,198	52.9	2,022	13.0					15,501	15,796	295		64.4	35.8
1212	1928	5,231	33.7	8,262	53.3	2,024	13.0					15,517	15,847	330		63.3	34.9

Table 4 (continued)

| Ship | Date | Total Costs (% of total costs) | | | | | | | | | | Total cost | Price received | Profit | Loss | % Wages of Mat-erials | % Wages of Hull |
		Wages	%	Materials	%	Fixed charges	%	Mach-inery	%	Addi-tional	%						
1213	1928	5,121	31.7	8,916	55.3	2,105	13.0					16,142	17,616	1,474		57.4	30.6
1214	1928	As 1213												,,			
1215	1928	As 1213												,,			
1216	1928	5,519		5,801		1,730		3,617		215		16,936	17,300	364			42.3
1217	1929	47,503	39.2	66,181	54.7	6,411	5.3			1,000	0.8	121,095	121,095	Nil		71.8	40.9
1218	1929	64,318	31.9	108,500	53.8	29,023	14.3					201,841	220,225	18,382		59.3	33.9
1219	1928	1,109		1,426		379		3,957				6,871	7,800	929			38.1
1220	1928	879		1,141		303		3,285				5,608	6,166	558			37.8
1221	1928	1,414		2,112		528		4,900				8,954	9,374	420			34.9
1222	1928	3,385	39.1	4,152	47.9	1,132	13.0					8,669	10,308	1,639		81.5	39.4
1223	1929	41,651	34.9	65,282	54.6	12,531	10.5					119,464	124,940	5,476		72.5	37.3
1224	1929	2,171	37.1	2,871	49.0	814	13.9					5,856	7,005	1,149		75.6	35.9
1225	1929	As 1224												,,			
1226	1929	As 1224												,,			
1227	1929	5,786	32.8	9,394	53.3	2,455	13.9					17,635	18,204	569		61.6	33.0
1228	1929	5,583	32.7	9,141	53.4	2,372	13.9					17,096	18,002	906		61.1	32.6
1229	1929	24,087	41.6	32,546	56.2	1,292	2.2					57,925	53,968		3,957	74.0	44.0
1230	1929	2,438	31.7	4,180	54.4	1,071	13.9					7,689	8,885	1,196		58.0	32.3
1231	1929	2,367	31.3	4,141	54.8	1,051	13.9					7,559	8,885	1,326		57.1	31.5
1232	1929	As 1231															
1233	1929	56,447	35.3	86,401	54.1	17,839	11.2					159,687	170,271	10,584		65.3	36.1
1234	1929	51,280	33.5	85,552	55.9	16,158	10.6					152,990	170,200	17,210		59.9	35.5
1235	1929	1,727	33.0	2,784	53.1	726	13.9					5,237	6,888	1,651		62.0	32.8
1236	1929	As 1235												,,			
1237	1930	As 1235												,,			
1238	1930	As 1235												,,			
1239	1930	As 1235												,,			

Table 4 (continued)

Ship	Date	Total Costs (% of total costs)										Total cost	Price received	Profit	Loss	% Wages of Materials	of Hull
		Wages	%	Materials	%	Fixed charges	%	Machinery	%	Additional	%						
1240	1930	As 1235												1,651			
1241	1930	4,728	32.0	7,972	54.1	2,051	13.9					14,751	15,418	667		59.2	34.5
1242	1930	4,728	32.0	7,973	54.1	2,050	13.9					14,751	15,318	567		59.2	34.5
1243	1930	5,309	30.6	10,280	59.2	1,787	10.2					17,376	17,376	Nil		51.6	40.5
1244	1930	75,956	33.6	124,520	55.2	15,293	6.8			10,000	4.4	225,769	225,769	Nil		56.5	38.8
1245	1930	29,305	38.1	36,678	47.8	10,849	14.1					76,832	76,832	Nil		79.9	39.8
1246	1930	5,475		6,223		2,030		3,676		196		17,600	17,600	Nil			40.0
1247	1930	1,937	26.0	4,925	66.0	594	8.0					7,455	7,455	Nil		39.3	33.3
1248	1930	6,331	35.7	9,422	53.1	1,996	11.2					17,749	17,749	Nil		67.2	36.2
1249	1930	32,702	35.1	49,260	52.8	10,309	11.1			1,000	1.0	93,271	93,271	Nil		66.4	37.1
1250	1930	Error?										135,000	135,000	Nil			
1251	1930	6,699	32.9	11,619	57.1	2,042	10.0					20,360	20,360	Nil		57.7	29.7
1252	1931	53,145	30.7	97,622	56.3	17,494	10.1			5,000	2.9	173,261	179,446	6,185		61.8	33.9
1253	1930	2,712	33.0	4,373	53.1	1,149	13.9					8,234	9,680	1,446		62.0	34.1
1254	1930	1,058		620		325		2,138				4,141	4,638	497			52.8
1255	1930	889		605		286		2,054				3,834	4,638	804			49.9
1256	1931	13,510		15,367		3,780		25,609				58,266	60,945	2,652			41.4
1257	1931	47,922	33.4	79,373	55.3	14,688	10.2			1,613	1.1	143,596	161,253	17,657		60.4	34.1
1258	1932	25,783	30.9	46,824	56.2	7,832	9.4			2,886	3.5	83,325	88,225	4,900		55.1	32.2
1259	1932	49,819	31.3	80,593	50.7	26,958	16.9			1,697	1.1	159,067	169,650	10,583		61.8	33.4
1260	1932	4,835	49.9	4,863	50.1	—	—					9,698	9,458		240	99.4	35.2
1261	1933	28,666	36.8	42,197	54.1	7,086	9.1			2,500	4.4	77,949	81,792	3,843		67.9	36.7
1262	1933	22,399	39.2	27,295	47.7	4,970	8.7					57,164	61,806	4,642		82.1	42.4
1263	1934	105,260	42.5	122,232	49.4	16,001	6.5			4,075	1.6	247,598	247,598	Nil		86.1	53.4
1264	1934	98,520	39.8	122,132	49.3	23,108	9.3			4,075	1.6	247,835	247,835	Nil		80.7	49.0
1265	1933	48,175	30.5	92,443	58.4	11,000	6.9			6,683	4.2	158,301	158,301	Nil		52.1	34.4
1266	1934	20,985	44.9	21,538	46.1	779	1.6			3,468	7.4	46,770	46,770	Nil		97.4	48.4

Table 4 (continued)

Ship	Date	Wages	%	Materials	%	Fixed charges	%	Mach-inery	%	Addi-tional	%	Total cost	Price received	Profit	Loss	% Wages of Mat-erials	of Hull
				Total Costs (% of total costs)													
1267	1934	12,399	29.3	23,465	55.5	6,400	15.2					42,264	45,500	3,236		52.8	35.6
1268	1934	In 1267															
1269	1934	3,231	24.9	8,062	62.1	1,694	13.0					12,987	14,008	1,021		40.1	41.0
1270	1934	In 1269												''			
1271	1934	In 1269												''			
1272	1934	17,402	43.7	18,385	46.1	665	1.7			3,398	8.5	39,850	39,350	Nil		94.7	46.5
1273	1934	Error										45,437	46,000	563			
1274	1934	26,362	54.6	45,984	54.6	8,475	10.1			3,342	4.0	84,163	84,163	Nil		57.3	32.1
1275	1934	23,212	33.8	36,584	53.2	6,236	9.1			2,673	3.9	68,705	68,705	Nil		63.4	38.3
1276	1934	62,475	32.9	95,881	50.5	25,814	13.6			5,583	3.0	189,753	158,889	Nil		65.2	32.6
1277*		180,615	35.8	243,031	48.2	43,076	8.5			7,600	1.5	504,322	508,616	4,294		74.3	41.1
1278*		In above												''			
1279		14,352	25.4	35,059	61.9	5,987	10.6			1,214	2.1	56,612	47,632	Nil		40.9	32.6
1280		7,431	22.4	20,562	61.9	3,075	9.3			2,126	6.4	33,194	35,181	1,987		36.1	36.7
1281		1,084	31.3	1,886	54.5	471	13.7			18	0.5	3,459	3,552	93		57.4	46.0
1282*		71,064	40.2	69,611	39.3	29,242	16.5			7,026	4.0	176,943	152,005	Nil		102.1	41.3
1283		3,022	23.9	8,285	65.5	1,262	10.0			77	0.6	12,646	15,493	2,847		36.5	40.4
1284		In 1283												''			
1285		In 1283												''			
1286		5,163	35.6	7,207	49.6	2,057	14.2			93	0.6	14,520	18,479	3,959		71.6	33.2
1287		In 1286												''			
1288		In 1286															
1289		70,514	34.9	98,694	48.8	28,695	14.2			4,243	2.1	202,146	149,944	Nil		71.4	34.4
1290		2,487	34.1	3,770	51.7	997	13.7			42	0.5	7,296	8,362	1,066		66.0	32.4
1291		3,753	35.9	5,144	49.1	1,501	14.3			68	0.7	10,466	13,564	3,098		73.0	33.8
1292		In 1291												''			
1293		27,435	30.7	47,473	53.1	11,177	12.5			3,267	3.7	89,352	91,725	2,373		57.8	31.6

Table 4 (continued)

Ship	Date	Wages	%	Materials	%	Fixed charges	%	Machinery	%	Additional	%	Total cost	Price received	Profit	Loss	% Materials	% Hull
					Total Costs (% of total costs)											*% Wages of*	
1294		2,517	29.1	3,991	52.5	1,095	14.4					7,603	10,014	2,411		97.5	40.6
1295		67,433	33.1	103,149	50.6	27,812	13.6			7,584	3.7	203,978	222,332	18,354		65.6	33.3
1296		2,317	26.8	5,259	60.9	1,007	11.7			52	0.6	8,635	10,945	2,310		44.1	51.6
1297		4,567	32.9	7,486	53.9	1,832	13.2					13,885	17,000	3,115		61.0	34.3
1298	In 1297																
1299		26,333	29.0	49,859	54.9	10,774	11.9			3,795	4.2	90,761	96,636	5,875		52.8	30.2
1300*	n/a													''			
1301*	n/a													n/a			
1302*	n/a													n/a			
1303		5,976	33.5	9,152	51.3	2,380	13.3			335	1.9	17,843	19,460	1,757		65.3	28.6
1305		23,755	25.0	58,196	61.3	9,461	10.0			3,569	3.7	94,981	109,573			40.8	35.7
1305		2,629	21.9	8,314	69.4	1,047	8.7					11,990	12,118	128		31.6	30.7
1306		16,649	38.1	19,254	44.0	6,631	15.2			1,200	2.7	43,734	46,800	3,066		86.5	38.8
1307		57,840	29.4	107,972	54.8	23,037	11.7			8,155	4.1	197,004	227,093	30,089		53.6	30.1
1308		5,180	24.6	13,787	65.6	2,063	9.8					21,030	21,854	829		37.6	30.7
1309	In 1308																
1316	In 1308																
1310		7,113	34.9	10,413	51.2	2,833	13.9					20,359	20,88⁴	525		68.3	34.8
1311	In 1310													''			
1312	In 1310													''			
1313	in 1310													''			

4. Lord Beaverbrook and the Supply of Aircraft, 1940-1941

A. J. Robertson

THROUGHOUT the period from the first world war until well after the second, Lord Beaverbrook was generally close to the centre of great events in Britain. For most of that time, he stood in the front rank of newspaper ownership and management, making his *Daily Express* into the most widely-circulating newspaper in the country. He also had political ambitions, but in that sphere he operated chiefly in the role of observer or as a minor participant rather than as a major directing or controlling influence. In British political life Beaverbrook was, for the most part, a member of the supporting cast in the dramas in which men like Asquith, Lloyd George, Baldwin, Chamberlain and Churchill played the starring roles. It may be doubted if he will enjoy any enduring prominence in British history in respect of his activity in politics and government, except for the brief episode in his career which forms the subject of this study. Occupying less than one year of Beaverbrook's long working life, this bids fair to guarantee him a permanent place in the annals of the Empire on behalf of which he was such a tireless campaigner. The question is whether that place is really deserved.

The episode began on 14th May 1940, when Beaverbrook accepted office as Minister of Aircraft Production in the government then being formed by his friend Winston Churchill. It ended on 1st May 1941, when he resigned from that office.[1] The episode, therefore, covered that crucial phase of the second world war which encompassed the fall of France, the Battle of Britain, and what came to be called the Blitz. Throughout this period, the key to Britain's ability to stay in the war and avoid defeat by Germany was perceived to be air power, above all the defensive air power exercised by R.A.F. Fighter Command but also the striking power of Bomber Command which represented Britain's only direct way of carrying the war to Germany itself. The supply of aircraft (together with the supply of pilots to fly them) was absolutely crucial to the British position, and Beaverbrook was now the man politically responsible for maintaining it. For this brief period he was at the centre of the stage, capable of exerting an active and significant influence upon great events. It is now generally believed that Beaverbrook did indeed exercise just such an influence. He is placed on a par, in most modern writing on the Battle of Britain, with Churchill himself and Sir Hugh Dowding as one of the architects of victory in that struggle. It is A. J. P. Taylor's view, for instance, that by reason of his activities as Minister of Aircraft Production Beaverbrook is entitled to be numbered 'among the immortal few who won the Battle of Britain . . . At the moment of unparalleled danger, it was Beaverbrook who made survival and victory possible'.[2] Christopher Dowling, in a recent study of the battle, pinpoints Beaverbrook's contribution more exactly: 'The British, however, had the greater reserves and, *thanks to the forceful methods of Lord Beaverbrook,* the Minister of Aircraft Production, were producing more than twice as many aircraft as the Germans'.[3] And in a popular account which may be more influential than all the academic studies in preserving the image of Beaverbrook's heroic role in the public mind, Len Deighton puts precise figures on his achievement: 'In that same week when Göring thought the R.A.F. had about 300 fighters serviceable, the true figure was over 700 . . . And the energies of Lord Beaverbrook were providing Hurricanes and Spitfires in ever increasing numbers. By the end of August he would be able to report that 1,081 fighters were immediately available, and another 500 were undergoing repair'.[4] Other such comments abound among the plethora of studies inspired by the Battle of Britain (to serve a popular interest in the event which seems not to have diminished much even after forty years), but further citation is unnecessary.

I

The heroic view of Beaverbrook's part in the battle, as expressed by Taylor, Dowling, Deighton and others, rests upon a firm foundation of comment by people with whom Beaverbrook was closely associated at the time. Especially telling perhaps was the observation of Air Chief Marshal Dowding in his official dispatch published at the end of the war. 'The effect of Lord Beaverbrook's appointment,' Dowding wrote, 'can only be described as magical and thereafter the supply situation improved to such a degree that the heavy aircraft wastage which was later incurred during the Battle of Britain ceased to be the primary danger.'[5] Equally authoritative is the view expressed by Beaverbrook's chief in the government of the time, Winston Churchill. As early as 3rd June 1940 — only about three weeks after appointing his new Minister of Aircraft Production, and before the Battle of Britain had even begun — Churchill wrote to the Secretary of State for Air (whose ministry had previously discharged the responsibility now exercised by Beaverbrook's department*) that 'Lord Beaverbrook has made a surprising improvement in the supply and repair of aeroplanes, and in clearing up the muddle and scandal of the aircraft production branch'.[6] Churchill held fast to this view after the war, and paid handsome tribute to Beaverbrook's work at the Ministry of Air-

---

* The office of the Air Member for Development and Production (A.M.D.P.) in the Air Ministry supervised military aircraft production up to May 1940. It is usually referred to as the Air Ministry production branch.

craft Production (M.A.P.) in his war memoirs: 'During these weeks of intense struggle and ceaseless anxiety Lord Beaverbrook rendered signal service. At all costs the fighter squadrons must be replenished with trustworthy machines. There was no time for red tape and circumlocution, although these have their place in a well-ordered, placid system . . . This was his hour. His personal force and genius . . . swept aside many obstacles. New or repaired aeroplanes streamed to the delighted squadrons in numbers they had never known before.'[7]

Beaverbrook's heroic standing, however, was by no means universally accepted among those who saw him in action at M.A.P., though the criticisms have tended to cut no ice with recent commentators. Indeed, they have hardly been noticed, and then only to be dismissed out of hand as the carping of 'disgruntled critics'.[8] This seems rather too off-handed and facile a way of dismissing witnesses of real standing. Their testimony cannot really be passed over simply as sour grapes. One critic who actually worked in M.A.P. during its formative months was the then Air Vice-Marshal Tedder. On leaving M.A.P. to take up an active command in the Middle East in November 1940, he passed on a scathing opinion of Beaverbrook's regime to the Air Minister, Sir Archibald Sinclair. '. . . the present organisation and working of the Ministry [of Aircraft Production] are such', Tedder maintained, 'as gravely to threaten the efficiency of the Service and consequently the safety of the country.'[9] Tedder's colleague, Air Vice-Marshal Slessor — serving in mid-1940 in that section of the Air Staff with responsibility for procuring equipment for the air force — was equally unwilling to subscribe to the Beaverbrook legend. In his memoirs, he commented on the 'widespread impression that . . . the appointment of Lord Beaverbrook came in the nick of time to bring about an industrial miracle and save this country from the disastrous consequences of the inefficiency of the Air Ministry'. Slessor dismissed this impression as entirely untrue, then went on to say that '. . . one of the oldest methods of acquiring merit upon taking over a new job is to create the impression that one has inherited chaos. To describe the state of the aircraft production in June 1940 as "muddle and scandal" is a grotesque travesty'.[10] The antipathy that existed between Beaverbrook and certain senior R.A.F. officers is well-known,[11] and the views of Tedder and Slessor cannot perhaps on that account be regarded as detached or dispassionate. But then neither, where his friend Max was concerned, could Churchill. Tedder and Slessor were in positions at least as good as the Prime Minister's for coming to a well-informed appreciation of the impact on aircraft production of the new ministry on Millbank and its chief.

II

There may of course be some question as to whether a Minister of Aircraft Production could have any influence of a direct and substantial kind on the activities of the aircraft industry. Certainly, in the circumstances prevailing in the summer of 1940, the answer would be very definitely in the affirmative. Even before the outbreak of the war, the Air Ministry was already exercising a considerable measure of direct control over aircraft production. It did this, not just through being the principal source of the orders which determined what aircraft should go into quantity production, but also by actively involving itself in the creation of new large-scale factory capacity under the 'shadow' scheme initiated in 1936. The Air Ministry determined which firms should be given access to this new capacity on an agency basis, and what they should manufacture with it. The Ministry could compel its main contractors to sub-contract work to other firms when increases in production were called for that exceeded the main contractors' own capacity. It also purchased and held stocks of raw materials for aircraft manufacture.[12] Beaverbrook enjoyed all these powers at M.A.P. after May 1940 and more besides. Legislation like the Emergency Powers (Defence) Acts of 1939 and 1940 had massively increased the powers of the state in wartime over individuals, companies and whole industries.[13] A large apparatus of direct state control of industry, based on the power to commandeer basic factors of production such as factory-space, capital equipment, raw materials, and even manpower itself was rapidly erected. An actively interventionist minister like Beaverbrook could make use of these powers (on his own initiative or in concert — though in Beaverbrook's case not always in tune — with other ministers) to exert a very powerful direct influence on the scale and make-up of production.

There is little doubt that Beaverbrook did so use his powers. Indeed, even before the formal establishment of his ministry, it seems to have been he who decided, after consultation with Sir Charles Craven (the Air Council's Civil Member for Development and Production), that productive capacity should be concentrated upon that limited range of aircraft types which would con-tribute most immediately to meeting the military crisis that was then un-folding. This decision has been described as the most important single incident in the history of war production, and it was very much of Beaverbrook's own making.[14] Once he had taken up his appointment, Beaverbrook threw himself energetically into badgering and browbeating officials and the managers of air-craft firms to inspire them to greater activity. He imperiously commandeered buildings, plant and other resources for purposes connected with aircraft pro-duction — on one occasion threatening, not wholly seriously, to take over a medieval cathedral for storing planes — in a way that frequently caused clashes with other departments of state. He inveighed constantly against bureaucratic procedures of all kinds, and bypassed them whenever possible. His dynamism was undoubted, but whether even an enthusiastic inter-ventionist like Beaverbrook, with all his far-reaching powers of control and direction over the aircraft industry, could revolutionise the state of production within the space of three weeks (as Churchill claimed) may remain open for the moment.

G

III

The claims and counter-claims surrounding Beaverbrook's impact on the aircraft industry ought, one might think, to be susceptible to some kind of empirical testing, by reference for instance to the detailed production and delivery statistics relating to aircraft that have been freely available since about 1950 with the publication of the official histories of the British war economy.[15] But the assessment of Beaverbrook's achievements at M.A.P. has been conducted largely upon an anecdotal basis, augmented occasionally by conveniently isolated production figures. Little attempt has been made to present a coherent body of statistical data on aircraft production for assessment, still less to relate this to serious consideration of the development of the aircraft industry's capacity and production processes. Recent comment on Beaverbrook at M.A.P. has been more within the context of political and military than economic affairs. In this study, his achievements will be examined, rather more rigorously than they have been hitherto, more in the economic context, and as far as possible (*pace* Lord Tedder) *without* prejudice.

IV

The record of British aircraft production in the years after the Great War was not very impressive. In November 1918, the recently constituted Royal Air Force possessed large numbers of then-modern machines, and there seemed little need to place substantial orders for more in subsequent years. The basic assumption that underlay all matters of British military procurement until 1932 was that no major war was likely within the next ten years. The economic situation of much of the post-war period was also influential: governments were trying to reduce expenditure where possible, and reductions in all kinds of military expenditure seemed eminently defensible so long as the 'Ten Year Rule' held sway. Starved of military orders, British aircraft constructors received little compensation from an expansion of civil aviation, which was slow to make progress in Britain against a fast and comfortable system of rail transport. By 1930, the British aircraft industry — which had been the biggest in the world in 1918 — was in the doldrums. Employing only some 30,000 people altogether, it was a small industry based on quite a large number of small firms. These lived from hand to mouth and were sometimes driven to seek survival by the production of items unrelated to the aeroplane.[16] Aircraft production was largely a matter of handicraft methods and highly skilled labour: existing as they did on 'penny packet' orders, the firms had no need of mass-production technology. By 1935, indeed (when rearmament officially began in Britain), even the recollection of large-scale production as practised during the Kaiser's war must have been fading from the industry's collective memory. It was not a situation from which large numbers of new aircraft embodying the latest developments in design and construction[17] could readily be conjured up, no matter how generous the scale of the state's financial provision for their purchase.

Expenditure on the R.A.F. increased nearly twelve-fold between April 1934 and April 1939; and of the £208 millions that were allocated to the service in the 1939 estimates, over half was devoted to the procurement of 'warlike stores', meaning primarily aircraft and their weapons-systems.[18] With this massive injection of funds, the aircraft industry certainly expanded, but the Air Ministry — which, as we have seen, took an active part in promoting the expansion — found it extremely difficult to obtain levels of production to match its plans for the growth of the air force's front-line strength. The lack of skilled labour and adequate plant-capacity were perhaps most to blame for the shortfall, though inadequate management within aircraft firms and technical problems arising out of innovations in design and construction were also involved.[19]

In spite of these difficulties, production increased impressively in the later thirties, if not quite on the scale that the Air Staff thought it needed. Deliveries of aircraft to the R.A.F. in the first six months of 1939, for example, were more than three times greater than they had been in the first half of 1938. By mid-1939, production had caught up with the plans of the Air Ministry for the growth of the R.A.F.[20]

What the aircraft production figures do *not* indicate is that Beaverbrook's appointment as minister and the establishment of M.A.P. in mid-May 1940 generated any new, dramatic upsurge in the level of aircraft production. Figure 1 shows that there was a period of stagnation through the winter of 1939-40, and that aircraft deliveries then began to climb steeply in the spring of 1940, during the three months or so before M.A.P. was set up. This upsurge continued only for a very short time after Beaverbrook took office: deliveries fell off after July, some time before the Battle of Britain reached its climax. By December 1940, aircraft deliveries were some way *below* the level that had been achieved in the month of Beaverbrook's appointment, though they picked up again in the early part of 1941. In any event, the galvanising effect that he is reputed to have had is not clearly substantiated by the figures. Aircraft deliveries (and by implication aircraft production) certainly grew for a time under his direction, but only in continuance of a trend that was already well-established.

The strategic circumstances of the summer and early autumn of 1940 dictated that special attention be devoted to the defensive arm of the R.A.F., Dowding's Fighter Command. It had to be kept up to strength in men and material to prevent the assertion of German air superiority over southern England which might pave the way for an invasion. To Beaverbrook, this obviously meant giving priority in the allocation of plant, materials and manpower to the production of fighter aircraft. In doing so, he was continuing a policy which had already evidently been put into effect by the Air Ministry

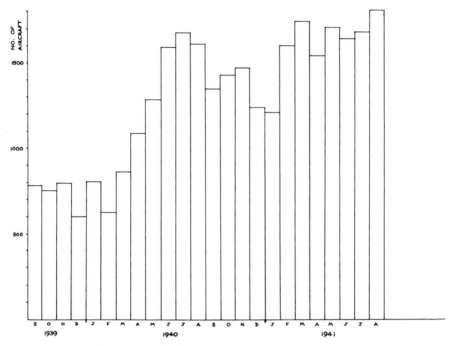

Figure 1. Total deliveries of new aircraft in U.K. (monthly).

production branch. The production of fighters had come to exceed that of bombers in February 1940 and continued to do so through March and April into May.[21] That the gap then widened probably had less to do with any heightened priority accorded to fighters by Beaverbrook than with the coming on stream in June 1940 of new industrial capacity created by the Air Ministry for the production of fighters.[22] As Figure 2 shows, deliveries of fighter aircraft had been improving markedly for some months before Beaverbrook's appointment in any case. After he took office, the rate of increase was not sustained beyond July, when fighter production reached a plateau with, if anything, a slight downward inclination to the end of 1940.

Measuring the level of activity in the aircraft industry in terms of the number of aircraft wheeled out of the factories is to employ a crude and potentially quite misleading yardstick. It puts the simplest small training-plane on the same footing as a large and complex multi-engined bomber. There exists, however, a more precise and sophisticated method of gauging aircraft production which irons out many of the problems created by the varying size and complexity of different types of aircraft. This employs a calculation based upon the weight of structures built and the number of man-hours employed in their construction. Developed by M.A.P. itself, this yardstick is still by no means perfect; but it is much more accurate and sensitive as an indicator of productive activity than a crude count of the number of disparate units manu-

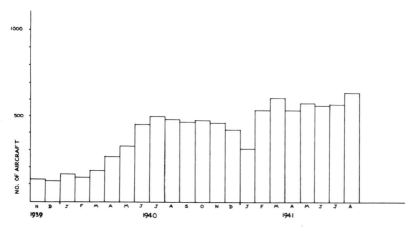

Figure 2. Fighter aircraft deliveries in U.K.

factured.[23] Applied to the British aircraft industry of 1939-40, however, this more refined method of measurement only serves to confirm the patterns exhibited by the cruder count of total numbers. Productive activity, as Figure 3 indicates, began to rise fairly steeply in the months immediately preceding the establishment of M.A.P. It reached a peak in June 1940, very early in the Beaverbrook period, and was already falling quite steeply as the Battle of Britain arrived at its climax. Again, the early months of 1941 witnessed a recovery.

None of the principal production indicators, then, seem to provide convincing evidence that Beaverbrook's direction brought about a dramatic expansion in British aircraft production from the middle of May 1940. Nor do

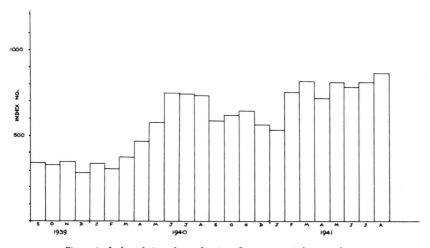

Figure 3. Index of aircraft production: Structure weight/man-hours.

they suggest, as far as the earlier months of that year were concerned, that output had been flagging at the hands of an inept Air Ministry subsidiary, as Churchill seems to have believed.

V

Whatever his effect on production itself, Lord Beaverbrook certainly made an impression on the state's machinery for administering it. Both he and Churchill regarded the existing system for supervising production through the Air Ministry's production branch as cumbersome and stultifying in its impact on the aircraft industry. Beaverbrook was appointed by his friend as the new broom which would sweep out this bureaucratic machinery, installing new men and new methods by which production would be gingered up. The Air Ministry production branch had developed by spring 1940 into an organisation much like a fully fledged ministry in size and intricacy. In the process, it had undoubtedly evolved a highly structured organisation — dominated by senior air force personnel and professional civil servants — within which committees flourished, set procedures existed for carrying out the work, and the functions of staff were clearly defined. Beaverbrook was hostile to this well-ordered way of doing things: *his* guiding maxims were 'Committees take the punch out of war' and 'Organisation is the enemy of improvisation'.[24] And he believed that production should be administered, not by servicemen and bureaucrats, but by practical men of industry with proven records of success in promoting the growth of output.[25]

There is a belief that from the very outset Beaverbrook ignored the Air Ministry production branch and started from scratch in developing M.A.P. in accordance with his own principles.[26] This does not square, however, with the official record of war production, which shows that he simply took over as a going concern the existing Air Ministry machine, lock, stock and barrel: 'at the beginning of its existence the new ministry was simply A.M.D.P.'s department carrying out its usual tasks under a new name'.[27] Beaverbrook began almost at once to introduce his own nominees — senior industrial managers like Patrick Hennessy of Ford and Trevor Westbrook of Vickers. But the established ways of doing things, carried over from the Air Ministry days, took time to break down. It was probably not until the autumn of 1940, with the departure of men such as Tedder and Air Marshal Sir Wilfred Freeman (who had been A.M.D.P. until May),[28] that the Beaverbrook set-up was established in a pure form.

With its establishment, the old clear-cut division of responsibility for supervising aircraft production was replaced by the allocation of work to senior staff by the minister himself on an *ad hoc* basis. The new regime was characterised by informality, an atmosphere of hectic activity, and above all by the autocratic attitudes of Beaverbrook himself. The break with the Air Ministry was almost complete. What is interesting about these administrative changes as far as aircraft production is concerned is that, having begun to increase markedly under the Air Ministry production branch, it continued to do so under the aegis of M.A.P. only so long as the old regime remained in the ascendant. As the influence of Beaverbrook's protégés grew, the momentum seems to have been lost.

Perhaps too much should not be read into the decline of production so soon after the establishment of M.A.P. The new ministry had to contend with problems in the high summer of 1940 and beyond which its predecessor had not had to face. First among these — or at least most obvious — was the disruption of the aircraft industry by German bombing, for which its factories were a prime target. Between the beginning of August and the end of December 1940, serious damage was caused both by raids specifically aimed at aircraft factories and by more generalised attacks like that on Coventry on 14th November (much of Coventry's engineering industry being by then involved in aircraft components).[29] The physical destruction of plant resulting from the bombing of aircraft factories does not seem to have been very great. Even badly damaged factories could evidently be restored to something like normal levels of output in a remarkably short time. A much bigger problem seems to have been the loss of working time occasioned by air-raids and the declining efficiency of a workforce regularly subjected to loss of sleep or even more severe disturbances to their personal lives.[30] One way or another, though, bombing was quite clearly a factor of some significance in the decline of British aircraft production from July 1940 to January 1941.

Before the supporters of the Beaverbrook legend take too much comfort from the direct effects of German bombing, it has to be said that Beaverbrook's reaction to the bombing itself had a deleterious effect on production levels in the aircraft industry. He adopted in the autumn of 1940 a general policy of dispersal for large units of production which occupied key positions in the industry and which, by reason of their size and the concentration of productive capacity they represented, made tempting targets for attack. But dispersing these large units meant sacrificing economies of scale, foregoing production while equipment was being moved from one site to another, and stretching scarce resources of managerial talent and skilled labour even thinner than before — all to the detriment of the volume of output. In the long run, the negative effects of dispersal could be overcome: indeed, once the immediate threat of air attack receded in the summer of 1941 (with the diversion of German strength to the east), both the dispersed plant and the original centralised factories could operate side by side. Dispersal, therefore, had the unenvisaged long-term effect of adding significantly to the aircraft industry's total capacity, though not in the most efficient manner. But as the official history of war production noted, 'Its "short term" effects . . . were most unsettling, and there is no doubt that for a time output suffered to a far greater extent than the public realised'.[31] Beaverbrook was aware of this and acknowledged the damage to production in a report to the War Cabinet in October 1940.[32] He seems to have regarded the increased security of production that dispersal assured as worth the short-term cost in volume of output, and in this his judgment seems to have been vindicated by experience during later attacks on Birmingham in the spring of 1941.[33] But there is no getting away from the fact that, however sensible the policy of dispersal may have been as a response to the danger of attack, its immediate effects were not comparable with the urgent need to maximise production.

VI

Dispersal stemmed from Beaverbrook's own initiative, and was one of several policies which enjoyed his enthusiastic backing. Another was the concentration of resources upon the manufacture of what are sometimes described as the 'priority types' — three bombers (Wellington, Blenheim and Whitley V) and two fighters (Hurricane and Spitfire) — the origins of which have already been outlined.[34] Reservations can certainly be stated about the quality of some of these types of aircraft. The Blenheim and Whitley bombers had both shown up unfavourably on active operations before the summer of 1940, and it is recorded that a large proportion of the Whitleys built during the war never left the aircraft storage units. The tragedy, one critic of wartime aircraft production policy observed, lay with those that did.[35] Beaverbrook may be open to criticism for permitting the continued, indeed the increased, production of obsolescent and operationally dubious types of plane which absorbed substantial quantities of skilled labour, light alloys, machine tools and aircraft engines (all of which were in chronically short supply). On the other hand, the deficiences of these aircraft could hardly be laid at his door. He had to make the best of what was actually available by way of types currently in production, and plant could not easily be switched from the manufacture of one aircraft to that of some other. Concentrating resources on a small range of designs — the best front-line aircraft, for all their faults, that Britain had at the time — was as obvious and sensible a policy in the circumstances as dispersal. It was a policy, however, that was not calculated to bring about a rapid and large-scale upswing in total output, since the more generous provision of acutely scarce raw materials, labour and plant for the priority types could only be achieved in the short term at the cost of declining production of other, less favoured designs.

Perhaps because of his long-standing connections with North America, Beaverbrook was from the outset as Minister of Aircraft Production a zealous advocate of calling in the productive capacity of the New World to redress the inadequacies of the Old. He did not initiate the policy of exploiting American potential to supplement British resources. The British aircraft industry was already heavily dependent on American machine-tools, metals and certain aircraft components long before May 1940. British orders for complete American military aircraft had been placed as far back as the summer of 1938, though America was never regarded before Dunkirk as more than a marginal source of finished aircraft for the U.K.[36] In June 1940, however, Beaverbrook stepped up the British commitment to American sources of supply to an enormous extent, with an undertaking to purchase up to 3,000 American planes per month — a figure which represented nearly twice the existing British output.[37] But it is hard to account this aspect of Beaverbrook's activities a success as far as the urgent need to maximise deliveries of operationally effective aircraft to the R.A.F. in 1940 was concerned. Large sums of Britain's perilously depleted dollar resources were, it is true, spent between May 1940 and March 1941 (when Lend-Lease solved the British dollar problem) on orders to American aircraft manufacturers and on the construction of plant in the U.S.A. for aircraft production on British account. Beaverbrook's activities in this sphere got him into trouble with the British and American authorities, as he tried to expedite matters by ignoring established procedures for drawing on American supplies. But the short-term results were disappointing. The American military aircraft industry had been extremely run down in the thirties, and had begun to emerge from this slough of inactivity even later than its British counterpart.[38] Its installed capacity in June 1940 was small and incapable of very rapid expansion to large-scale production. Thus, in the three months following Beaverbrook's undertaking to buy up to three thousand American planes per month, deliveries from America averaged less than two *hundred* per month.[39] And the aircraft themselves were frequently not up to the rigours of air warfare as practised in Europe in late 1940 and early 1941.[40] In the long run, of course, the qualitative and quantitative problems of American aircraft supply were largely overcome, and this success owed much to Beaverbrook's pioneering work. But while he remained Minister of Aircraft Production, America remained a marginal source of aircraft for the R.A.F

VII

Beaverbrook's distrust of formal procedures was well-known. As far as production was concerned, he was suspicious of formal programmes, such as the Air Ministry production branch had been operating since the spring of 1938. At that time, Sir Ernest Lemon (the newly-appointed civilian Director General of Production at the Air Ministry) had begun to develop a centralised method of planning aircraft production in a way that took account of a number of often conflicting considerations, such as strategic requirements, finance, productive capacity, technical feasibility, and so on.[41] This development was one of the first casualties of the new M.A.P. regime. As far as the new minister was concerned at that stage, 'The only programme was "all that can be done"'.[42] By the autumn, however, with the passing of the immediate threat of invasion, even Beaverbrook acknowledged that something other than frenetic, hand-to-mouth improvisation was needed if he was to maintain the initiative in controlling the aircraft industry's activities. Accordingly, he instructed Hennessy to draw up a new basis on which the industry's efforts could be ordered. The Hennessy scheme[43] appeared in October 1940 and embodied a basic principle dear to Beaverbrook's heart in that it set production targets at extremely high levels and thereby (as he saw it) provided a powerful stimulus to the greatest possible productive effort. The scheme came to be known as the 'target programme' or 'carrot programme'. It was not simply a crude exercise in plucking large and random numbers from thin air, but had some basis in the extrapolation of existing output figures and in the calculation of factory floor-space available within the industry. But its essence was to set targets a long way beyond the practical capacity of the industry on the assumption that, by striving to reach the impossible, firms would actually achieve the maximum possible output. Unfortunately, the fact that the targets set were impossible to attain quickly came to be recognised, by the production directors within M.A.P. itself as well as in the factories themselves, and all sorts of problems followed from this recognition. Firms often rapidly ceased to try to meet their targets, knowing they were beyond their practical capabilities, the more so when they realised that M.A.P. did not really expect the targets to be met in full anyway. The extent to which targets *were* met varied widely from firm to firm, according to their individual circumstances. The results — in an assembly industry which depended upon the careful organisation of component supplies — were to be seen in the dislocation of the flow of materials and components, with knock-on effects on the activities of airframe constructors and others further along the chain of production.

There were also political problems connected with target programming in M.A.P.'s relations with other departments of state controlling such vital factors to the aircraft industry as imported raw materials and labour. Beaverbrook's relations with the Minister of Labour, Ernest Bevin, were never particularly cordial at the best of times. The problem was that M.A.P. claimed allocations from these other departments based upon the target programme. But when the other departments realised that the targets were never met — worse, were never intended to be met — arbitrary cuts began to be made, and interdepartmental relations soured. Target planning fitted in well with Beaverbrook's style of management, but its shortcomings had to be recognised. It had not led to the smooth and rapid acceleration of production that had been expected of it. A short time before Beaverbrook's final resignation as Minister of Aircraft Production, the first steps were taken towards the replacement of target programming by a more elaborate but more realistic system of centralised planning based on the recommendations of the Manchester economist, Prof. John Jewkes, and in essence very similar to the system which had been developing under the old Air Ministry regime. 'Realistic' programming (as the new system was called) also tended often to fall short of fulfilment, but the margin of unreality was much narrower than with target programming. Failure to meet the planned level of production seems to have been less demoralising under the new scheme, and the degree of disruption it caused within the industry was therefore less severe.[44] The abandonment of target programming in favour of a return to something resembling the Air Ministry system of production programming was not, as we shall see,[45] the only respect in which M.A.P. under Lord Beaverbrook backtracked on its initial hostility to Air Ministry practices.

VIII

An important factor in maintaining the strength of the Royal Air Force during the Battle of Britain (and thereafter), over and above the provision of newly built aircraft, was the return of damaged aircraft to service after repair. Nearly thirty per cent of the aircraft delivered to squadrons between May and August 1940, for instance, came into this category, and Beaverbrook is widely credited with the development of the industrial mechanisms that made this possible.[46] Credit is indeed due to him, in so far as his ministry was responsible for running the repair shops from May 1940, and in so far as the structure of organisation under which the shops operated from that point was much influenced by his ideas on management. Administrative informality and the expansion and dispersal of facilities were as much the order of the day for M.A.P.'s repair shops as for the factories engaged in the production of new air-craft. But the M.A.P. repair set-up did not represent a completely new development, and the claim that 'Repair languished under the Air Ministry'[47] before M.A.P. took over does not seem to stand up to serious examination. It is true that in the early stages of rearmament during the thirties Air Ministry calculations about the maintenance of air force strength in wartime had revolved around the availability of new aircraft alone. But in 1938 it had been recognised that repaired planes could make a substantial contribution towards keeping up the front-line strength. A large-scale repair organisation combining service and civilian resources was accordingly built up by the Air Ministry between 1938 and 1940. This organisation seems to have coped with the volume of work it had to face before May 1940, when it was taken over and administratively much modified by M.A.P.[48] Whether in its original shape it could have coped with the greater volume of repair work that arose after that point, there is really no way of knowing, since it was never put to the test in that form. But Beaverbrook built his achievements in the matter of repairs on a substantial foundation laid by his predecessors.

IX

Building military aircraft, even in 1940-41 when both the machines themselves and the processes by which they were manufactured were much simpler than they are now, was a fairly complicated business. It required, then as now, large amounts of factory space, the deployment of a highly trained labour force and a sophisticated and expensive technology of manufacture, the organisation of the supplies of the myriad of large and small components that go to make up a complete aeroplane, and the co-ordination of the activities of the component producers so that all the bits and pieces were ready for assembly in the requisite volume and in the right order. Bringing together all the requirements for aircraft production in order to accomplish the growth of output on a substantial scale was not something that could be achieved overnight, or even in a period of a few weeks or for that matter a few months. The heightened pressures of war might speed up the expansion of productive capacity, but it still took time even then to build factories, install machinery, recruit and train workers, and create in general a going concern. New plant could not be conjured out of thin air, even by the most energetic of ministers. The Minister of Aircraft Production (or earlier the Air Member for Development and Production) could take steps to increase capacity, of course, but he had to accept lengthy delays before actual additional output resulted.[49] To meet the military emergency in the second half of 1940 and keep up the front-line strength of the air force, Lord Beaverbrook had to rely on plant that already existed or was nearing completion. This meant, in effect, that the level of aircraft production that he could achieve was in the first instance dependent on the plant developed by his Air Ministry predecessors. Fortunately for him, Sir Wilfred Freeman and Sir Ernest Lemon had between them promoted the development of aircraft production from a glorified cottage industry based on small-scale workshop methods to high-volume output based on large modern factories. As with the repair of damaged aircraft, the Air Ministry had laid the foundations for M.A.P.'s achievements, in the form of the industrial capacity in airframe, aero-engine and component manufacture which produced the steep rises in production graphs that marked the period between February and July 1940. By the end of 1939, the Air Ministry production branch — that scandalously muddled institution — was vigorously pursuing the creation of the industrial capacity to manufacture 2,300 planes per month.[50] The main component of this expansion programme took the form of three huge 'shadow' aircraft factories, which were complemented by large-scale engine and component factories. Begun between October 1938 and March 1939, this activity bore fruit in the spring and early summer of 1940, just at the time when those who had brought it about were deprived of control over it by the formation of M.A.P. under Beaverbrook. It was this new capacity which generated the substantial rise in output (particularly of fighter aircraft) in the first half of 1940 which sustained the R.A.F. during the Battle of Britain. Without it, Beaverbrook's energy would have been unavailing. Indeed, with this massive addition to the aircraft industry's potential coming into operation when it did, one may reasonably wonder if all of Beaverbrook's much-vaunted dynamism really made much of a difference to the industry's level of activity.

In the very short term, it may have made some impact: even Beaverbrook's sternest critic concedes that he was successful for a brief period in promoting a greater sense of urgency in the industry than had existed before May 1940.[51] It might, of course, be argued that this owed more to the shock of defeat in France, the political upheaval that brought Churchill to power, and the imminent threat of invasion than to any prompting from Beaverbrook. Quite apart from his exhortations, the other circumstances of the time must have been calculated — like the threat of impending execution — to develop a wonderful concentration of mind. Whatever the inspiration, though, there does seem to have been for a time a greater intensity of effort in the aircraft industry. This could not be sustained, however, over any great length of time before exhaustion and declining efficiency set in. The limitations began to be felt from July, and M.A.P. itself was soon advising firms to slacken off the pressure on their labour forces.[52] The effects of the spurt on output seem in any case to have been fairly marginal.

In the longer run, the effects of Beaverbrook's individualist, anti-bureaucratic approach to the management of aircraft production turned out in some respects to be unfortunate. Evidence of this comes from within M.A.P. itself, in the form — for example — of a powerful complaint in January 1941 from the Director General of Engine Production that the lack of a coherent and organised development programme for new types of aircraft and engines was creating duplication of effort on a serious scale, resulting in the wasteful use of industrial capacity and needlessly hindering production.[53] That M.A.P. recognised the difficulties arising from Beaverbrook's rejection of settled bureaucratic procedures for developing greater cohesion in the activities of its own sections (to say nothing of co-ordinating M.A.P.'s activities with those of other ministries, above all the Air Ministry) may be seen in the events of spring 1941. At that juncture, in spite of Beaverbrook's antipathy to committees and all they stood for in his view, there was a creeping resurrection within his ministry of procedures resembling those which had been followed by the supposedly discredited Air Ministry production branch. A case in point is the shift from 'target' to 'realistic' production programming, to which reference has already been made. Another such was the apologetic introduction in February 1941 of what was called — to avoid using the dreaded term 'committee' — a 'little group' of representatives from both M.A.P. and the Air Staff for the purposes of formulating a coherent policy for the development and production of engines, following the Director General's complaint.[54] It looks very much as if M.A.P. was turning away from the informal arrangements of its early days to something that increasingly corresponded with those of the body it had replaced, with its orthodox bureaucratic methods and its formal hierarchy following clearly defined lines of responsibility, some time before Beaverbrook ceased to be in charge.[55]

X

Beaverbrook's final resignation from M.A.P. has been described as the event which 'signalised the end of the great crisis in aircraft production which he had done so much to overcome . . .'[56] The statistics of aircraft production for 1940-41, however, do little to support this conventional image of Beaverbrook the industrial wizard, transforming a disorganised and sluggish aircraft supply position in the nick of time to save the country. It might be argued that 'the great crisis in aircraft production' existed only in the imaginations of some of Britain's leaders, notably Churchill himself. His political position in the middle and later thirties had been based on a critique of Britain's unpreparedness to meet the German threat, especially in the air. In 1940, on becoming Prime Minister, he seems to have assumed that nothing had happened to alter the position significantly and that a radical change of direction was needed. Churchill seems particularly to have been influenced in his decision to create a new department to supervise aircraft production by a deep-rooted belief that military agencies were congenitally incapable of the effective management of production. This belief stemmed, not from any close familiarity with what was going on in the field of aircraft production in 1940, but from his recollection of the supply problems that had plagued the military situation in the early part of the first world war.[57] The military agencies, especially the War Office, had then been judged to have mismanaged the business of munitions production, so that it had been taken out of their hands in 1915 and handed over to a specially created Ministry of Munitions headed initially by Lloyd George and dominated by civilians with relevant industrial experience.[58] Churchill saw in the situation of May 1940 an exact parallel with the events of twenty-five years before, calling for an exactly similar solution. Beaverbrook was to be his Lloyd George for aircraft production.

Beaverbrook evidently shared, on the same basis of Great War precedent, Churchill's views on the necessity to take control of the production of military equipment out of the hands of those who would actually use it. 'He did not believe,' says the official historian of war production, 'that people he described generically as "air marshals" were suited by temperament or training to the running of aircraft production.'[59] The aircraft industry could only be expected, in Beaverbrook's view, to respond to the demands of the military crisis of 1940 if brought under the control of practical men of business who, like himself, were not bureaucratically hidebound. But the 'air marshals' seem to have managed things fairly well, at least from 1938, and it is significant in this connection that Beaverbrook, having swept into office at M.A.P. with a determination to break with the methods of his predecessors, should preside over the re-establishment of so many of them before his departure. A consideration of the policies particularly identified with his administration of aircraft supply seems to confirm that here was no magician. Some were sound enough, others were less so: none seems to have been decisive in promoting the rapid growth of aircraft deliveries towards or during the Battle of Britain.

Beaverbrook came into office just in time to preside over an aircraft industry in which the really acute problems of creating the productive capacity to match German strength in the air — and so to safeguard Britain's security in the direct confrontation that followed the fall of France — were already well on the way to being solved thanks to the Air Ministry production branch.[60] He took over when the priority accorded to fighter production had already been raised above that given to bombers, and after the actual trends of production had come to reflect this change in priorities. And he took charge of an industry in which the volume of output was already rising fast towards the peak of July. Indeed, viewing things from an industrial rather than a political or military standpoint, the record of the 'air marshals' looks not at all bad. One is left wondering whether Beaverbrook really faced a 'great crisis in aircraft production' at all in May 1940.

Beaverbrook's activities as Minister of Aircraft Production may, especially in his early days in office, have created the impression of a crisis in aircraft production where no real grounds for it existed. His flair for 'drama' was well-known[61] and he ran his ministry accordingly, with a barnstorming verve and in a blaze of publicity. He generated an air of hectic activity in the capital which must have contrasted sharply with the discreet activities of the Air Member for Development and Production's office, especially after the latter moved to its wartime base in Harrogate. There may indeed be something in the claim made by Slessor that Beaverbrook created the impression that he had inherited chaos in aircraft production. It would have served his need for dramatisation to do so: his dynamic approach would be seen to have solved a crisis, even if that crisis had to be — in a sense — manufactured to begin with.

To suggest this is not to imply that there was anything consciously cynical or self-serving in Beaverbrook's behaviour. Creating an *atmosphere* of crisis served the useful purpose of helping to create a greater sense of urgency among people in production, thereby raising them to a greater pitch of effort. Having created the spirit of crisis, he may well have come to believe it had real substance. For, as his most recent biographer has noted, it was often the case with Beaverbrook that 'the imaginary became more real than the reality'.[62] The political circumstances in which he was operating may have helped in the process. Beaverbrook was conscious that his new ministry would have a hard time establishing in the eyes of the Air Ministry and other settled departments of state its right to exercise in an independent fashion functions over which the Air Ministry had previously enjoyed full control. To do this, and to justify the belief that his creation was superior to the regime of the 'air marshals', perhaps he had to convince himself and others that a crisis existed in aircraft production that only he and his administrative methods could solve. 'History,' Len Deighton has remarked, 'is swamped by patriotic myths about the summer of 1940.'[63] It is time perhaps that the myth of Beaverbrook the industrial miracle-worker was recognised for what it is and added to the others.

NOTES

1. One feature of Beaverbrook's term of office at M.A.P. was the frequency with which he expressed the wish to be relieved of the job. His first attempted resignation came only about six weeks after his appointment: K. Young, *Churchill and Beaverbrook: a Study in Friendship and Politics* (1966), p. 149.

2. A. J. P. Taylor, *Beaverbrook* (1972), pp. 413-4.

3. N. Frankland and C. Dowling (eds), *Decisive Battles of the Twentieth Century* (1976), p. 119. My italics.

4. L. Deighton, *Fighter* (1977), p. 226.

5. Quoted in Taylor, *op. cit.*, p. 415.

6. Minute to Sir Archibald Sinclair: reproduced in W. S. Churchill, *The Second World War: vol. II — Their Finest Hour* (1949), p. 561.

7. Churchill, *op. cit.*, pp. 286-7.

8. Taylor, *op. cit.*, p. 414.

9. *With Prejudice: the War Memoirs of Marshal of the R.A.F. Lord Tedder* (1966), p. 14.

10. Sir John Slessor, *The Central Blue; Recollections and Reflections* (1956), p. 307.

11. See, e.g., M. M. Postan, *British War Production* (History of the Second World War, U.K. Civil ser., 1952), p. 137.

12. The powers enjoyed by the Air Ministry before the war are discussed in J. D. Scott and R. Hughes, *The Administration of War Production* (History of the Second World War, U.K. Civil ser., 1955), chap. III.

13. The Emergency Powers (Defence) Act of 1940 was particularly sweeping. It gave the government, in effect, 'complete control over persons and property, not just some persons of some particular class of the community, but of *all* persons . . . and all property' (C. R. Attlee, Lord Privy Seal, on introducing the Bill in the Commons, 22nd June 1940).

14. The matter is described in Scott & Hughes, *op. cit.*, p. 293: see also Postan, *op. cit.*, p. 116, from which the quotation comes.

15. There are two principal published sources for wartime aircraft statistics: Postan, *op. cit.*, appendices 3-4, pp. 472-85; and Central Statistical Office, *Statistical Digest of the War* (History of the Second World War, U.K. Civil ser., 1951), tables 130-6, pp. 152-7. All production and delivery statistics cited here are drawn from these sources, and Figures 1-3 are based upon them.

16. The Westland Aeroplane Co., for example, kept itself going at one stage by making beer barrels; Postan, *op. cit.*, p. 5.

17. The fundamental design-change was from biplane/fixed undercarriage to monoplane/retracting undercarriage configuration. With this was associated a change in the method (and materials) of construction, involving essentially the decline of fabric-covered wooden or metal frameworks and the adoption instead of all-metal stressed-skin construction.

18. Expenditure on the Royal Air Force (£ millions):

Fiscal Year	Warlike Stores (Vote 3)	Total
1934-35	7.2	17.7
1935-36	11.6	27.5
1936-37	25.3	50.0
1937-38	43.4	81.8
1938-39	72.2	126.4
1939-40	114.9	208.6

Source: *Air Estimates* (annual).

19. The problems of the pre-war aircraft industry are quite fully discussed in Postan, *op. cit.*, chap. II. For a more recent discussion of relations between the state and the industry, see P. Fearon, 'The British Airframe Industry and the State, 1918-35', *Economic History Review*, 2nd ser.

XXVII (1974), and *Economic History Review*, 2nd ser. XXVIII (1975) for comment by A. J. Robertson and reply by P. Fearon.

20. For Air Ministry plans, see Postan, *op. cit.*, p. 472. Deliveries (which are usually taken to indicate production levels) are given in the same work, p. 484.

21. The Air Staff had given increased priority to fighter procurement in 1938, under what was known as Scheme L.

22. In particular the Castle Bromwich 'shadow' factory, which was intended to be given over to Spitfire production. It was one of the three biggest 'shadow' aircraft factories, and was complemented by a new Rolls Royce factory at Hillington, Glasgow, to produce the Merlin aero-engines used in both Spitfire and Hurricane fighters. Hillington came into operation slightly before Castle Bromwich. On the 'shadow' system, see W. Hornby, *Factories and Plant* (History of the Second World War, U.K. Civil ser., 1958, pp. 199-203 and 395).

23. The technique is explained in Postan, *op. cit.*, pp. 169-72.

24. On Churchill's reasons for creating M.A.P., see above, p. 96. The state of the Air Ministry production branch on the eve of the Beaverbrook take-over is discussed in Postan, *op. cit.*, pp. 137-8, and Scott & Hughes, *op. cit.*, p. 291. Beaverbrook's slogans are quoted in Taylor, *op. cit.*, p. 421.

25. Above, p. 96.

26. See Taylor, *op. cit.*, p. 415.

27. Scott & Hughes, *op. cit.*, p. 291. They note in addition that A.M.D.P.'s department 'even apart from the creation of M.A.P., was undergoing a rapid development at this period'.

28. Freeman's responsibilities were much diminished after the changeover to M.A.P., where his continued presence was probably an embarrassment. After a period as Deputy Chief of Air Staff, he returned to M.A.P. after Beaverbrook's departure: Scott & Hughes, *op. cit.*, pp. 291 f., 305.

29. The effects of bombing are discussed in Postan, *op. cit.*, pp. 164-5; a full study of the Coventry raid is provided by N. Longmate, *Air Raid: the Bombing of Coventry, 1940* (1976).

30. Scott & Hughes, *op. cit.*, p. 192; A. Calder, *The People's War* (1969), p. 169.

31. Postan, *op. cit.*, p. 166.

32. C. M. Kohan, *Works and Buildings* (History of the Second World War, U.K. Civil ser., 1952), p. 320.

33. Kohan, *op. cit.*, p. 321.

34. Above, p. 83.

35. Storage of Whitley bombers: M. M. Postan, D. Hay and J. D. Scott, *The Design and Development of Weapons* (History of the Second World War, U.K. Civil ser., 1964), p. 12; D. Divine, *The Broken Wing* (1966), p. 196.

36. R. D. Hall, *North American Supply* (History of the Second World War, U.K. Civil ser., 1955), p. 105.

37. Hall, *op. cit.*, pp. 171-3.

38. Hall, *op. cit.*, pp. 105-7.

39. C.O.I., *Statistical Digest*, table 135, p. 156.

40. American land-based fighter aircraft bought by Britain in 1940-41 were in particular greatly inferior in performance at normal combat altitudes to their British and German counterparts, and generally more lightly armed. They were either assigned to alternative roles in Europe or employed as fighters in theatres where their lack of performance was less of a handicap (e.g. the Middle East). A good number were more or less given away to Russia and China.

41. On Lemon's activities, see Scott & Hughes, *op. cit.*, pp. 386-9.

42. Scott & Hughes, *op. cit.*, p.389.

43. The Hennessy scheme is outlined in Scott & Hughes, *op. cit.*, pp. 390-1, and Postan, *op. cit.*, pp. 123-4.

44. The problems of 'target programming' (and of other varieties) are examined at length in E. Devons, *Planning in Practice: Essays in Aircraft Planning in Wartime* (1950), chap. II. Prof. Devons was a colleague of Prof. Jewkes in the University of Manchester and worked in the

H

planning division of M.A.P. for four years. On the Jewkes Report and the abandonment of 'target programming', see Scott & Hughes, *op. cit.*, p. 392.

45. Above, p. 95.

46. Taylor, *op. cit.*, p. 430.

47. Taylor, *op. cit.*, p. 418.

48. For the Air Ministry repair organisation, see Postan, *op. cit.*, pp. 316-9.

49. In the case, for instance, of the earliest shadow factories authorised in 1936, construction started early in 1937, but the first finished aircraft were not rolled out until about the time war broke out in September 1939. Hornby, *op. cit.*, pp. 199-203.

50. On the achievements of Freeman and Lemon, see Postan, *op. cit.*, p. 464. Also Slessor, *op. cit.*, p. 308, which quotes Lord Hives (managing-director in 1940 of Rolls Royce, one of Britain's chief aero-engine manufacturers) to the effect that 'It was the expansion which was carried out under Freeman's direction in 1937 to 1939 which enabled the Battle of Britain to be won. Without that foresight and imagination no efforts in 1940 would have yielded any results'.

51. Tedder, *op. cit.*, p. 14: he reckoned that Beaverbrook managed to ginger things up for only about four weeks.

52. Postan, *op. cit.*, p. 164.

53. Scott & Hughes, *op. cit.*, p. 343.

54. Scott & Hughes, *op. cit.*, p. 344.

55. Scott & Hughes, *op. cit.*, p. 297, records that M.A.P. 'was in fact returning to a more unified and orthodox form of control' before May 1941.

56. Scott & Hughes, *op. cit.*, p. 391.

57. Churchill, *op. cit.*, p. 12.

58. Churchill was closely involved in the creation of the Ministry of Munitions in 1915, and later served as Minister.

59. Taylor, *op. cit.*, pp. 415-6, shows that Beaverbrook too was influenced by the Great War precedent. The quotation is from Postan, *op. cit.*, p. 137.

60. British production had come to match German late in 1939 and to exceed it in 1940; see Postan, *op. cit.*, p. 471, for German output.

61. Taylor, *op. cit.*, pp. 414-5.

62. Taylor, *op. cit.*, p. 142.

63. Deighton, *op. cit.*, p. 21.

PART TWO

Studies in Banking History

5. Banking and Industrialisation in Britain in the Nineteenth Century

Rondo Cameron

THE title of this study, which was suggested by the editor of the volume, suggests in turn a number of questions. What was the relation between the banking system and industrialisation in nineteenth century Britain? Did the former play a positive, growth-inducing role? Did it merely respond passively to the needs of industrial finance? Or did it, as some historians of banking have asserted, have little if anything to do with industrialisation as such?

In an earlier volume on this subject I wrote:

> From a broad spectrum of possible forms of interaction between the financial sector and the other sectors of the economy that require its services, one may isolate three type-cases: (1) the case in which inadequate finance restricts or hinders industrial and commercial development; (2) the case in which the financial system is purely permissive and accommodates all 'credit-worthy' borrowers; and finally (3) the case in which financial institutions either actively promote new investment opportunities or encourage applicants for finance to come forward, provide them with advice and extra services, etc.[1]

In view of the obvious fact that Britain was the 'first industrial nation' it is difficult to make a convincing argument for the first type-case; at the least, inadequate finance did not actually stifle industrialisation, although it is possible that with a different banking system industrialisation might have proceeded more smoothly and rapidly. In the work previously cited I concluded that 'it seems likely that in . . . England . . . the banking system was essentially passive or permissive, responding fully to the demand for financial services but not inducing growth directly', whereas the Scottish banking system received the highest marks of all the systems studied.[2]

In an extended review of *Banking in the Early Stages of Industrialisation* Professor Checkland took me severely to task for the judgments restated above (as well as on several other matters). In his words, 'Cameron's contrast between the Scottish and English systems is overdone, and rests, in part, upon false grounds . . . It is realistic to regard the English and Scottish banking systems as being essentially similar'.[3] The verb tense is significant. I agree that in the twentieth century it *is* realistic to regard the two systems as 'essentially similar'; indeed, except for the now trivial difference of the Scottish note issue, they form a single system. But I was writing about the 'early stages of industrialisation', specifically the period before the middle of the nineteenth century. With all due respect to Professor Checkland, I still maintain that there were significant differences in the two systems at that time, and that the Scottish system was markedly superior. I shall even call on evidence from Professor Checkland's magisterial history of Scottish banking (completed after he wrote his review) to substantiate my view.

Professor Checkland also chided me for my 'gratuitous remarks' concerning the relative economic decline of Scotland in the twentieth century.[4] It is quite true that in a parenthetical statement I remarked that the decline 'has been accompanied by an increasing assimilation of Scottish educational and banking policies and practices into those of England'.[5] I will not attempt to defend my assertion about education in this study (nor will I retract it), but I will undertake to demonstrate when, why, and how the Scottish banking system was assimilated to the English, and with what results.

First, however, I would like to emphasise the large measure of agreement between us on most matters of interest. This will become evident when I quote what he has actually written about banking in England and Scotland.

I

Both Professor Checkland and I prefer a structural-functional approach to banking history and analysis.[6] That is, we believe that the effectiveness with which a banking system performs its functions is determined in large measure by its structural characteristics. 'Whether or not the banking system makes a positive and substantial contribution to economic development does not depend primarily upon the personal qualities of the bankers . . . The structural characteristics of the system, and the laws, regulations, and customs that govern its behaviour, will normally be far more important determinants of its effectiveness.'[7] Thus the first step in ascertaining whether or not the English and Scottish banking systems in the first half of the nineteenth century were 'essentially similar' is to review their structural features.

The most obvious feature of English banking structure was the pre-eminence of the Bank of England. Until 1826 it was the only joint-stock company permitted in the banking business; all other banks, whether in London or in the provinces, were either single proprietorships or partnerships not exceeding six persons. In 1826 the law was modified to permit joint-stock banks outside a 65-mile radius of the City, and in 1833 within that radius provided the bank did not issue notes; the growth of joint-stock banking clearly met a felt need, but did not seriously challenge the pre-eminence of the Bank. In quantitative terms, the Bank controlled approximately 58 per cent of all banking assets in England and Wales in 1800, about 36 per cent in 1844.[8] Despite its great size, however, the Bank contributed little to industrial finance. Its primary concern — at the time of its founding, during the Napoleonic Wars, and even in the long period of peace that followed — was governmental finance. Its share capital was permanently immobilised in government securities, and in the first half of the nineteenth century well over half of its short-term advances went to the government.[9]

A second notable feature of the English banking structure early in the nineteenth century was the large number of small private banks scattered throughout the provinces. These, the 'country banks', had originated in the eighteenth century in response to both the inadequacy of the circulating currency and the shortage of credit facilities.[10] Many of them grew out of industrial or commercial enterprises with which they maintained close ties, and issuing banknotes for local circulation was their *raison d'être* and principal source of profit. Already numbering more than three hundred at the beginning of the century, they doubled in the first decade of the century, when the suspension of specie payments by the Bank of England greatly facilitated entry into the industry; after a slight decline in the immediate postwar years, they rose to a new peak in the boom year 1825.

Constrained by the privileged position of the Bank of England, the country banks were mostly quite small and frequently undercapitalised in relation to their ambitions; they also had difficulty in attracting professional management. As a result bankruptcies occurred with alarming frequency. The country banks were often accused of causing or at least contributing to the financial panics that occurred at irregular intervals, although in fact they were more often the victims than the perpetrators of the crisis. In any event, the crisis of December-January 1825-26, during which more than sixty country banks and several London private banks closed their doors, precipitated the emergency legislation of 1826 which, among other things, allowed the formation of joint-stock banks.

The response to the new legislation was sluggish at first, but after the recharter of the Bank of England in 1833, which explicitly provided for joint-stock banks in London if they did not issue banknotes, activity stepped up. (By that time bankers had discovered that they could carry on a profitable business with deposits subject to cheque, in place of the formerly almost ubiquitous banknotes.) By 1844 about 150 joint-stock banks had been established which, with their branches, accounted for almost 600 bank offices. Some of the new banks resulted from the conversion or absorption of formerly private banks, which accordingly began a long-term and ultimately (in the twentieth century) final decline; others were totally new creations, brought into existence by the need for their services and the profit orientation and perspicacity of their founders. The functions of the joint-stock banks did not differ appreciably from those of the private bankers whom they replaced or competed with (except for the matter of note issue, which many of the new banks either did not exercise or relinquished voluntarily), but their larger size and numbers of branches gave them at least the appearance of greater security and stability.

When Professor Checkland wrote of the English banking system in the post-Napoleonic period he was, I presume, referring to the functions of both the private and joint-stock banks. It is a description with which, in general, I agree. He wrote that the banking system financed 'textiles, metal goods, and industrial products generally', but 'it was the financing of the *movement* of goods, and the holding of stocks, rather than their production, that constituted the bankers' major contribution. This is not to diminish its importance — rather the contrary. Though the bankers provided mainly finance of this kind, and that for only some portion of total transactions, their attitude was crucial to the level of activity'.[11] Again, 'though the business world was finding its own resources and allocating them over the area of opportunity, the bankers were still crucial to the process. They could aid particular projects by supporting their credit, but their most important function was still to control the total supply of short-term credit made available very largely for the movement of goods and the holding of stocks'.[12]

The English banking structure in the first half of the nineteenth century was therefore characterised by one large, legally privileged institution concerned primarily with government finance, and a large number of much smaller institutions whose main business was the extension of short-term credit for commerce and industry. The latter facilitated but did not, to any significant extent, promote industrial growth. Professor Checkland rightly stresses the spontaneous initiative of private entrepreneurs in industry, whose firms grew mainly by the reinvestment of profits. The bankers assisted in this process with their short-term credits but, constrained by the structure of the system to insure first and foremost their liquidity, could not afford to engage in long-term commitments to industrial enterprise.

The structure of the Scottish system differed in several respects from that of England. Instead of a single large privileged institution, Scotland had three 'public banks' (i.e. with royal charters but operating as private enterprises), all dating from before the middle of the eighteenth century: the Bank of Scotland (1695), the Royal Bank of Scotland (1727), and the British Linen Company (1746). In addition, by the beginning of the nineteenth century more than a score of banking companies, operating like joint-stock companies but without charters or limited liability, had set up shop in Glasgow and a number of smaller cities. (All of the public banks were headquartered in Edinburgh.) All of these, both the public banks and the banking companies, issued their own banknotes, and most of them had one or more branches in other cities. There were as well a few private banks that did not issue notes, but they were of marginal significance.

When the Bank of England suspended specie payments in 1797 the Scottish banks spontaneously followed suit, though without legal authorisation until after the fact. As in England, suspension favoured the establishment of new banks; by 1810 there were more than forty, a number maintained with little fluctuation for more than a decade. (One reason for the growth in numbers, in addition to the ease of entry, was popular dissatisfaction with the policies of the public banks. During the Napoleonic Wars the latter invested heavily in government securities, thereby curtailing their ability to support domestic commerce and industry.) In the 1820s and 1830s a process of consolidation began, with the creation of new, larger joint-stock banks that absorbed the smaller banking companies. By 1845 the total number of issuing banks had been reduced to nineteen, of which five each were headquartered in Edinburgh and Glasgow; but with their branches they gave Scotland a total of almost 400 bank offices, or about one office per 7,200 persons — almost double the bank density of England and Wales.

A few other quantitative measures, made possible by the meticulous work of Professor Checkland, will add precision to these brief remarks on Scottish banking structure. In 1802 the three public banks controlled 54 per cent of all bank assets in Scotland; twenty-one banking companies disposed of 37 per cent; and seven private banks had the remaining 9 per cent.[13] In 1825 the same three public banks' share had fallen to 46 per cent; three new joint-stock banks controlled 26 per cent; twenty-four smaller banking companies had 24 per cent, with the remaining 4 per cent in the custody of private bankers.[14] By 1850 the public banks had only 33 per cent, twelve joint-stock banks 64 per cent, and the two remaining banking companies 3 per cent; the private bankers had disappeared.[15]

Some explicit quantitative comparisons reinforce the impression of the superiority of the Scottish system. In 1801 the banking density of England and Wales, measured by the number of bank offices per 10,000 inhabitants, was 0.48; in Scotland in 1802 it was 0.56. In 1841 the English density was 0.71; in Scotland it was 0.78 in 1825, 1.41 in 1850.[16] The ability of a banking system to mobilise capital is one of the most important indicators of its effectiveness. Scotland, in spite of its smaller population and income, inferior resources, and later start in industrialisation, greatly outdistanced its neighbour in this respect. This was already evident at the beginning of the century, when the Scottish banking system had £7.46 in assets per inhabitant, compared with only £5.97 in England (or £7.19 if one includes the share capital of the Bank of England). By 1844 the English figure had risen to only £9.00, whereas Scotland reached £11.07 in 1825 and £18.05 in 1850.[17]

Thus the Scottish system was not only superior; it was precocious as well. Indeed, as Professor Checkland has written, as early as 1772 the Scottish system 'was perhaps the most developed in Europe, ready to respond to the demands of industrialisation'.[18] Moreover, it responded to those demands not merely by financing the movement of goods or the holding of stocks, but by making advances on plant and equipment and other non-liquid securities.[19] The banks did, of course, provide short-term finance, but 'they continued to be involved to a significant degree in medium and even longer-term advances both in industry and agriculture'.[20] They were able to do this because the structure of the system relieved them of the intense, almost pathological concern with liquidity that plagued English bankers. The combination of a relatively small number of substantial banks, each with a large number of branches, provided the benefits of competition without the constant threat of bankruptcy.

The record of the Scottish banks with respect to stability of the system, and the presence or absence of panics and crises, is remarkably good in comparison with that of the English. Professor Checkland once contrasted the goals of stability and growth for a banking system (or an economy as a whole) as though they were antithetical, and charged me with favouring the latter over the former.[21] But stability is not the same as stagnation. As we have discovered again since World War II, a healthy growing economy can achieve stability more easily than one in which growth occurs by fits and starts. This phenomenon was first demonstrated historically for industrialising nations by the more rapid, more stable growth of Scotland than of England in the late eighteenth and first half of the nineteenth century.[22]

The contribution of the banking system to this achievement has best been summarised by Professor Checkland:

> In the formative period of modern banking, before 1850, the Scottish system was a good deal more important than its absolute size would suggest, for it was more advanced relative to its economy than was the English, or indeed any other; qualitatively, it was in many ways more intensive and more progressive. Indeed, Scotland for several generations between the 1740s and 1850s held a unique place in world banking development. The Scots pioneered in many areas, including banking on the limited liability principle, the early adoption of and extension of the note issue to the point at which gold and silver virtually disappeared, the elaboration of an agency/branch system, the invention of the cash credit (later to become the overdraft), the vigorous development of deposit-gathering reinforced by the payment of interest, the early adoption of joint-stock banking, experiments in exchange stabilisation (made between Edinburgh and London), and the practice among banks of being willing, in times of stress, to hold each other's notes, a principle now being applied by central banks in the international field . . . Scotland also began the Savings Bank movement and the investment trust; it formed the first Institute of Bankers; it exported trained young bankers all over the world, many of them rising to top positions and extending Scottish usages.[23]

II

Structure affects function. Since one of the most important determinants of banking structure is legislation, it should come as no surprise that the Bank Acts of 1844 and 1845, which fundamentally altered the banking structure of England and Scotland, respectively, also affected the performance of their functions.

The Bank Charter Act of 1844, which renewed the privilege of the Bank of England, had, according to some interpretations, three objectives: to insure the convertibility of the note issue; to prevent 'speculation'; and, most importantly, to prevent financial panics.[24] The means by which the Act sought to achieve those ends were separation of the note issue from the 'banking' function of the Bank; centralisation of the note issue in the newly created Issue Department; and the gradual demise of the note issues of the existing private and joint-stock banks. In practice, the Act totally failed in its last two objectives, and had only qualified success in the first. In terms of means, the Act eventually achieved the last two, and nominally the first as well but that was really an illusion. In addition, however, it had several quite unanticipated results.

One immediate consequence of the Act was to slow the formation of new banks. The private country banks were already in decline, as they converted to the joint-stock form or were taken over by new joint-stock banks; but the number of the latter had increased dramatically — 114 in all — in the twelve years preceding the Act. In the following twelve years only seven new banks came into existence, and one of those failed shortly.[25] The effect of this was to lessen competitive pressure at a time when the increasing pace of commerce and industry demanded more credit facilities.

A secondary consequence, directly contrary to the stated intentions of the Act, was to prolong the existence of the private note-issuing banks; since amalgamation into larger units in either private or joint-stock form would automatically terminate the issues — still a source of profit — many of the small local bankers doggedly hung on even when their amalgamation into larger units would have been beneficial to their regions.

Yet another unanticipated consequence, also contrary to the principles of the Currency School on which the Act was based, was to hasten the replacement of currency transactions by those settled by cheques. The non-issuing joint-stock banks naturally pursued an aggressive policy of gathering deposits, by payment of interest and other inducements, and within a few years deposits subject to cheque overwhelmed other means of payment. Whereas in 1844 specie and banknotes together constituted 45 per cent of the money supply (narrowly defined) and deposits 55 per cent, by 1865 the latter accounted for almost three-fourths of the total; banknotes had fallen to a mere 7.4 per cent.[26]

In the longer run it is probable that the Act also contributed to the movement towards amalgamation and concentration in English banking. Many other factors contributed to this movement, of course, but as deposit banking eclipsed the note-issue function in importance, the economies of scale to be obtained in the former gained in significance. With concentration and consolidation came changes in the structure and functions of the banking system. Three times in the quarter-century following the Bank Act, in 1847, 1857, and 1866, its principal provision — that for 100 per cent specie reserve for all notes in excess of the fixed fiduciary issue — had to be suspended in conditions of financial panic. As the concentration movement accelerated after 1870, however, no similar panics recurred, not even during the Baring crisis of 1890. A system dominated by the Bank of England and a few large joint-stock banks with nationwide chains of branches had at last found stability. But it was stability bought at a price. Lending policies became more conservative, routinised, bureaucratised. Local initiative by the branch offices was subordinated to general policies laid down in London, where the executives were out of touch with and unsympathetic to local needs, especially the needs of industry: 'the City to a large extent had its back turned to industry'.[27]

The counterpart of the neglect of domestic industry was the cultivation of foreign investment. In effect, the banking system and the stock market were draining the provinces of their savings to invest them abroad. 'If the City was perhaps too cautious in participating in the domestic industrial sector, it was excessively generous in its foreign loans.'[28] This situation has been frequently commented upon in discussions of the relative decline of the British economy prior to World War I, but has not yet been investigated in detail and with the rigour that its importance merits.

III

The Bank Act of 1844, like most other English banking legislation, did not extend to Scotland. Peel's government, however, determined to extend to all parts of the United Kingdom the basic principles that underlay that Act, and in 1845 the Parliament obediently passed 'an Act to regulate the Issue of Bank Notes in Scotland'. The most important provision of the law prohibited the formation of new banks *with right of issue.* In principle, new banks devoted solely to deposit banking could have been created, but the fact that there were no new banks after 1845, in contrast to the numerous new starts before that year, is eloquent testimony to the importance of freedom of issue in promoting bank competition.

The law made no explicit provision for a fiduciary issue, as in the case of the Bank of England, but it did require a 100 per cent specie reserve for all note issues in excess of the average issue of the period immediately preceding enactment. In some respects the law was less restrictive than the Bank Act of 1844. For example, in deference to Scottish public opinion it allowed retention of the £1 notes. (Notes smaller than £5 had been prohibited in England by the emergency legislation of 1826, but fervent protests by Scottish spokesmen secured an exemption for Scotland.) In the event of amalgamation by formerly independent banks, they could sum their 'authorised issues' instead of forfeiting both, as in England.

Professor Checkland has written that 'The English system moved in the Scottish direction as England took up the Scottish examples of the joint-stock principle, the branch system, and the payment of interest on deposits'.[29] That movement occurred mainly between the legislation of 1826 and that of 1844-45. Thereafter the movement was in the opposite direction. Although the Scottish banks continued vigorous and active for some three or four decades after the Act of 1845, they came to resemble their English counterparts more and more. No doubt the spectacular failures of the Western Bank in 1857 and the City of Glasgow Bank in 1878 influenced the system as a whole in a more conservative direction, but the reduction of competitive pressure as a result of the Act of 1845 was already working in the same direction. In fact, the concentration of Scottish banking preceded that of England, as the twenty banks existing in 1845 were reduced to ten in 1885. As Professor Campbell has written, 'with the amalgamations of the banking institutions within Scotland came a greater assimilation to English ways'.[30]

In the 1870s Scottish industry entered a phase of relative decline even more marked than that in England. The reasons are many and complex, and probably no two people could agree on the weight to be assigned to each. Almost without question, however, some weight must be given to the changes in the structure and performance of the banking system. In Professor Checkland's words, 'the Scottish banking system, from being the most open and competitive in the world before 1830, had become by 1880 one of the most tightly controlled'.[31] Such a drastic change could not but affect the course of industrial progress.

The questions raised at the beginning of this study recur. Can a banking system play a leading, growth-inducing role in economic development? Can it, on the other hand, hinder or retard industrialisation and economic growth? What role does banking structure play in either case? Although positive proof for either proposition is probably unattainable, it seems to me that the financial and industrial history of England and Scotland in the nineteenth century offers overwhelming evidence for a positive answer to the first two questions, and highlights the role of banking structure as a key variable.

I trust that Professor Checkland will agree.

NOTES

1. Rondo Cameron *et. al.*, *Banking in the Early Stages of Industrialisation: A Study in Comparative Economic History* (New York and London, 1967), p. 2. Much of my part of the work on this book was accomplished during my tenure as Fulbright Visiting Research Professor in the University of Glasgow in 1962-63, where I enjoyed both the hospitality and the inspiration of Professor Checkland.

2. *Ibid.*, pp. 290, 304.

3. S. G. Checkland, 'Banking History and Economic Development: Seven Systems', *Scottish Journal of Political Economy*, XV (1968), pp. 153-54.

4. *Ibid.*, p. 150.

5. Cameron, *Early Stages of Industrialisation*, p. 97.

6. S. G. Checkland, *Scottish Banking: A History, 1695-1973* (Glasgow and London, 1975), pp. xix-xx; *id.*, 'Banking History', p. 146; Cameron, *Early Stages*, pp. 291 ff.; *id.*, ed., *Banking and Economic Development: Some Lessons of History* (New York and London, 1972), pp. 8-9.

7. *Banking and Economic Development*, p. 8.

8. *Id.*, *Early Stages*, pp. 34, 42-5.

9. Arthur D. Gayer, W. W. Rostow, and Anna Jacobson Schwartz, *The Growth and Fluctuation of the British Economy, 1790-1850: An Historical, Statistical, and Theoretical Study of Britain's Economic Development*, 2 vols. (Oxford, 1953), II, p. 893.

10. L. S. Pressnell, *Country Banking in the Industrial Revolution* (Oxford, 1953).

11. S. G. Checkland, *The Rise of Industrial Society in England, 1815-1885* (New York, 1964), p. 202.

12. *Ibid.*, p. 204.

13. *Id., Scottish Banking,* p. 240.

14. *Ibid.*, p. 424.

15. *Ibid.*, p. 426.

16. Scottish figures from *ibid.*, pp. 240, 424, 426; English figures from Cameron, *Early Stages,* p. 28.

17. Scottish figures as in n. 16; English calculated from Cameron, *Early Stages,* pp. 33-35.

18. Checkland, *Scottish Banking,* p. 92.

19. *Ibid.*, pp. 416-18.

20. *Ibid.*, p. 416.

21. *Id.*, 'Banking History', pp. 148, 151, 164.

22. Cameron, *Early Stages,* pp. 60, 63-64.

23. *Scottish Banking,* pp. xvii-xviii.

24. S. Evelyn Thomas, *The Rise and Growth of Joint-Stock Banking* (London, 1934), p. 391.

25. *Ibid.*, p. 398 and Appendix M. In his text Thomas states eight banks in eleven years, but that is contradicted by the details of the appendix.

26. Cameron, *Early Stages,* p. 42.

27. Peter Mathias, *The First Industrial Nation: An Economic History of Britain, 1700-1914* (New York, 1969), p. 353.

28. Checkland, *Rise of Industrial Society,* p. 205.

29. *Scottish Banking,* p. xviii.

30. R. H. Campbell, *Scotland Since 1707: The Rise of an Industrial Society* (Oxford, 1965), p. 147.

31. *Scottish Banking,* p. 715.

32. Several items have come to my attention since I submitted my manuscript to the editors that reinforce the argument made above and in *Banking in the Early Stages of Industrialisation* that banks in *both* Scotland and England made a greater contribution to industrialisation than traditional accounts credited them with. These include Pat Hudson, 'The Role of Banks in the Finance of the West Yorkshire Wool Textile Industry, c. 1780-1850', *Business History Review,* 55, Autumn 1981, pp. 379-402, and Charles W. Munn, *The Scottish Provincial Banking Companies, 1747-1864* (Edinburgh, 1981), as well as several articles that I have not yet been able to examine. I look forward to reading Dr. Munn's contribution to this volume.

6. The Development of Joint-Stock Banking in Scotland, 1810-1845[1]

C. W. Munn

WHEN the reports of the Lords and Commons Committees on small notes in Scotland and Ireland were completed in the early summer of 1826, they revealed a consensus of opinion which was highly favourable to the system of banking which had evolved in Scotland. The Commons Commissioners felt that Scottish banking was

> a system admirably calculated, in their opinion, to economise the use of Capital, to excite and cherish a spirit of useful Enterprise, and even to promote the moral habits of the people, by the direct inducements which it holds out to the maintenance of a character for industry, integrity and prudence.[2]

So great was the vote of confidence in Scottish banking that the legislation which had been proposed to abolish one pound and one guinea notes, thus bringing Scotland into line with England, was abandoned.

Nor were these committees alone in their high opinion of banking north of the border. Thomas Joplin, the Newcastle merchant, company promoter and pamphleteer, had published his pamphlet on the subject of banking in 1822 in which he claimed that the Scottish system was worthy of all praise and imitation.[3] Joplin's initiative was partially responsible for the legislation passed in 1824 and 1825 for Ireland and 1826 for England and Wales, which dented the monopolies of the Bank of Ireland and Bank of England and so permitted the formation of joint-stock banks throughout the United Kingdom.

Yet despite the high esteem in which the Scottish system was held, it underwent a metamorphosis of structure and, to some extent, of function which, by the time the Bank Charter Act was passed in 1844, and legislation was being planned for Scotland and Ireland, had produced a banking system which bore little resemblance to that which had been found so successful and worthy of imitation in 1826.

This study is concerned with the nature of the change which took place and with the reasons for the transition.

I

Table 1 sets out the scale of the transition between 1826 and 1845. In addition, ten banks were formed and disappeared in the intervening years

TABLE 1

The Structure of Scottish Banking, 1826-1845[4]

	1826	1845
Public Banks	3	3
Joint-Stock Banks	3	12
Private Banks	7	1
Provincial Banks	23	3
	36	19

together with an unquantifiable number of abortive schemes. There is, however, despite these figures, no suggestion that the banking system was contracting, quite the reverse. This was in fact the most explosive period of growth in the history of Scottish banking up to this time. Professor S. G. Checkland calculated that in 1825 the total liabilities of the whole system were £24,419,000 and that by 1850 they had more than doubled to £51,866,000. This growth is also reflected in the number of offices (head offices and branches) which increased from 173 (1 per 12,800 of population in 1825) to 407 (1 per 7,000 of population in 1850), and in the figures for bank assets measured per capita, which were £11.07 in 1825 and £18.05 in 1850. The implication of these figures is clear: the size of the average bank rose fourfold from the 1820s to the late 1840s, although it must be stressed that the banks were structurally a much more homogeneous group at the later date.

The years between the enquiry of 1826 and the Bank Act of 1845 were, then, a period of great change in the structure of Scottish banking. Similar trends were visible in England and Wales, where there was also a move towards joint-stock banking, although the relative scale of change was probably not so great. In Ireland, however, the change was even more dramatic as many joint-stock banks were formed with extensive branch networks. These movements in other parts of the British Isles were partly derived from Scotland, as the model for the structures of English and Irish joint-stock banks was often the Commercial Bank of Scotland or one or other of the Public Banks, and the manner of conducting business was derived more generally from the Scottish system. Scottish bankers were recruited in substantial numbers to work in the new banks of England and Ireland,[5] while other Scots were active in new promotions south of the border and across the Irish Sea.

Evidently a great transformation, which was not without its traumas, was taking place in the world of banking, and the reasons for these changes are to be sought in the conditions which underpin the stability of a banking system, i.e. society itself, the general level of activity in the economy, and the profitability and business practice of the banks themselves.

The years between the mid-1820s and the mid-1840s saw great changes and dramatic events in the society of the time. The very ethos of society was changing with the development of ideas about laissez-faire, commercial freedom and expansion. There was political reform at national and local level.

It was the age of Chartism, Factory Reform, the Anti-Corn Law League, Poor Law reform, Trade Union activity and the collapse of the handloom weavers' craft. There were also great outbreaks of cholera and, at the end of the period, the potato famine. In short, it was a period of great ferment in every sphere of life — when solutions were sought, although not always found, to a great variety of social and political problems. All of these events affected Scotland to quite a marked extent.

In the economy, too, there were a number of marked changes of direction and increased levels of activity. The general trend was certainly expansionary although the trade cycle caused a number of stops to growth. More particularly, this was the age when steam technology made its greatest strides forward, both in the factory and in the realm of transport. These years witnessed the beginning of the railway and steamship age which, apart from their domestic impact, had great implications for overseas trade. It was also the time when urban growth proceeded with great pace.

In all of these developments the Scottish economy was intimately involved, but perhaps the most dramatic event in Scotland was the coming of the hot blast furnace in 1830 which, together with large reserves of black band ironstone, was to transform the iron industry from its almost moribund state in 1830 to being the producer of about 30% of the whole UK output in 1850. From having 27 furnaces in blast in 1830, the industry developed to have over 100 furnaces in blast by 1844. Indeed it is arguable that, unlike England, the Scottish economy had not attained self-sustaining growth by 1830 but by 1845 the twin growth industries of cotton and iron had achieved this.

Given the very great changes which were taking place in the economy, it becomes easier to appreciate why the financial sector in general, and banking in particular, underwent such a dramatic change over these years. For banking is a service industry and as such, if it is to be successful, must at least be responsive to the demands placed upon it by its customers, although it also has a more positive role to play. It is to the nature of these demands and to the response of the banks that we now turn.

II

Down to 1830 the main demand placed upon banks by their customers was for credit, and this was satisfied by the dual credit devices of the bill of exchange and the cash credit. The cash credit has been compared to the modern overdraft, but the analogy is not quite perfect, as holders of cash credits were required to sign a bond acknowledging their obligation and to have two or more friends or business associates guarantee the advance by adding their names to the bond. The security was therefore a personal one, although of course all signatories to the obligation were liable to the full extent of their personal fortunes for the sums borrowed.

Most holders of cash credits (accounts) would also have discount facilities at their bank, and it seems likely that these were used to finance stocks and trade debtors while cash credits were used to draw notes from the bank to pay wages and incidental expenses. It is, however, possible to demonstrate how cash accounts could become long-term loans; borrowers drew their credits to the full extent and met their bank's requirement for note turnover by rapid withdrawal and repayment of about 25%, never letting the outstanding balance fall below 75% of the authorised limit. The amounts authorised varied from bank to bank and often depended upon the size of the borrower. Credits between £1000 and £2000 were quite common, although the average was probably nearer £800 by the 1820s.[6] Bills of exchange and cash credits were therefore complementary aspects of bank credit provisions which combined to meet the main part of a firm's external requirements of working capital and some part of the need for fixed capital.

By 1830, however, the system of bank lending had begun to show signs of strain, and as the decade progressed cracks appeared. The major problem was that industry's needs for credit were changing. More specifically they were becoming larger — a reflection of the general growth of scale in the economy. It gradually became clear that the cash credit for £800 or even £2000 together with regular discount facilities were no longer adequate for many business organisations. Yet many of the provincial banking companies were aware that they would be overexposed if they were to lend larger sums to individual customers. Warnings about this from Gilbart and Rae later in the century were merely reiterations of an already well learned lesson. The provincial banking companies, then, because of their relatively small size, were not well equipped to meet the increased demands from industry and commerce being placed upon the banking system.

The Public Banks — Bank of Scotland, Royal Bank of Scotland and British Linen Bank[7] — were better able to respond to the new requirements and did so with some energy. But there remained a gap in the provision of credit facilities, a gap which was to be filled by a new breed of bank — the joint-stock bank. Tables 2 and 3 set out the date of formations and subsequent experience of these companies down to 1845.

These new concerns were similar in size and structure to the Public Banks and differed from the provincial banking companies in a number of minor ways and in one important respect, that is, they were bigger and therefore were better placed to meet the growing requirements of volume lending to their customers — many of whom were lured away from the provincial banking companies. A few of the provincial banking companies failed, but most took the easier way out of merging their entire interests in the office of a joint-stock bank. Indeed not a few, when their contracts came up for renewal, took the opportunity of relaunching themselves on a large scale, sometimes with new names as joint-stock banks. This was obviously important for the provincial bankers because they lost nothing and avoided failure, but it was

TABLE 2

Scottish Joint-Stock Banks Created 1810-1845

Name of Bank	Date of formation	Remarks
Commercial	1810	
National	1825	
Aberdeen Town & County	1825	
Glasgow Union	1830	became Union Bank of Scotland 1843
Ayrshire Banking Company	1830	
Western	1832	
Central (Perth)	1834	
North (Aberdeen)	1836	
Eastern (Dundee)	1838	
Southern (Dumfries)	1838	to Edinburgh and Leith 1841
Clydesdale	1838	
Caledonian (Inverness)	1838	
Edinburgh and Leith	1838	became Edinburgh and Glasgow 1844
Paisley Commercial	1838	to Western 1844
City of Glasgow	1839	
Greenock Union	1840	to Clydesdale 1844
Glasgow JSB	1843	became Edinburgh and Glasgow 1844—with 13
Bank of Glasgow	1843	to National 1844
Glasgow Banking Company	1843	to Western 1844
Glasgow Bank (2)	1844	to Clydesdale 1844
Edinburgh and Glasgow	1844	13 and 17

TABLE 3

Scottish Joint-Stock Banks in operation, 1845

1	Commercial	8	North
2	National	9	Eastern
3	Aberdeen Town and County	10	Clydesdale
4	Union	11	Caledonian
5	Ayrshire	12	City of Glasgow
6	Western	13	Edinburgh and Glasgow
7	Central		

Scottish Public Banks in operation, 1845

1	Bank of Scotland	3	British Linen Company
2	Royal Bank of Scotland		

Scottish Provincial Banking Companies in operation, 1845
(all large co-partneries)

1	Dundee Banking Co	3	Aberdeen Banking Co
2	Perth Banking Co		

also important for the joint-stock banks because they gained the personnel and accumulated experience of bankers whose expertise had been so generously acknowledged in the Parliamentary enquiries of 1826.

It would, however, be naive to argue that the great changes which were taking place occurred without tension or trauma, or that all joint-stock banks were founded to fill a readily identifiable gap in the provision of financial services. It is clear that the arrival of the joint-stock banks injected into the banking scene a further element of competition for business. Scottish banking had from the 1770s been a competitive activity, with local banking companies often vying for business with a local competitor and/or with branches of one or more of the public banks; and from the mid-1820s another element of competition entered into the scene with the coming of the joint-stock banks.[8] One result, the demise of the majority of the provincial banking companies, has already been mentioned, but there were other consequences, not the least of which was the erosion of banking profits — already low compared with England (see below).

The other major result of the heightened competitive situation was the attempt by all banks, joint-stock especially, to meet the growing scale of credit needs and other requirements of their customers. But before the problem of larger advances could be tackled, the banks became aware that traditional forms of security for advances would prove inadequate to meet the changed situation. The personal security of the cash credit, it was felt, would not be sufficient for larger advances, and so the story of the 1830s and 1840s is one of continued experimentation with larger advances and new forms of security, including ships, bank shares, railway shares, land, minerals, turnpike tolls, insurance policies, and goods, especially cotton. It was also the time when the unsecured advance, the overdraft, became common.[9] There were many problems associated with these new methods of business, not the least of which were the questions of how a bank could obtain effective security over an asset and how much of a margin should be left between the market value of the asset over which security was to be taken and the amount of the advance. Only trial and error provided the answers to these questions, and solutions were seldom achieved without some mistakes being made. Nevertheless, what is evident in all this is a marked degree of responsiveness on the part of the banking system to the needs of industry.

This responsiveness was also evident in other ways. The growth in the number of offices (branch banking) has already been mentioned. In part this is a reflection of the search for deposits, and in part a search for lending outlets; but it is also an indication of the response to the need for a greater flexibility in the payments mechanism. As the scale of businesses increased and a national market developed, it became necessary to have a rapid and inexpensive means of remitting money. The extensive branch networks developed by many of the joint-stock banks served this purpose. The need to make payments in other parts of the United Kingdom, on the Continent, and in other parts of the world was met by a system of correspondence agreements entered into with banks in places where it was likely that customers had need of them. As this facility matured, and other banking systems developed branch networks, the correspondence agreements were extended, on a reciprocal basis, to the branches, so that branches of one bank could draw bills on branches of other banks virtually anywhere that there were banks and agreements had been reached.[10] In this is to be found the kernel of the modern documentary credits form of international finance. The facilities thus provided added greatly to the ease with which payments could be made, both within the United Kingdom and internationally. It must also be argued that the availability of these services encouraged merchants to incur debts in many parts of the world, and so extended the breadth and size of markets for manufacturers. They also had the effect of encouraging the growth of deposits.

The corollary of the growth of business and the competitive nature of the banking system was that charges, already low, were further reduced, especially in the 1830s. The reduction of the charges and the narrowing of interest differentials between lending and deposit rates had a regional dimension, being greatest in the rapidly industrialising West of Scotland and less pronounced in Edinburgh and the agricultural areas of the country. The reduction of charges was especially welcome to customers and often determined where business was placed, but from the banker's point of view there were dangers in that profits were reduced and therefore all earning assets had to be managed with fine attention to detail. There was no room for error or even slackness if dividends were to be maintained.

III

Bank profits generally were put under severe pressure in the 1830s. This was such a source of concern to the Bank of Scotland that an enquiry was begun into the causes, and the results were published as a pamphlet.[11] Four factors were identified as causing the downturn in profits. These were (1) a reduction in the yield on Government Securities; (2) a reduction in the par of exchange on London; (3) the abandonment of some commission charges and the increase of stamp duty on notes; and (4) the note circulation, which had formerly been the major source of profit, had decreased due to the increased competition for business and the growing use of cheques. The effect of these factors can also be seen in the archives of the provincial banking companies, which goes some way to explain why they all but disappeared in the 1830s and 1840s. The new joint-stock banks were not exempt from the pressures, although most, because of their scale of operation, were better equipped to withstand them; for example, the Aberdeen Town and County Bank directors recorded in 1838 that in consequence of the increased competition in Banking the circulation of this Bank in common with others has suffered a diminution but that is the only department of the Bank's business in which there has been any falling off.[12]

Two years later they recorded that '. . . competition is now so great and the efforts of those connected with other establishments so vigorous . . .'[13] The vicissitudes of trade and the regular return to the downswing of the trade cycle further exacerbated the pressure. Some of the smaller joint-stock banks felt very badly exposed, for example the Southern Bank of Scotland, based in Dumfries, which was essentially an agricultural bank. It was founded in 1838, opened seven branches in Dumfriesshire and Galloway, and paid a dividend of five per cent in 1840, but passed on dividends in the following two years before seeking release in a merger with the Edinburgh and Leith Bank in 1842.[14] Clearly even joint-stock banks without a broad base were vulnerable in a very critical way.

A few of the provincial banking companies tried to resist the march of progress; for example, the Ship Bank and the Glasgow Banking Company joined forces in 1836 to form the Glasgow and Ship Bank which was to be a 'private firm of the old type',[15] although there were members who wished to convert the concern into a joint-stock bank. The conservatives, however, argued that the discussions before Parliament rendered a decision on the matter ill-advised until the intentions of the legislature were more certain, and nothing was done.[16] This concern also tried to resist the reductions of charges; for example, in 1841 the manager claimed with respect to commission on money transmissions that 'we adhered to that long after our neighbours had abandoned it'.[17] The result was that the bank lost deposits at an alarming rate and was subsequently taken over by the Union Bank in 1843, having paid the price of its conservatism.

Many bankers realised that there were four organisational options open to them which, if adopted, would help them to meet or limit the competitive pressures. The first of these was the extension of the branch network. All public and joint-stock banks attempted this in order to meet the challenge of competition and broaden their deposit base. The second was to take over other provincial or joint-stock banks and so enlarge their business in a fairly simple way. The third was to seek mutual agreement with all other banks on a scale of charges appropriate to modest profits. The fourth was to reduce their reserve assets and lend a higher proportion of their resources in an attempt to earn a higher rate of return. All of these options had inherent dangers, but some were more dangerous than others.

Many banks were conscious that the main solution to the competitive pressures was to extend the size of their business and to take advantage of the economies of scale which were available; for example the directors of the Western Bank thought it 'evident from the low range of profit, business must be conducted on a large scale'.[18] The principal means by which they extended the scale of their business was the opening of branches. The Western set up 23 branches in the 1830s and a further 49 in the 1840s, and as a result had the largest branch network of any of the Scottish banks.[19] Others were almost as adventurous. The Commercial had 54 branches by 1850. Scottish banks had had branches since the 1770s, but the experience of the 1830s and 1840s brought new dimensions to the system. The opening of branches tended to follow the trade cycle, with the largest numbers appearing at the peak, but there were very few closures in the slumps.

The founders of the Clydesdale Bank in Glasgow were sure that this 'great City and Neighbourhood afford an ample field for the operations of another Banking Company. It is intended that (the Bank) shall be chiefly a local bank — having few branches'.[20] It did not take long, however, for the promoters to recognise the trends in banking, and very soon the Clydesdale had a broad sweep of branches from Campbeltown in the West to St Andrews in the East.[21]

The early branches of Scottish banks had been lending agencies first and deposit gatherers second, but those set up in the 1830s and 1840s reversed this ranking. There had been a time, even as late as 1830, when the directors of the National Bank could claim that small branches were good for keeping the bank's notes in circulation, but as the 1830s progressed and the note issue became relatively less important and deposits more important, it was the latter which came to dominate the logic of branch extensions. Perhaps this change is one reason why the National and Commercial — both Edinburgh-based — kept out of Glasgow for so long. They knew that any offices in the West would be bound to be dominated by demands for credit rather than offers of deposits; for it was in the West that the greatest developments of the industrial revolution were taking place and consequently that the greatest demands for credit were made. Only an Edinburgh or Northern bank with considerable difficulty in placing any surplus funds would find it necessary to open branches in the West. The experience of the National Bank is particularly interesting in this respect. By 1826 its thirteen branches formed a crescent through Scotland covering North, East and South, but the only branch in the West was at Airdrie. No Glasgow office was opened until 1843.[22]

There is no disputing the fact that the greatest competition for deposits was in the rapidly industrialising West and to a lesser extent in the Dundee area. One manifestation of this competition was the rate of interest. The National had to pay $\frac{1}{2}$% more for its deposits at Airdrie, to conform to West of Scotland rates, than it did at its other branches or in Edinburgh.[23] This state of affairs was not likely to recommend itself to a bank based in the East which was already having difficulty keeping up its profits. Yet the realisation eventually came to those who had so assiduously kept out of the West that it was in that 'district the principal banking business is done'[24] and, if growth was to be sustained, then there was no alternative to opening offices in Glasgow, Paisley and other centres. In this way funds deposited throughout Scotland were lent in Glasgow.

One of the spin-off benefits derived from the spread of branches was the increasing professionalisation of banking. The traditional practice was to recruit local men, often lawyers, who would conduct the bank's agencies often in conjunction with their legal practice or other business. Increasingly, however, the banks found it difficult to recruit men of the right calibre who would conduct their business with the required blend of prudence and neutrality. The solution was to appoint career bankers to vacant agencies, and so began the slow transition to professional banking. Allied to this development was the formation of inspection departments and the related attempt to standardise branch practice throughout the bank — 'uniformity of system for all the Branches or Agencies appearing to be of great consequence'.[25]

Although the extension of branch networks was seen by some as an answer to the problems of competition and low profits, it very soon became clear that if everyone saw branches in that light, then the result would be, not a lightening of the burden of competition, but an intensification of the problem. As early as 1833 Hugh Watt, one of Scotland's most experienced bankers, and by then manager of the Huddersfield Banking Company, thought that

> the branch bank system has been carried too far, and the competition for business which has taken place, by the increase of agents of banks, has been productive of injurious consequences, especially to the trade of the district where such competition has taken place.[26]

Such warnings, however, were bound to go unheeded until the real cause of the problem, low profitability, could be solved.

Other banks sought a solution to the problem of low profits in taking over other banks. The Commercial, National, Western and British Linen were all involved in take-overs of provincial banking companies and private banks as these concerns failed to face up to the challenge of increased competition.[27] The most active concern in this respect was the Glasgow Union Banking Company[28] which, between 1836 and 1850, took over the businesses of five provincial banking companies, including their branches, and one private bank in Edinburgh, thus achieving a countrywide spread of branches. Yet this seemingly simple route to growth was not without its problems, for the taking over of other banks often involved the assumption of obligations and the employment of staff which, in different circumstances, might not have been undertaken, and which subsequently caused a drain on profits. This tactic, however, enabled the Union to become one of the biggest Scottish banks.

It was, however, not just the old provincial and private banking companies which were taken over; many of the smaller joint-stock banks also disappeared in the name of rationalisation at this time. Several of the smaller, more localised and younger joint-stock banks, which had not had time to become well established before succumbing to competitive pressures, for example the Southern Bank and Paisley Commercial Bank, were taken over by large joint-stock banks.[29]

The outcome of all this was, by 1845, a greater homogeneity amongst banks than had existed before. Even if the remaining banks did not have national branch networks, most were at least supra-regional.[30]

The third solution to the problem of low profits was to attempt to minimise the worst effects of competition by trying to reach an agreement amongst all the banks on appropriate rates of interest for deposits and advances, and charges for services. The nature of competition, however, made agreement difficult to achieve, and any success in this area was at best regional and often short-lived. The directors of the Commercial felt that

> the Banks have been compelled to conduct many most laborious and responsible parts of their business without any recompense at all but at the expense of increased establishments for the purpose.[31]

As a solution to this, three possibilities were considered over a number of years from the mid-1830s to the early 1840s. The first was to widen the margin between lending and deposit rates; the second was to vary the manner in which interest was applied on deposits — the traditional daily balance method was to be replaced by the minimum monthly balance; and thirdly some forms of commission charges for services and accounts could be instituted. All of these were tried with varying degrees of success, but it was evident that all banks in direct competition would have to be in agreement, lest those who had the lowest charges or highest deposit rates attracted too much business away from the others. The lead in all this came from the Edinburgh public and joint-stock banks, principally the Bank of Scotland, British Linen, Commercial and National.[32] The Royal Bank found itself in a difficult position, for it had not yet chosen to have an extensive branch network and depended very heavily for its profits on its large branch in Glasgow.

Despite a relatively late start in joint-stock banking, the Glasgow bankers had developed in a dramatic way in the 1830s, so that by 1841 the Glasgow Union was able to write to the Bank of Scotland indicating its broad agreement

> to any arrangement which the other banks would adopt; on the other hand anything like a threat from your side of the country would be met with defiance as we think ourselves quite a match for you in the race of unrestrained competition should such unhappily be resorted to by any of the Edinburgh banks.[33]

Such agreements as were reached were exceptionally fragile, and efforts were made to force the new banks, which were still being formed at the turn of the decade, to conform to agreements on charges and rates of interest as a condition of their being admitted to the note exchange.[34] Those banks which had already been admitted, however, proved more troublesome.

The problem seems to have been that where there was a greater demand for money, that is, in the areas of greatest economic development — Glasgow and, to a lesser extent, Dundee — the price of money, or rate of interest on deposits, was likely to be greater. The outcome of this was a stand-off. There was some little success in introducing charges and commissions on accounts and money transfers, but no lasting agreements on these or on interest rates — with those in the West, and often Dundee, being consistently higher than in Edinburgh.[35] The directors of the National Bank got round this problem by instructing branches that whenever branches of the Edinburgh banks are met by those of the Glasgow local banks the Glasgow rates are to be adopted.[36]

Similarly eight years later (1847) the Commercial Bank

> authorise the Agents when met by the Western Bank and Clydesdale Bank who now pay 4 per cent interest on Current Accounts to allow the same rates so as to preserve our customers.[37]

No lasting agreement was reached.

The fourth possible solution to the problem of low profits was to engage in risk banking, that is, lending a larger portion of total assets than was the normal practice of the Edinburgh banks. Such practice would enable banks to advance more to customers, and as advances produced a higher return than that obtainable on conventional reserve assets, that is, Government securities, then the result would be higher profits although lower liquidity. The existence of banks with low reserves was a great worry to the Edinburgh bankers, and Alexander Blair of the Bank of Scotland was in favour of making a reserve ratio compulsory for all banks.[38] Risk banking was not a new phenomenon in Scottish banking, having been carried on for many years with great success by the provincial banking companies. But these were moderately sized banks who, because of the local nature of their proprietorship and business, could depend upon their customers not to make runs upon them.[39] The new joint-stock banks with their national or cross-regional branch networks could not be so dependent upon the goodwill of their customers and note holders. Reserves were essential to the new-style banks. The directors of the Commercial were fully aware of this when they stated that

> it is a sound principle in our trade, that a distinct relation must always be preserved between the Deposits of the Bank and that proportion of its funds which must be kept freely at its command and therefore comparatively unfruitful, whilst however, the interest payable on the former is increased the latter are not rendered more productive.[40]

The National Bank directors were similarly prudent but were aware that

> a portion of the sound principles which should regulate the Banking operations have not been uniformly adhered to. Instances have not been wanting to illustrate the evil consequences of a disregard of prudent management, in the zeal to realise greater returns and speedily to declare large dividends.[41]

Not unexpectedly the prime offender in this respect was a Glasgow concern, the Western Bank of Scotland. As a result of overdrawing their London account in 1834, Jones, Lloyd and Company — the London agent — had refused further drafts, forcing the Western to try to borrow elsewhere, as it had no appreciable liquid or near-money reserves. When these events became public knowledge, the other Scottish banks refused all Western notes in payments. The Bank of Scotland as senior bank and policeman of the system lectured the Western on proper practice and demanded guarantees before re-admitting the Western to the exchange. In particular, attention was drawn to the absence of any investment in stock, Exchequer bills or other marketable securities, which would be an immediate tangible fund in case of pressure on your means.

The public and private banks in London and Edinburgh are in the practice of investing a sum equal to their whole circulation and one third of their deposits in securities of a marketable description.[42]

An opinion, however, seems to be hazarded that a Joint-Stock Company assumed to be composed of individuals of undoubted credit, may dispense with the rules which are considered essential to the safety and right conduct of Chartered and Private Banks because as it is contended the public is ultimately safe.[43]

The Western's logic had argued that the limited liability which was generally assumed to be a feature of the constituting Act or Charter of the Public Banks rendered a large reserve necessary in the interests of the public, but because joint-stock banks had no such advantage and instead all proprietors were liable for the debts of the bank to the full extent of their personal fortunes, then a large reserve was unnecessary as all debts could ultimately be paid in full. The Bank of Scotland, however, was unimpressed by this argument, insisting instead that other banks and the public

neither have, nor can be expected to have, such information regarding the individual credit of a large proprietary as to warrant them to act upon the assurance that dealings with them to an unlimited extent are safe . . . yet the greatest loss and inconvenience may be sustained by the banks and the public dealing with them from the temporary derangement of their affairs, caused either by mismanagement or by political or commercial panic.[44]

Although the behaviour of the Western improved, it was never entirely satisfactory to the Edinburgh banks who, when the Western applied for a Royal Charter in 1838, objected to the granting of it on the grounds that the Western remained 'a threat to the entire credit structure'.[45] Such caution seems to have been well founded, for the Western failed in the crisis of 1857. The Western was the only major bank which engaged in risk banking. Evidence on some of the smaller joint-stock concerns is rather scanty, but it seems likely that others, mostly the smaller concerns like the Dundee-based Eastern, were also guilty. Most banks, however, were well aware of the need for good reserves.

IV

When the Scottish Bank Act was passed in 1845, the average Scottish bank was a large-scale Public or joint-stock concern with many branches, that is, the system was radically different from that of 1826. Despite fragmentary evidence, it does seem that the banks had passed the worst of their competitive excesses, although the drive for branch extensions continued, with periodic bursts of activity, for many more years. From the evidence available, it appears that the attempt to restore profitability to the system bore fruit, for the dividends of nearly all Scottish Public and joint-stock banks increased from 1840 to 1856 and 1864 (see Table 4). This table does seem to demonstrate

TABLE 4

Dividends of Scottish Banks, 1840, 1856 and 1864/5, [46] *as percentage of issued capital (nominal values)*

Edinburgh-based banks	1840	1856	1864/5	Glasgow-based banks	1840	1856	1864/5	Others	1840	1856	1864/5
Bank of Scotland	6	8	10	Union	7	9	10	Aberdeen Town and County	7½	6+	10
Royal	6	6	7½	Western	6	9	—	North	6	10	10
British Linen	8	9	11	Clydesdale	6	7	9	Caledonian	—	8	10
Commercial	7	10	10	City	—	6½	7	Central	6	8	12½
National	6	7	10								

that profitability had been restored, although dividends are not always the perfect guide to this as some concerns may have paid larger dividends than were warranted by profits, by drawing on reserves, while others may have preferred to pay dividends lower than might have been expected, and to supplement these with occasional bonuses. Nevertheless the figures are sufficiently all-encompassing to suggest a general trend to higher profits, although they were still lower than in English banks.[47]

Much of this age of high competition had passed against a backdrop of threatened Government legislation to control the banking system, which was itself reflected in the great debate of the Banking and Currency schools. The Scots had remained relatively aloof from all this except when it seemed likely that their system would be threatened. The defensive mechanism which had proved so effective in 1826 began to gather its strength in the early 1840s. The Directors of the Commercial earnestly hoped that the legislature would

> see cause to respect the almost unanimous voice which on this subject has been expressed and pause before they venture to lay a rude hand on that which hitherto has wrought so beneficially for the Country or introduce change which may eventually tend to the disjointing of a system which has become incorporated with the progress and prosperity of this portion of the United Kingdom.[48]

Similarly the Caledonian directors in Inverness stated in August 1844 that

> the measures now introduced into England affect the currency without materially affecting the system of Banking while in Scotland the one is so intimately connected with the other that any attempt to interfere with the Currency must materially affect the whole system of Banking as pursued in this Country. It need hardly be stated that any diminution of the circulation will also diminish the profits of the Scotch Banks and necessarily lead to the introduction of the English system of Charges which press more heavily upon business transactions than what we have been accustomed to in this country.[49]

The concern of these Northern businessmen for circulation reflected the geographical isolation of Inverness. Elsewhere in Scotland the note circulation was much less important than it had been in 1826, having been partly superseded by cheque transfers.

When the final proposals for Scotland were drafted, most of the opposition to the measure melted away although there remained some heartfelt misgivings. The more prescient, however, felt that there was some advantage in the Bill. The Court of the Aberdeen Town and County Bank thought that the

> measures . . . though restricting the Banks to their average Circulation of the last 13 lunar months will yet secure them the great boon of the monopoly of Banking in Scotland.[50]

This prediction proved correct. No new banks were founded in Scotland after the passing of the Act in 1845, and so the threat of more new banks bringing more competition into the system was removed. This fact alone must have been the major reason why opposition to the Bill was so muted.

V

The transition in Scottish banking from the four-tier structure of 1826 to the relatively homogeneous structure of 1845 was not accomplished without trauma. Yet what had been achieved in this relatively short period was of immense significance for the Scottish economy. The banking system which had been so successful in the industrial revolution had given way to a system which in its scale of operation and manner of doing business was more appropriate to a maturing industrial economy. Although progress in this regard had also been made in England, the situation there was not strictly comparable with that of Scotland. The new English joint-stock banks, according to a recent writer, were 'in size and nature very much like their private counterparts, having small capitals, few branches, and parochial outlooks'. Other attempts to assess the differences between Scotland and England have also shown that by 1850 the Scots had achieved a system of banking which was relatively more extensive and pervasive than its neighbour's.[51]

NOTES

1. I am very grateful to the University of Glasgow and the Carnegie Trust for financial assistance for the research of this paper.

2. Parliamentary Papers, Report from the Select Committee on Promissory Notes. 1826, page 12.

3. T. Joplin, 'An Essay on Banking in England and Scotland' (1822).

4. S. G. Checkland, Scottish Banking: A History 1695-1973 (1975) and C. W. Munn, The Scottish Provincial Banking Companies 1747-1864 (1981).

    (1) Public Banks — founded by Act or Charter — Bank of Scotland, Royal Bank of Scotland and British Linen Company — note issues, branch networks.

    (2) Joint-Stock Banks — large-scale, note-issuing, multi-ownership banks with (usually) extensive branch networks.

    (3) Private Banks — Edinburgh-based — usually non-note-issuing, no branches, tend to act as retailers of credit from public banks but gradually developing their own deposit base. Small partnerships.

    (4) Provincial Banks — country banks. Note-issuing, some with a few branches. Some small partnerships but some quite extensive co-partneries, similar in structure to joint-stock banks but much smaller.

5. C. W. Munn, 'The Coming of Joint-Stock Banking in Scotland and Ireland 1810-1850', in T. M. Devine and D. Dickson (eds.), Ireland and Scotland, 1600-1850 (forthcoming).

6. C. W. Munn, 1981, Chapter 6.

7. Called Public Banks because their constitutions derived from Government authority and their shares were freely traded. See Checkland, 1975, Chapter 2.

8. C. W. Munn, 1981, Part 1.

9. S. G. Checkland, 1975, pages 385-386. For the industrial counties of England see M. Collins and P. Hudson, 'Provincial Bank Lending: Yorkshire and Merseyside 1821-1860', Bulletin of Economic Research, 1979.

10. See especially Union Bank of Scotland archives.

11. T. Gourvish, 'The Bank of Scotland 1830-1845', Scottish Journal of Political Economy 1969, and Bank of Scotland pamphlet 1840.

12. Aberdeen Town and County Bank, Court Minute Book, 6/8/1838.

13. *Ibid.*, 25/2/1840.

14. J. M. Reid, *The History of the Clydesdale Bank 1838-1938* (1938), pages 90-94.

15. R. S. Rait, *The History of the Union Bank of Scotland* (1930), page 210.

16. C. W. Munn, 1981, page 91.

17. Bank of Scotland Archives, 1/518/1, Minutes of meetings of treasurers of Banks, 31/1/1841.

18. M. A. Whitehead, 'The Western Bank and the Crisis of 1857'. Unpublished M.Litt. thesis, University of Strathclyde, 1978, page 73.

19. S. G. Checkland, 1975, pager 328.

20. J. M. Reid, 1938, pages 36-37.

21. *Ibid.*, page 63.

22. National Bank of Scotland Minutes.

23. *Ibid.*, 28/5/1827.

24. Commercial Bank of Scotland Minutes, 29/4/1844.

25. *Ibid.*, 18/6/1811.

26. H. Watt, *The Practice of Banking in Scotland and in England* (1833), page 19.

27. C. W. Munn, 1981, pages 85-94.

28. Formed in 1830 as the Glasgow Union Banking Company, it changed its name to the Union Bank of Scotland in 1843.

29. See Table 2.

30. See Table 3.

31. Commercial Bank of Scotland Minutes, 17/12/1840.

32. National Bank of Scotland Minutes, 21/8/1839.

33. Bank of Scotland Archives, 20/1/15 Currency and Banking. Letter from Glasgow Union to Bank of Scotland, 27/2/1841.

34. *Ibid.*, 1/518/1. Minutes of meetings of treasurers of Scottish Banks 16/1/1839.

35. A parallel can be found to this in Ireland where rates in the industrial North were higher than in the agricultural South.

36. National Bank of Scotland Minutes, 22/5/1839.

37. Commercial Bank of Scotland Minutes, 6/5/1847.

38. PP Evidence of Committee on Banks of Issue 1841 Q 1949.

39. C. W. Munn, 1981, conclusion.

40. Commercial Bank of Scotland Minutes, 4/12/1834.

41. National Bank of Scotland Minutes, 4/12/1834.

42. Western Bank of Scotland Minutes, 18/10/1834.

43. *Ibid.*, 23/10/1834.

44. *Ibid.*

45. M. A. Whitehead, 1978, page 67.

46. Bank of Scotland Archives, 20/1/12 and 20/1/18.

47. M. Gaskin, 'Note Issue in Scottish Banking'. Unpublished M.A. thesis, University of Liverpool (1955), page 27.

48. Commercial Bank of Scotland Minutes, 17/12/1844.

49. Caledonian Bank Minutes of General Meetings, 6/8/1844.

50. Aberdeen Town and County Bank Minutes, 7/5/1845.

51. P. L. Cottrell, *Industrial Finance 1830-1914* (1980), page 16. See also R. Cameron, *Banking in the Early Stages of Industrialisation*, 1967, ch. 3 and M. Collins, *The English Banking Sector and Monetary Growth*, University of Leeds Discussion Paper, No. 102, 1981.

7. London, Paris and Silver, 1848-1867

P. L. Cottrell

ONE of the features of the world economy during the third quarter of the nineteenth century was the substantial international flows of the monetary metals. Most attention has been paid to the movement of the 'new' gold from the mines in California and Australia, initially to London but then disseminated throughout the international economy as a result of Britain's import surplus. Equally of note was the transfer of silver along with gold out of Europe to the Orient, but this considerable flow has aroused only the spasmodic interest of historians.[1] The purpose of this paper is to look at some of the effects of this transfer of bullion and specie especially upon the two major quasi-central banks of the period — the Bank of England and the Bank of France.

I

There has been some controversy over the forces responsible for the drain of treasure to the Orient during the 1850s. Sayers has argued that the reason for the bullion flow was a growing import surplus with China and India caused by differentials in the rate of inflation between the West and the East. With the arrival of the 'new' gold in Europe, the prices of locally produced goods rose faster than those imported from the Orient, because the 'new' gold-induced inflation did not spread as rapidly to the silver standard countries. The relative cheapening of oriental luxuries such as silks and teas and the like on Western markets increased demand for them, producing a worsening of the trade balance and a rise in the drain of treasure. More recently Hughes has demonstrated that not only did prices of cotton, silk, tea, indigo and sugar increase more than those of Western-produced goods, but also the quantity imported rose. There was a price inelastic demand for Eastern produce on the markets of Western Europe during the 1850s. The Hughes analysis can also be applied to the first half of the 1860s when, as a result of the Civil War, there was a price inelastic demand for raw cotton from the Middle East and Asia in Western Europe. In both the 1850s and the 1860s the main source of silver to meet Western Europe's trade imbalance with the Near and Far East was the French bimetallic currency.[2]

The demand for silver during the middle decades of the nineteenth century led to an appreciation in its gold price. The price of silver had been extraordinarily steady during the first half of the nineteenth century, but between 1848 and 1851 it rose from 4s 11½d per standard ounce to 5s 1⅝d on the London market and remained above its 1848 price until 1875. Silver production had been increasing from the 1830s and output was expanded with the market appreciation especially during the late 1840s. But this appears to have been a once-and-for-all response as production thereafter hardly grew during the 1850s.[3] During the cotton famine caused by the Civil War, some silver was drawn out of the German States to feed the drain, while silver mined in Mexico and South America was shipped directly to India. The introduction of the greenback currency in the United States led to flows of gold and silver from North America to Europe which also fed the drain to the East.

While it is generally accepted that the drain to the Orient was the corollary of Western Europe's trade deficit with that area, it is difficult to support this statement with any statistical precision. The nexus of the flows of goods west-ward and bullion and specie eastwards was Britain's entrepôt trade. British imports until 1854 were valued at 'official prices', and although 'computed real values' were introduced in that year, the 'declared' system was not extended to imports and re-exports until 1871. China merchants maintained that the Board of Trade seriously undervalued imports from the Celestial Empire throughout the 1850s and 1860s.[4] The problem is further complicated by the transshipment of goods overland at the Suez isthmus until the opening of the canal in 1869. This resulted in Indian silks together with Chinese silks and teas exported initially to India being listed in the British trade returns as imports from Egypt. The 'point of origin' problem also affects the eastward flows, as bullion was noted simply in the trade returns as British exports, either to Egypt, or more generally to 'the East'. As a result the quantification of the import surplus with the East even for Britain alone is exceedingly difficult. Davis's recently pub-lished estimates show that Britain's net import surplus with Asia and China, after allowing for re-exports, fluctuated considerably during the first half of the nineteenth century. During the mid-1820s and mid-1830s it averaged £6.5m but then fell to £3.6m in the mid-1840s before increasing to £11.4m in the mid-1850s.[5]

Western European trade with the East was moving towards being multi-lateral and this had an effect upon the eastward drain of bullion. One counter-vailing item which tempered the drain was opium shipped and smuggled from India to China. These opium shipments increased sharply during the late 1820s and the late 1830s.[6] In the decade 1854 to 1863 China's trade deficit with India averaged £8.25m while opium accounted for 84.8 per cent of Indian exports to China in 1856 and 85.1 per cent in 1866.[7] The actual size of the opium trade is difficult to gauge because of smuggling, while Europe's deficit with India sharply worsened in the 1850s. Britain's average annual deficit with Asia swung from £470,000 in the mid-1840s to £3,748,000 in the mid-1850s. The Indian deficit became more adverse with raw cotton shipments during the 1860s, while British imports of Chinese silks and teas declined after 1864 due to supply shortages caused by the Taiping rebellion.

The volume of the silver drain from Western Europe to the East, like the other flows involved, is difficult to quantify with any precision. A fairly reliable contemporary estimate by Sir H. M. Hay[8] of the bullion dealers Moccatta and Goldsmid reveals two peaks — one of £20.15m in 1857 with a second and smaller peak of £16.85m in 1864. It was believed that most of the silver that went east was shipped to China whereas the gold involved in the Oriental drain went to India. The flow of the yellow metal to the sub-continent rose steadily during the 1850s and the first half of the 1860s to reach a peak of £9.84m in 1864/5. Statistical evidence assembled in the late 1870s and mid-1880s would appear to support the thesis of gold to India and silver to China for the 1850s. However in the 1860s, with the cotton famine, most of the gold and silver went to India alone.

The appreciation of silver in terms of gold had monetary effects in Western Europe. Silver became undervalued at the French mint from 1848 with the result that silver in France was either hoarded or exported. After 1848 the French franc became *de facto* a gold currency, although nominally France remained on the bimetallic standard which had been established by Napoleon in 1803.[9] During the first half of the 1850s the Bank of France's total bullion holdings fell from £17.2m to £7.9m with the proportion in appreciating silver declining from 99.1 per cent to 50.1 per cent.[10] The Bank of England generally refused to hold silver in its reserve from 1848.

The problems faced by the Bank of England and the Bank of France caused by the drain of 'treasure' to the 'East' during the 1850s and 1860s were exacerbated by other changes arising from the evolving world economy which increased the international sensitivity of the money markets of London and Paris. Capital exports, some to India and China, from Britain and France rose substantially during the 1850s and 1860s. The pattern of world trade and its associated payment system, partly as a consequence, began to shift from a segmented mosaic of independent payment systems to a fully multilateral system. With these processes sterling, but also the franc to some extent, became an important world reserve currency. However, at the same time the reserves of the Bank of England and the Bank of France were no longer protected by distance. The expansion of railway networks, the growth of steam shipping and the laying of international telegraph cables speeded up global communication. The world's money markets became knitted together with a consequent increase in arbitrage operations. London and Paris were in any case physically close, and by 1861 an interest rate differential of more than two per cent was sufficient to cause gold to cross the Channel. These developments during the mid-century were powerful but there were also a series of strident shocks which jarred against the underlying mechanisms. These primarily arose from war, in particular the Crimean and the American Civil Wars, which dislocated international intercourse and caused uncertainty.

The bank most subject to pressure was the Bank of France, from whose

K

vaults the majority of the silver to feed the drain was obtained. How the Bank of France reacted affected other financial markets, especially London. The Bank of France alternated between two policies. At times, and especially during domestic booms, the French institution competed aggressively for the 'new' gold in order to try and maintain her reserve. On other occasions the Bank of France co-operated with her Anglo-Saxon counterpart in order to resolve the problems that they both faced.

II

Co-operation between Threadneedle Street and the Rue de Petits Champs was not a new development. The two banks had worked together, albeit indirectly for reasons arising from their statutes, during periods of stringency and crisis since the 1820s.[11] By the early 1850s co-operation, at least of an intermittent form, was a well-established practice. The two banks exchanged information and by 1854 telegraphed each other news of changes in their discount rates on a regular basis.[12] Other knowledge, and sometimes requests, came to Threadneedle Street by letter, occasionally brought by a personal representative. The ties between the two banks were reinforced by the personal and business links of their directors and *regents*. This informal relationship was actually more important than the formal which tended to be concerned with the technical problems of counterfeit coins, the suitabilities of differing papers for bank notes, and mercantile and banking law. The strength of the informal ties can be clearly seen in their influence upon Bonamy Dobree, who was Deputy Governor and then Governor of the Bank of England between 1857 and 1861. His major source of Parisian information was his friend Charles Mallet, the merchant banker, whose son Alphonse was a *controleur* of the Bank of France. Dobree and Mallet conducted an extensive personal correspondence, and the French protestant banker visited London frequently. Dobree kept a private record of monetary changes, noting in his day diary the course of the sterling/franc exchange, the movement of *rentes* and, at sensitive periods, details of the Bank of France's balance sheet, information which occasionally appears to have been sent privately and directly to Threadneedle Street.[13]

The extent of co-operation between the two banks was also affected by the political relationship between Britain and France. During the Crimean War a common problem was perceived — the drain of precious metals — which it was thought was caused 'by the vast foreign expenditure of our respective governments for the purpose of carrying on the war in the East'. Hankey, then the Deputy Governor, went further, writing, 'it is thus apparent that unity of action is most desirable on the part of both Banks and that which I have the honour to represent would deem nothing gained to its own reserves which should detract from those of the Bank of our Ally'.[14] However, after the Treaty of Paris this common cause disappeared, and for the next decade the two banks were in varying degrees of conflict as a result of their individual efforts to sustain their reserves. There was one exception, which was a series of transactions in 1860 which may have been due to political factors as well as the personal and business ties of the individuals involved.

Wartime co-operation between the two banks broke down before hostilities with Russia had ceased. During the crisis of the autumn of 1855 the Bank of France sent bills for discount to the Bank of England, buying gold with the proceeds although the London/Paris exchange was well above the gold export point.[15] Between 31 August and 18 October, Bank Rate was raised from $3\frac{1}{2}$ to 6 per cent as the reserve of the Bank of England fell by £5.1m. Hankey wrote to the Governor of the Bank of France explaining that the rate changes had been caused by the increased demand for discounts coupled with a decline in the 'treasure' and that they were not a hostile measure directed against the French institution.[16] However, with the continuing falling level of its reserve, the Bank of England by the middle of October was inspecting bills presented for discount in order to see if they would lead to further gold exports across the Channel.[17] The alliance brought about by the Crimean War was broken by the effects of the drain to the East. Gold was being shipped to Paris in order to obtain silver at below its market price from the Bank of France to be exported to the Orient. The Bank of France had required gold in order to shore up its reserve.[18]

Despite falling reserves in the first half of the 1850s, the Bank of France was reluctant to depart from past practice and vary its rate of discount. This time-honoured policy of allowing fluctuations in its normally large reserves to compensate for demands for specie and discounts was given official sanction when the French government in October 1855 empowered the Bank to pay a premium on gold. Actually this costly policy, which involved purchases of between £70m and £100m, mainly on the London market, proved to be self-defeating, as Hughes has shown, for it actually augmented the silver flow.[19] One effect of the Bank of France's gold-buying policy was increased difficulties for the Bank of England as the import surplus widened with the upswing of the trade cycle.

The *regents* of the Bank of France faced a dilemma in trying both to minimise the bank's reserve losses and maintain the silver proportion. It is probable that interest rate changes would have had little effect, given the underdeveloped nature of France's financial sector, especially in the 1850s. It has been estimated that specie made up 82 per cent of the French money stock in 1845 as opposed to 25 per cent in England. Forty years later specie probably still accounted for more than half of the Gallic money supply. Cheques were not recognised by French law until 1865, and even then post-dating and over-drafts were specifically forbidden.[20] These disparities in financial conditions were well known to contemporaries.[21] In such an environment Anglo-Saxon remedies would probably have had little effect upon French monetary problems. Further, Anglo-Saxon techniques were not yet that well founded. In Threadneedle Street it was only with the 'new' policy of competitive discounting after 1844 that Bank Rate fluctuated widely. The old traditions died hard and Weguelin at the Bank of England in the 1850s still favoured the *écheance* weapon as opposed to changes in Bank Rate,[22] a preference shared by other Bank directors.

The gold premium policy did not solve the Bank of France's problem and it faced extreme difficulties again in the autumn of 1856, caused on this occasion by an internal gold drain. An approach to the Bank of England for co-operation in the purchase of £2m to £3m of bullion was declined.[23] Its English counterpart was also trying to stem a fall in its reserves and consequently Bank Rate was increased from 4½ per cent to 5 per cent on 1 October, and then on 6 October to 6 per cent for bills less than 60 days, and to 7 per cent for bills up to 95 days, the latter change a mixture of dear credit and the *écheance* weapons. Both banks got through the 1857 crisis, but with difficulty. Despite the extreme pressure that was exerted on both their reserve positions, no joint action was considered although there was some private contact.[24]

The experience of the mid-1850s led the Bank of France to abandon its policy of keeping changes in its discount rate to an absolute minimum, there having been one rate change in 1853 and two rate changes a year in 1854, 1855 and 1856. A further problem allied to the interest rate question was that until 1857 the Bank of France had been restricted to a ceiling of 6 per cent under the Usury Laws.[25] A new approach became possible in 1857 when the Bank received a new charter and the Comte de Germiny succeeded Comte d'Argout as Governor. A new policy of varying the rate of discount inversely with the level of the reserves was introduced. There were to be thirty rate changes during de Germiny's six years as Governor as opposed to the twenty which had occurred during the previous fifty-seven years. Bopp has attributed this change of policy to 'a change of generation', as by 1855 over half of the Bank's executives were new compared with 1850.[26] Undoubtedly fresh thinking was occurring in Paris, and this was not just due to new minds but also new problems. There had been a major burst of domestic investment, especially in railways, during the boom of the decade while formal financial intermediaries had been established to channel savings. Operating with these domestic factors was the increase in the Parisian market's international sensitivity and above all the drain of silver to the East. The Bank of France needed to increase the range of its armoury to maintain the convertibility of the franc, as the experience of the autumnal drains of 1855 and 1856 had revealed, but, given the dualist nature of the French economy and the small size of the modern sector, there were definite limits on the effectiveness of an Anglo-Saxon interest rate policy.

III

The Cobden-Chevalier Treaty of 1860 and the political rapprochement that it involved may have encouraged another bout of co-operation between the Bank of England and the Bank of France. However, the main bond between the two institutions during the difficult year of 1860 was the well-established one of the personal ties between members of international banking houses, in particular the friendship of Dobree and Mallet. After a post-crisis year of relative ease, the eastern flow of silver had resumed in 1859 at almost full spate. The dimensions of the flow contracted in 1860 but to a level still above that of the first half of the 1850s. This difficult international monetary situation was made worse during the second half of 1860 by a poor European grain harvest. Consequently there were large imports of North American grain to be financed, together with the largest southern cotton crop on record. The vagaries of nature were responsible for the first act of the financial crisis of the autumn of 1860. The second act consisted of the financial consequences of the election of Lincoln as President of an increasingly disunited republic. International monetary metal flows during the second half of 1860 were broadly made up of the Eastern drain coupled with a growing flow of gold to the United States, the latter a reversal of the normal flow across the Atlantic.

In spite of de Germiny's different policy with respect to reserve problems, the Bank of France began to purchase gold at a loss during October 1860 to augment its reserves, just as it had done in the mid-1850s. These London purchases were initially camouflaged, and the French demand for gold appeared to be the result of the needs of the establishment of a branch of *Comptoir d'Escompte* at Shanghai together with the payment of French troops in China, Rome and Syria.[27] The real cause of the disruption of the London money and bullion markets with its effects for the Bank of England's reserve was further complicated by a French loan in gold to the Viceroy of Egypt. *The Economist* reported that £20,000 in bar gold and 50,000 sovereigns were taken from London by France for the loan.[28] Dobree, now Governor of the Bank of England, received a report on the loan from Goschen and wrote to Alphonse Mallet for verification.[29] During the first three weeks of October the Bank of France lost £3m in bullion and the Bank of England experienced a withdrawal of £1.647m.

By the beginning of November 1860 it was clear in London that the Bank of France was the ultimate buyer of much of the gold that had crossed the Channel. Dobree learned from Alphonse Mallet that the Bank of France was purchasing gold at a 1 per cent premium in London through Raphaels, which confirmed the suspicions of Baring.[30] The Governor of the Bank of England explained the situation at a meeting of the Committee of the Treasury on 6 November. He had ascertained positively that £20,792 in bar gold purchased from the Bank the previous day by Haggard & Co., bullion dealers, was for the Bank of France. Further, all available gold on the London market had been bought by Hambro & Son at a price above £3 17s 10½d per standard ounce, the Bank's selling price. It was clear that these transactions were connected with the execution of a contract between the Bank of France and the *Comptoir d'Escompte*. The Committee was recalled the following day before the weekly Court in order to consider whether to recommend raising Bank Rate to either 4½ or 5 per cent. Dobree did not favour a change, noting in his diary: 'The whole Mercantile World to be punished to protect 14 millions of bullion when there is no pressure for discounts is to my understanding quite unjustifiable'. He also knew from Sampson of *The Times* that the French gold operation was at an end.[31] On Thursday, despite Dobree's opposition, the Committee did recommend a rise to 4½ per cent. To put this decision into some perspective, it is probable that other directors were worried by the Bank's bullion holdings having fallen by £230,788 over the previous week while £43,952 in bar gold was sold to three firms of bullion dealers on the day of the Court meeting.

While the Bank of England was beginning to feel the first signs of the pressure of the autumn of 1860, the Bank of France was in a graver situation. *The Economist* argued that it ought to raise its rate, 'but it was its custom to purchase gold at a loss rather than disturb the money market'.[32] Later Bagehot commented: 'to do so would, it is true, cause a great outcry, for here the majority of the public understand financial matters so ill, that they think the Bank can fix what discount it pleases, and that consequently a high one is little better than robbery'.[33] However, there were parallel English provincial complaints against either high interest rates or the lack of credit at any price because of international gold flows.[34]

The Bank of France did follow *The Economist's* advice, for on Monday, 12 November it raised its rate from 3½ per cent to 4 per cent,[35] but this may have been a response to the Bank of England rather than a positive attempt to control its internal position. The Parisian bank could not afford losses arising out of Paris/London arbitrage rates in addition to the strains of the eastern drain, and the consequences of American grain and cotton imports. Its action heralded the beginning of what was to be a very difficult week. The *Swiftsure* from Melbourne had delivered £282,246 of gold the previous Friday, but £35,908 had been bought immediately by the bullion dealers. There were no bullion transactions at the Bank of England on Monday but on Tuesday, when the *Ethiope* from Africa discharged only £13,945 in bar gold, Raphaels bought £302,124 in bar gold. It was these circumstances which led to an unusual meeting of the Court in the Governor's room on Tuesday. Dobree began the meeting by reading a letter from Alphonse Mallet which explained why the Bank of France had raised its rate together with a further communication detailing the Bank of France's gold loss. The London bankers and merchants decided to raise Bank Rate to 5 per cent, voting nine to three, and the decision was telegraphed to the branches and the Bank of France.[36] The Bank of England sold £346,716 of gold on Wednesday, and while there were no bullion sales on Thursday, Raphaels commented that they were merely deferring purchases. The week's *Economist* contained a report that the Bank of France on Wednesday had ordered its London agents to buy and ship £1m in gold of which £0.635m had come from the vaults of the Bank of England.[37] At the normal weekly Court meeting of the Bank of England on Thursday the motion to raise Bank Rate to 6 per cent had been carried unanimously.[38]

After the Court meeting the Treasury Committee was convened and the question of assistance to the Bank of France was considered. It was decided that the Bank of England would not object to swapping gold for silver from the Bank of France if such an operation was pressed on Threadneedle Street. Following the decision, Dobree wrote to Alphonse Mallet and had an interview with the Chancellor of the Exchequer who thought that the proposed swap was highly desirable. It is clear that the initiative for this central bank swap had come from Governor Dobree. He had a clear view of both Parisian problems and the needs of the Bank of France through his connection with the Mallets, while the operation would help calm the London market and possibly allow a reduction in Bank Rate. The need for some form of stabilisation was emphasised during the following Friday and Saturday when gold shipments arriving in London were sold immediately.

The details of the operation were soon settled and the whole matter was placed before the Court of the Bank of England on 20 November. The directors decided to purchase 50m francs of silver bullion at 4s 10½d per standard ounce, paying in gold bar at 77s 1½d per standard ounce, prices determined partly by the 1844 Charter Act but also much closer to those of the French mint than in the free market.[39] This proved acceptable to the Bank of France, which had already agreed in outline, and by 22 November Alphonse Mallet and his fellow *controleur* Leon Charzal had arrived in London.[40]

At the end of November 1860 the bullion holdings of the Bank of France amounted to £17m, of which £4m was in silver. The French bank would only sell gold because if it released silver at the legal ratio it could be resold on the Paris market at a premium of 15 to 16 francs per mille for gold. Bagehot, after explaining the situation, noted that there was no foundation to the rumour that the Bank of France had agreed to discontinue its private buying of gold in London at a premium as a condition for the operation.[41] The swap was rapidly put into effect and the Bank of England sold some of its recently acquired silver at 5s 1½d per standard ounce. There was not an immediate direct replacement of gold by silver in the 'Old Lady's' balance sheet, as the Bank of France took the opportunity to settle some of its indebtedness to the London gold market.[42] The transaction was completed by mid-January 1861 and the Bank of England sold £0.5m out of the £2m of silver that it bought from its French counterpart.[43] In London, Bank Rate was reduced to 5 per cent on 29 November 1860 because the swap initially did reduce the pressure on the market.[44] The Bank sold only £5,184 in gold during the last week of November.

IV

The difficulties stemming from the silver drain and the financing of abnormal imports from North America continued until the Spring of 1861. However, a second monetary problem developed from the end of November 1860 which was an effect of political uncertainty in the New World. Lincoln's election resulted in the sterling/dollar exchanges falling due to American eastern bankers buying gold. By the first week of December the trans-Atlantic exchange had dropped to $104½-106 from a par of $109½.[45] With the abnormally large exports of cotton and grain the exchanges were in any case in America's favour, but the political crisis led American exporters to sell bills on the east coast 'at what they would fetch'. This panic selling of flood proportions resulted in the price of bills falling 3 or 4 per cent below the par specie point. Furthermore Americans were drawing sooner than was usual upon English and French importers, they were suspending orders for English and French exports, and were attempting to dump their own exports upon Western European markets. Consequently there were few American mercantile buyers of English bills and sterling paper was bought in New York 'by those willing to advance the value of bills till the equivalent in gold be procured in England'.

The Bank of England's first intimation of this new problem came on 30 November; the position of the sterling/dollar exchange was unclear but sovereign shipments amounting to £102,000 had been announced and there were rumours of other large amounts going to the United States.[46] The situation was clarified during the first week of December. Letters from New York dated 21 November arrived at Threadneedle Street on 3 December giving a rate on London of $104 but subsiding. Various estimates of probable sovereign exports were made including one by Cross of Dennistoun, Cross & Co. who thought that 30,000 had gone with a further 500,000 to be shipped for exchange purchased at $100. The Liverpool branch of the Bank, which was running out of sovereigns, announced on 6 December that 117,000 would be shipped, while on the following day news of further movements, including bar gold, reached London. The *Persia* was getting ready to sail from Liverpool with 540,000 sovereigns on board, of which 510,000 had come from the Bank.[47] *The Economist* estimated that the total movement of gold to New York over the previous week including the *Persia's* cargo to be £70,000.

The trans-Atlantic shipment of bullion continued but the volume of the flow did eventually subside. The Boston steamer took £211,000 on 15 December and the Bank's Liverpool branch lost £60,000 on 21 December and £81,000 on 26 December for export to America.[48] The Bank of England's weekly returns showed that it had lost £218,561 during the second week of December and £115,835 during the following seven days. Bagehot's staff estimated that £1.4m in bullion had been shipped across the Atlantic by 22 December. Gold was also moving out of England to India and France, despite being the same price on the Paris market.[49] The financial difficulties arising from the American drain reached a climax during January 1861. Bank Rate was increased to 6 per cent on 31 December and to 7 per cent on 7 January 1861. At this level the tide was turned and pressure on the Bank slackened. In late January its return was still showing a fall in bullion holdings but the reserve had increased by £109,307. The Bank had been borrowing on stock on the London Stock Exchange, something *The Economist* regarded as an innovation, while the New York/London exchange had risen to $105½ for first-class paper. The Bank's reserve position was also assisted by domestic flows. English farmers had begun threshing during January and the London money market expected money to return from the provinces as advances made by country bankers were repaid. But in early January the country balances of the London correspondent banks had 'never been so low . . . as at the present time'.[50] By early February, with the continuing fine weather 'large sums' were flowing into Lombard Street from the country banks. The Bank's return for the last week of January showed an increase of £90,036 in its bullion holdings. Gold arriving from Australia was now going straight to the Bank with some £260,000 having been refined.[51] It was calculated that £3,161,800 in gold was shipped to New York between 26 November 1860 and 9 February 1861, but with the exchange at $106½ by mid-February this was now expected to return.[52]

The Bank of France was also affected by the Atlantic drain, with the result that it began competing again for the supply of newly mined gold. Its swap gold was exhausted by mid-January 1861, and in London it was thought that the French bank would resume private gold purchases at a premium in order to protect its silver holding. The Bank of France did raise its discount rate, increasing it to 7 per cent on 8 January, but these changes were primarily responses to movements of Bank Rate in London.[53] Throughout January it was thought likely in London that the Bank of France would have to suspend specie payments due to the withdrawals of gold and the demand on it for discounts. By mid-January the Bank of France was buying bills directly and indirectly, and sending them to London for discount. There were rumours of new negotiations with the Bank of England which proved to be groundless,[54] while an arrangement to exchange £1.25m of silver for gold with the Bank of St. Petersburg was vetoed by the Czar for political reasons.[55] The Bank of France did obtain £160,000 in gold through a direct German purchase together with 'large sums' from other sources including Constantinople.[56] In this piecemeal fashion the French bank survived. By the beginning of February its position had improved; its bullion holdings, which had fallen to 13m, increased sharply, while the Parisian open market rate fell to 5 per cent.[57]

France had a visible trade deficit in 1861 caused principally by the poor harvests of 1860 and 1861.[58] This import surplus led to a decline in the cash reserve of the Bank of France. A new monetary factor was a fall in the price of silver from 5s 1¼d per standard ounce, November 1860 to 5s 0d-5s 0¼d by July 1861. This led the Bank to prefer to meet its liabilities in depreciating silver rather than gold. Although the Bank since 1857 was more prepared to vary its rate of discount, it still in 1861 used the devices of the mid-1850s. It made a contract in October 1861 with Rothschilds under which they were to draw three months' bills on London amounting to £1m which were to be placed in circulation on the Bourse. This action would prevent gold flowing to England as it would depress the premium on London bills. If any of the bills reached the English metropolis, then they would enable gold to be drawn to Paris. Similar arrangements were made with Barings, and the Bank of France also arranged loans in Paris and London on French government stock.[59] In November 1861, as imports of grain rose, the Bank of France negotiated with the Bank of Prussia for a loan of £2.25m.[60]

Rist has maintained that the Bank of France responded vigorously to the decline in its cash reserve by raising short-term interest rates which, possibly, accelerated the fall of domestic incomes resulting from the adverse trade balance. The average rate of discount was 5.52 per cent during 1861 as opposed to 3.63 per cent in 1860, while the Bank's reserves averaged £14.74m in 1861 compared with £20.54m in 1860.[64] It is evident that the Bank under de Germiny was more prepared to vary its discount rate in accordance with its reserve position. However, according to contemporary English observers, the Bank of France during the autumn of 1860 and throughout 1861 was still not prepared to change its rate frequently enough. The Bank did not pursue a 'pure' discount rate reserve policy but instead used an amalgam of the premium on gold, swap operations, and changes in its rate. This 'mixed' policy continued, with changes in emphasis, until 1867. Indicative of this is that during 1862 the Bank's reserve averaged £14.76m, only £0.024m higher than in 1861, but its average rate of discount was only 3.77 per cent as opposed to 5.52 per cent in 1861.

V

Although the American cotton harvest of 1860 produced a bumper crop, the outbreak of the Civil War led to an immediate search for alternative supplies of raw cotton. In February 1861 'wild orders' were being placed in Bombay. The easing of monetary conditions in London and Paris in February 1861 proved to be a temporary respite. This speculative buying of Asian cotton resulted in a new drain of silver and gold to the East. During the first six weeks of 1861, £1,521,901 was exported to India and China as opposed to £3,703,903 over the previous six months.[62] The Bank of England sold £0.35m of silver during the first week of February and Bank Rate was raised to 8 per cent on 14 February. This increase did attract money to London, with gold 0.5 per cent dearer in London than in Paris, and during the week ending 27 February the Bank's bullion holdings increased by £315,465 and its reserve by £315,435. These events were a portent of monetary conditions in 1863 and 1864. However, in 1861 there was only a short flurry of speculative cotton buying, with the result that the Bank of England was able to reduce Bank Rate to 7 per cent on 21 March, to 6 per cent on 4 April, and to 5 per cent on 11 April.

The development of the raw cotton bullion drain to India in 1862 led to further intense bouts of competition between the Bank of England and the Bank of France for the supply of 'new' gold. The flow was substantial, though not as great as in the mid-1850s, and during the second half of 1862 the two banks lost £9,309,142 in bullion as a result of payments for cotton from Egypt and India.[63] This led between 1862 and 1865 to the Bank of France and the French government developing various methods to attract gold to Paris. In December 1862, for instance, the Bank of France's bullion holdings increased by £1m and it was 'believed by some well-informed persons [in London] that the gold had been procured by anomalous purchases in our market'.[64] This type of buying continued during January 1863 when the Bank of France raised its discount rate from 4 to 5 per cent and Bank Rate in London was increased from 3 to 4 per cent. There were further rumours of the Bank of France operations on the London market in July and August 1863, and on the latter occasion it was thought that they were connected with the Bank window-dressing its monthly return, the bullion in question having come from the stores of the London dealers.[65] It is possible that the Bank of England may have used what were subsequently called the 'gold devices' instead of raising Bank Rate to protect its reserve against the tactics of the Bank of France.[66]

The Bank of France continued to rely on London gold purchases as its main defensive weapon until 1864 and, only when these proved insufficient, did it raise its rate of discount, but then sharply and violently. When the cotton drain to the East was at its height in 1864, the Bank of France turned to changes in its discount rate but, as before, delayed alterations until the last possible moment. These violent fluctuations in the discount rate of the Bank of France comprised one of the main factors responsible for the frequent and sudden movements in Bank Rate in London.[67] *The Economist* commented forcefully: 'For some time past the occasional poverty of the Bank of France has been the most sudden and the most incalculable force in our money market, and it would be absurd indeed in us if we did not heedfully attend even to every slight symptom of its possible recurrency'.[68]

That one of the principal factors behind changes in Bank Rate was the movement of the Bank of France's discount rate constitutes grounds for reinterpreting an analysis undertaken by Nishimura. He found a fairly strong positive correlation between the amount of bills drawn in England and the London-Paris discount rate differential during the period 1861-1870. However, he concluded that the correlation was meaningless as Paris market rates were stable with the consequence that the London-Paris differential was only a disguised version of the movement of London rates.[69] This conclusion is certainly correct for the period 1868 to 1870, but before 1867 Paris market rates fluctuated considerably.[70] Therefore it would appear that the actions of the Bank of France, through the London-Paris interest rate differentials, had a strong

BULLION AND SPECIE FLOWS, 1848-1868 (£'000s)

Year	GOLD to France from U.K.[1]	SILVER to 'the East' from U.K.[1]	SILVER to India & China from U.K. & Mediterranean[2]	SILVER to China from U.K. & Mediterranean[3]	India Year	India: Net Import of GOLD[4]	India: Net Import of SILVER[5]
1848	840						
1849	246	13					
1850	1,367	97			1850-1	1,153	2,117
1851	1,211	1,563			1851-2	1,127	2,865
1852	685	2,892			1852-3	1,172	3,605
1853	5,327	4,571			1853-4	1,061	2,305
1854	13,388	3,254	4,580		1854-5	731	29
1855	9,865	5,630	7,980		1855-6	2,506	8,194
1856	9,657	10,929	14,120		1856-7	2,091	11,073
1857	10,863	17,295	20,150		1857-8	2,783	12,218
1858	10,530	5,088	5,690		1858-9	4,426	7,728
1859	14,902	16,003	16,350		1859-60	4,284	11,147
1860	10,400	8,124	10,800	4,902	1860-1	4,232	5,328
1861	998	7,274	8,860	1,222	1861-2	5,184	9,086
1862	6,356	10,708	14,600	2,830	1862-3	6,848	12,550
1863	3,502	8,815	15,130	3,076	1863-4	8,898	12,796
1864	7,775	5,708	16,855	2,199	1864-5	9,839	10,078
1865	4,263	3,808	9,740	1,034	1865-6	5,724	18,668
1866	8,465	2,538	7,070	757	1866-7	3,842	6,963*
1867	6,043	646	2,050	702	1867-8	4,609	5,593

* 11 months only.

1. *Statistical Abstract* (various years).
2. *British Parliamentary Papers*, 1876, VIII; Select Committee on the Depreciation of Silver, Appendix No. 6A.
3. *Ibid.*, Appendix No. 24C.
4. *British Parliamentary Papers*, 1888, XLV; Royal Commission on the Recent Changes in the Relative Values of the Precious Metals, Statement F.
5. *Ibid.*, Statement E.

influence upon the English demand for credit in the form of bill creations during the 1860s boom. As the volume of English bills, contrary to contemporary monetary theory, moved positively with changes in interest rates, they were a major destabilising cyclical factor.

VI

The outward flow of silver from Europe to the East during the 1850s and 1860s has been likened to a parachute in that in Europe it retarded the fall in the market price of gold. The effect was to overcome a dramatic price inflation while the enlargement of the money supply through the new gold, especially in Britain, France and the United States, had its impact upon the level of output.[71] However, the mechanism was not smooth and the replacement of silver by gold in the French currency led to a tussle, at times even a struggle, for the new gold between the Bank of England and the Bank of France, especially during the upswings of booms in the mid-1850s, 1860, and the mid-1860s. Bonamy Dobree noted carefully in his day diary at the Bank of England the arrivals of gold steamers and the exact amount of their precious cargoes. The London money market in the conduct of its business came to depend upon the arrival of the Australian steamers.[72] One effect of this struggle, this friction in the mechanism of the parachute, was to push up interest rates which in England between 1852 and 1867 were at their highest nominal levels for the longest periods of time for the whole of the nineteenth century.

NOTES

1. R. S. Sayers, 'The Question of the Standard in the Eighteen Fifties', *Economic History*, III (1933); J. R. T. Hughes, *Fluctuations in Trade, Industry and Finance* (Oxford, 1960); K. L. Wong, 'Anglo-Chinese Trade and Finance 1854-1914', unpublished Ph.D. thesis (University of Leicester, 1976); D. A. Martin, 'The Impact of Mid-Nineteenth Century Gold Depreciation upon Western Monetary Standards', *Journal of European Economic History*, VI (1977).

2. This was well recognised by contemporaries: see *British Parliamentary Papers*, 1876 (388), VIII: *Select Committee on Depreciation of Silver*, evidence of W. Bagehot, qq. 1410-12 and R. Giffen, q. 427.

3. See Martin, *loc. cit.*, p. 643.

4. *S.C. on Depreciation of Silver* (1876), Appendix No. 24C.

5. R. Davis, *The Industrial Revolution and British Overseas Trade* (Leicester, 1979), p. 59.

6. M. Greenberg, *British Trade and the Opening of China 1800-42* (Cambridge, 1951), p. 221.

7. Wong, *op. cit.*, pp. 122, 125.

8. *S.C. on Depreciation of Silver* (1876), Appendix No. 6A.

9. H. P. Willis, *A History of the Latin Monetary Union* (rep. New York, 1968), pp. 1-5.

10. Hughes, *op. cit.*, p. 253.

11. See Sir J. H. Clapham, *The Bank of England*, II *1797-1914* (Cambridge, 1944), pp. 101, 168-70, 200. There is some confusion in the literature regarding the transaction in 1847 as both Clapham and Morgan refer to a credit or loan of £1m while Hidy maintains that the Bank of

France borrowed £0.8m in silver. E. V. Morgan, *The Theory and Practice of Central Banking 1797-1913* (rep. 1963) and R. W. Hidy, *The House of Baring in American Trade and Finance* (Cambridge, Mass., 1949), p. 376.

12. Bank of England Archives, London (henceforth cited as BOE): Cou/B610 Deputy Governor's letters, 1851-1861, W. Hubbard to Comte d'Argout, 11.5.1854. I am grateful to the Governor and Company of the Bank of England for permission to consult the institution's archives and to the staff of the Museum and Historical Research section, especially the late Eric Kelly, for their help and assistance.

13. *Ibid.*, Cou/B614/3 5.4.1859 which contains an enclosure on Bank of France notepaper giving its reserve position.

14. *Ibid.*, Cou/B610 Hankey to Comte d'Argout, 9.10.1855.

15. Morgan, *op. cit.*, p. 160.

16. BOE, Cou/B610, 9.10.1855.

17. Hughes, *op. cit.*, p. 239

18. *Ibid.*, p. 253.

19. *Ibid.*, pp. 253-4. British Parliamentary Papers, 1857 (220) X, Pt 1, *Select Committee on the Bank Acts of 1844 and 1845*, evidence of W. Newmarch, qq. 1705, 1711; T. Weguelin, qq. 24, 24*, 564, 566-75; and W. Hubbard, q. 2838.

20. R. E. Cameron, 'England, 1750-1844', and 'France 1800-1870' in Cameron *et al.*, *Banking in the Early Stages of Industrialisation* (1967), pp. 42, 116 and 118-9.

21. See *The Economist* (1860), p. 1036.

22. *S.C. on the Bank Acts* (1857), evidence of T. Weguelin, q. 1236.

23. BOE Cou/B610, f152.

24. Clapham asserts that a concerted policy was proposed, referring to a volume of Deputy Governor's letters, but a search carried out by the Bank's archival staff failed to bring to light any substantiating evidence. Clapham, *op. cit.*, p. 229 but see BOE 917/1 Bonamy Dobree's letters, 16.10.1857, 9.11.1857 and 10.11.1857, Charles Mallet to Dobree.

25. The rate increases in 1855 and 1856 were accompanied by reductions in the *écheance:* K. Bopp, 'Bank of France Policy: Brief Survey of Instruments, 1800-1914', *American Journal of Economics and Sociology*, XI (1952-3), pp. 236-7. See also *S.C. on the Bank Acts* (1857), evidence of T. Weguelin, qq. 1231, 1233-5. The Bank of England changed its rate six times in 1853, twice in 1854, and eight times in both 1855 and 1856.

26. Bopp, *loc. cit.*, pp. 236-7.

27. *The Economist* (1860), pp. 1036-7, 1102, 1131.

28. *Ibid.*, pp. 1157-8, 1186.

29. BOE, Cou/B614/4 entry 17.10.1860. Goschen thought that the loan was for £4m and referred to it as secret, while according to *The Economist* it was for £0.8m.

30. *Ibid.*, 5.11.1860.

31. *Ibid.*, entry 7.11.1860.

32. *The Economist* (1860), pp. 1232, 1242.

33. *Ibid.* (1861), p. 38.

34. F. W. Fetter, *Development of British Monetary Orthodoxy, 1797-1875* (Cambridge, Mass., 1965), pp. 237-9.

35. BOE, Cou/B614/4, entry 12.11.1860.

36. *Ibid.*, entry 13.11.1860.

37. *The Economist* (1860), pp. 1257-8, 1264-5, 1270.

38. BOE, Cou/B614/4, entry 15.11.1860.

39. The swap ratio, silver:gold was 15.97:1 as opposed to the 1803 French bimetallic ratio of 15.5:1.

40. BOE, Cou/B614/4, entries 20.11.1860, 22.11.1860.

41. *The Economist* (1860), pp. 1301, 1309, 1314, 1316.

42. *Ibid.*, p. 1329.

43. *Ibid.* (1861), p. 44.

44. *Ibid.* (1860), p. 1343.

45. The sterling/dollar exchange was calculated on a mean specie point of $109\frac{1}{2}$ = £22 10s; see G. J. Goschen, *The Theory of the Foreign Exchanges* (16th ed., 1894), pp. 48-54, 92, 95-7, 105. On the long-term movement of the exchanges, see L. E. Davis and J. R. T. Hughes, 'A Dollar Sterling Exchange, 1803-1895', *Economic History Review*, 2nd ser., XIII (1960).

46. BOE, Cou/B614/4, entry 30.11.1860.

47. *Ibid.*, entries 3, 4, 5, 6, 7, 8.12.1860.

48. *Ibid.*, entries 15, 18, 21.12.1860 and inserted note 26.12.1860.

49. *The Economist* (1860), pp. 1344, 1430.

50. *Ibid.* (1861), pp. 98-100.

51. *Ibid.*, pp. 126-8.

52. *Ibid.*, p. 155.

53. *Ibid.*, pp. 10, 29, 36, 66.

54. *Ibid.*, pp. 29, 70.

55. *Ibid.*, pp. 70, 95, 126, 157, 730-1.

56. *Ibid.*, pp. 95, 100.

57. *Ibid.*, pp. 116, 165.

58. M. Rist, 'A French Experiment with Free Trade: the Treaty of 1860', in R. E. Cameron (ed.), *Essays in French Economic History* (Homeward, Illinois, 1970), pp. 292-5.

59. *The Economist* (1861), pp. 730-1, 1122-3, 1150-1, 1205.

60. *Ibid.*, pp. 1341-2.

61. Rist, *loc. cit.*, p. 293, converting at a rate of £1 = 25 francs.

62. *The Economist* (1861), p. 169.

63. *Ibid.* (1863), pp. 57, 64, 66-7.

64. *Ibid.* (1862), p. 1373.

65. *Ibid.* (1863), pp. 810, 869.

66. BOE, A Guard Book, Memoranda by George Forbes, Chief Cashier, f75, 'if France imports gold from England, what are the advantages to the importer in taking French coin instead of Bar Gold'. Forbes, in a calculation involving 250,000 ounces, found that the importer gained £4,264 through savings on seignorage, import duties, and time lost at the mint. A similar exercise may have been carried out in 1857; see f18.

67. Morgan, *op. cit.*, pp. 177-8.

68. *The Economist* (1863), p. 785.

69. S. Nishimura, *The Decline of Inland Bills of Exchange in the London Money Market 1855-1913* (1971), pp. 69-70. Discount rate differentials, London rate-Paris rate, annual averages, correlations with amounts of bills, 1861-70:

Inland bills and differentials, +0.62;

Foreign bills and differentials, +0.57;

Total bills and differentials, +0.60.

70. As Nishimura's own monthly series for the Paris market rate reveals. See *Ibid.*, pp. 115-7.

71. Martin, *loc. cit.*, p. 658.

72. *S.C. on the Bank Acts* (1857), evidence of D. B. Chapman, q. 5310.

8. The Social Costs of Mortality in the Victorian City

John R. Kellett

THE idea of placing a money value upon a person is particularly emotive, as the discussion amongst American historians over the slavery issue has demonstrated in the last decade or so.[1] In Western industrial society the use of the wage labour of free individuals meant that such considerations did not usually arise; although Robert Owen did suggest, in evidence to Parliament, that if individual workers were regarded as capital assets they might be better treated and maintained. The first serious attempt to quantify the value of what is now called 'human capital' or 'health capital' came not from industry, but, inauspiciously, from the early nineteenth century Poor Law Commissioners, themselves a subject of obloquy by many contemporaries.[2] But however hardhearted the idea of placing a price upon the life of an adult or child may be, it does at least ensure that *some* valuation is made, and to that extent it could be said to be anti-Malthusian. For the fatalistic doctrines propounded by Thomas Malthus, and widely accepted in the early nineteenth century, implied that preventive checks, 'wars — the silent though certain destruction of life in large towns and manufactories — and the close habitations and insufficient food of many of the poor — prevent populations from outrunning the means of subsistence'. Unless these 'and other deadly agents, carry off the excess of the numbers born — unless the outlets of life and blood be left open — the whole people must be exposed to a slow process of starvation'.[3] Attempts to interfere with this balance by tinkering with remedial public health measures would be pointless, and could only postpone marginally the point at which the toll of lives would be resumed. By the same token it was Utopian to suggest that civic policies should be based upon the ideal of reducing the urban death rates, of 25 or 30 *per thousand*, to the 17 *per thousand* returned in healthier districts.

If not firmly rejected, this doctrine made it impossible to place any permanent value upon lives saved. 'Hygienic improvements of every kind must have languished under the cold shadow of this doctrine,' wrote William Farr of the Registrar General's Office, in the course of a vehement attack upon both the methodology and the implication of Malthus's *Principles of Population*. 'Statesmen,' he urged

are not then, by alarming cries of increase of population in a faster geometrical progression, to be deterred from the noblest work in which they can engage; for it is certain that population as it improves in England, will not increase faster than the requirements of industry in all its forms at home or the new openings of colonial enterprise abroad.[4]

As early as his Fourth Annual Report, Dr Farr took issue with the dangerous fallacy which Malthus had disseminated

> which, if it cannot be employed by any but the most depraved to sanction the destruction of life, might slacken the zeal of some in ameliorating the public health, by lending a colour to the dreadful notion that the excess of population is the cause of all the misery incidental to our condition or nature; and that the population might at the same time be diminished and saved from starvation, by epidemic diseases, unhealthy employments, or pestilential localities.[5]

Three decades later, in his 30th, and his supplement to the 35th, Annual Reports, Farr was still reiterating the same basic argument. 'We have everything to hope, and nothing to dread from measures of public health and of public safety.' The population of Great Britain obviously could not exceed the subsistence it could command, but it was not necessary that the subsistence should itself be produced in this country. 'Other products of the same exchangeable value can in the present state of transport in the world always be converted into subsistence. Manchester lives as well as a county consisting of farmers and agricultural labourers.'[6] The British cities, in which the battle to save lives had raged in the 1850s and 1860s, were not parasitical growths, but earned their keep by productive industry. Restraint of population should not be accepted as the cornerstone of policy, Farr argued vigorously:

> Had this principle been accepted by the people, the population of the kingdom instead of amounting to thirty-two millions would have remained, as it was at the beginning of the century, sixteen millions. England, in the presence of the great continental states, would now (1875) have been a second-rate power; her dependencies must have been lost; her colonies have remained unpeopled; her industry crippled for want of hands; her commerce limited for want of ships.[7]

These were forceful words to issue from the Assistant Commissioner for the census. It might almost seem that he was stepping outside his official function to express such partisan views, and Farr was not afraid to repeat them in papers to the British Association and the Social Science Association. He felt the need to do so because even such responsible officials as Dr Henry Letheby, President of the London Health Officers' Association, wrote as if they actually believed the crudest form of Malthusianism. Finding that the death rate amongst children under five was 40% of the total deaths in England and Wales (still more in the industrial cities), Letheby had reflected, philosophically,

> If this were not so the increase of population would be prodigious . . . in 40 years the population of England and Wales would be over 45,000,000 . . . in 120 years it would be near 182,000.000 . . . in 240 years the population of England and Wales, unless it was exported in huge masses, would reach to rather more than 1,550 millions, and it would be as thickly placed over the whole country as it is in London at the present moment.[8]

Farr was justifiably disturbed that a Medical Officer of Health should evidently be persuaded by the statistical 'parlour tricks' to which the abuse of Malthus's geometrical ratio of population could give rise.

So the first thing to establish firmly was that there was some point in saving human life at all (and nowhere was there greater scope for doing so than in the larger mid-Victorian cities). The next was to justify the necessary expenditure by putting a monetary figure upon the lives saved. There should be nothing repugnant in such an exercise. 'As the artist for his purpose views the human being as a subject for the cultivation of the beautiful,' Chadwick argued to the Statistical Society, 'as the physiologist for the cultivation of his science, so the economist may well treat the human being solely as an investment of capital in productive force.'[9]

Earlier attempts to value individuals in money terms date back to the seventeenth century, to Sir William Petty's *Political Arithmetic*, if not earlier, but such calculations were given renewed interest by the long debate, and the concern shown over the mounting cost of late eighteenth and early nineteenth century Poor Law administration.[10] Anxiety about the cost of maintaining pauper families, or families who had lost their breadwinner through illness, accident, early death or chronic intemperance, suggested one rough and immediate fiscal guide — the burden of taxation to provide support which would not be required by the family of an adult in good health. 'Is it not expedient, even on the grounds of economy, to appropriate a part of the money expended on the poor in protecting them from fever?'[11]

The calculation which was thus advocated was crude in the extreme, although this should not detract from its potential effectiveness. A somewhat unrealistic comparison was made between the established death rate of the most favourable areas, in the deep countryside, or in favourable suburbs or neighbouring townships, Broughton for Manchester, Hampstead for London. Even as early as 1855 a calculation was made, for example, by a Manchester statistician, David Chadwick (no relation), along the lines which had already been suggested in his namesake's *Sanitary Condition of the Labouring Population*. Working upon the Registrar General's quarterly return for December 1854, David Chadwick produced the following simple table:[12]

TABLE 1

	Population in 1851	Total Deaths in 1854	Rate per Thousand	No. of lives lost in 1854 from preventable causes	Estimated annual pecuniary loss from preventable disease and mortality
Manchester	228,433	7,796	34.12	2,800	£168,000
Birmingham	173,951	6,022	34.61	2,200	£132,000
Liverpool	258,236	10,377	40.18	4,600	£276,000

The full table, in fact, extended to thirty-one town districts and covers a particularly bad year for urban health. In these thirty-one town districts a total of 61,000 deaths were, in the Registrar General's words, 'referable to the imperfect operations of the sanitary organization of our towns'. The financial assessment was David Chadwick's own, by rough rule of thumb. Each death cost directly £5 for the burial fees, coffin, mourning, etc. This was a minimum cost, and many workmen's clubs paid £10 commonly for burial. Funerals were an obsessional item of conspicuous expenditure in the view of many Victorians. Even the humane William Farr spoke of the unwise custom of 'squandering guineas lavishly on stones, or on lids of feathers, rich silk bands, porter's pages, feathermen and mutes', though he was presumably referring not to the £5 artisan undertaker's expenses but to the more pretentious funerals of the 'tradesmen of the first class' (£50) or 'gentry and the higher classes of people' (£100 and upwards).[13]

In addition to the cost of each *death*, it was assumed that there would be 25 cases of illness 'which Mr Lee of the Board of Health has shown to cost twenty shillings each for medicine and loss of time'; say 25 x 20 = £25.[14] The other £30 was estimated to come from the years of labour lost amongst those who were wage-earning adults (on average five years, at £19.10s per year or 7/6d per week). As a rough calculation David Chadwick's costing of £60 per death was obviously no more than inspired guesswork, but it did show some features of the modern methods of assessing human capital in that it included a figure not merely for deaths, but for what one might call the zymotic *casualties* (who lost a month's work through relapsing fever, etc.) and also gave a figure for loss of future income flow, by years of productive work forgone. It was extremely crude, but capable of much greater development and sophistication; and indeed James Kay Shuttleworth and William Farr produced elaborate tables showing the changing value of a labourer's future wages, offset against his prospective costs of maintenance, year by year, from childhood to old age.[15] On this scale the excess of a labourer's earnings over his maintenance costs rose steadily from his early teens (£116) to his late twenties (£246), and then gradually curved down, below £200 in his early forties, below £100 by his late fifties, and so on. This was the value of the work over and above the costs of his own keep which a victim of zymotic disease (or accident, for that matter) might be expected to have been able to contribute at various points in his life. It was a much more satisfactory yardstick than the simple pricing of each casualty at £60 (or £150, as in later estimates), and indeed became so detailed in William Farr's later essays as to become virtually Life Tables, the vigorous actuarial discipline of which was only marred, as Farr conceded, by 'the extreme hypothesis that the wages are as certain to be paid as Government Life Annuities at 3 *per cent* interest'.

The other half of the equation, after devising more realistic assessments of the value of individuals' future services, was to attempt to tie this *per capita* figure to the number of deaths which could be argued to be avoidable. Here the calculations were even more approximate, and often made, even by official statisticians, upon premises which were unrealistic in the extreme. Whether or not they intended to render their Death Rate statistics more graphic, and dramatically interesting, or to provide polemic ammunition, their reports were certainly used for the latter purpose. Their commonest way of working out the possible saving of life was to compare the miserable urban death rates with those achieved in the 51 to 53 healthiest registration districts, in which a fortunate million or so people lived, mostly engaged in agriculture, on low wages, and rarely tasting animal food, but on a salubrious soil and enjoying (if one can use such an expression) a death rate of 17 per thousand. This was the figure most frequently set out as an achievable goal. William Farr wrote:

> It will not, therefore, be pitching the standard of health too high to assert that any excess of mortality in English districts over 17 annual deaths to every 1,000 living is an excess not due to the mortality incident to human nature, but to foreign causes to be repelled, and by hygienic expedients conquered.[16]

In his 20th Annual Report (1859), Farr enclosed tables for the period 1849-53 which went still further, by making an allowance for the less favourable age balance of the country districts. The 'unnatural deaths' totalled by this calculation 21,403 of the 57,582 who died in London over these five years; 4,000 per year, or the difference between London's annual actual death rate of 24.2 per thousand, and the notional 15.24 which the Healthy Districts would have returned if they had had an equal proportion of people in the prime of life.[17] Dr E. H. Greenhow of St Thomas' Hospital, reporting for the General Board of Health at about the same period (1857-8), even suggested as a goal a figure as low as 12.5 per thousand for the death rate, if all men lived to their full term. 'Let local authorities do their utmost . . . they will be counteracting causes of death infinitely more powerful than those which, because of their suddenness, seem so terrible in the moment of epidemic visitation.' They should strive to 'give to human life the same security against the infliction of preventable disease as against the infliction of wilful violence'.[18] This was an argument echoed still more forcefully by James Morrison in *A few remarks on the high rate of mortality in Glasgow* (1874). After quoting a claim by the Medical Officer of the Privy Council, John Simon, that 120,000 died annually in England and Wales from preventable disease, he continued: 'Any deaths in a people exceeding 17 in a thousand annually are unnatural deaths. If the people are shot, drowned, poisoned by strychnine, their deaths would not be more natural than the deaths wrought clandestinely'.[19]

Yet it could be argued that it was unrealistic in the 1860s and 1870s to suggest that the great cities could seriously expect to reduce their death rates to those prevailing in the healthiest districts. And there was a Utopian element, even in William Farr's Reports. 'It cannot be questioned,' he observed in the course of his 23rd Annual Report (1862), 'that large populations have even now advantages of a nature favourable to health which villages do not possess. The highest attainable health is probably to be sought in a happy combination of both states — *rus in urbe.*' The Assistant Registrar then goes on to quote as no dream, but a well founded expectation, 'the words of an excellent popular writer' (Charles Kingsley) 'who predicted a complete interpenetration of city and country, a complete fusion of their different modes of life . . . and a combination of the advantages of both, such as no country in the world has ever seen'.[20] Of course in the long run he, and the other propagandist statisticians and sanitarians, were right; 17 per thousand, even Greenhow's 12.5 per thousand, were not impossible goals. But it was perhaps setting the sights rather high in the 1860s to raise such expectations, and led to disappointment and even recrimination, particularly in Manchester and Liverpool, which frequently figured as examples of the two towns with the very worst health records. William Duncan, the pioneer Medical Officer of Health in Liverpool, was particularly aggrieved by the invidious comparisons made between health in his own city and that prevailing in other places, indeed *any* other city. 'I think Dr Greenhow is very wrong', Duncan wrote to a friend, after reading Greenhow's third quarterly report to the Registrar General. There were two 'fallacies' which lay behind this unjust condemnation of the results of his decade of work:

> In the first place Greenhow takes the mortality of a *portion* of the borough, and that the most unhealthy portion, and represents it as the mortality of 'Liverpool' . . . Secondly, having taken the most unhealthy portion of the borough, he next selects a most unhealthy period within which he confines his calculations of mortality — a period of six years (1849-54) the first and last of which were signalized by visitations of epidemic cholera, increasing the mortality of Liverpool in these two years alone by upwards of 7,000 deaths . . . Even on Dr Farr's showing the mortality of the Parish has been reduced four per thousand, or 1,100 persons per annum; so that we have saved more lives in ten years than have been lost in battle in the last 40; and yet you theorists turn up your noses at such results.[21]

It must have been particularly galling for Britain's first Medical Officer of Health to find his efforts under very difficult circumstances denigrated by false comparisons. Greenhow's comparison with Ely, though well intended, was particularly annoying. 'It is impossible', Duncan protested, 'that any means within the compass of human ingenuity, aided by the most lavish expenditure, can ever succeed in placing the two towns on the same level in respect of mortality.' Yet three years later, in 1862, Edwin Chadwick repeated the comparison before the Statistical Society in London, though after Liverpool's protest he substituted Cambridge rather than Ely to point to a town in which measures had been taken 'which leave much to do but which yet give the inhabitants, as it were, a jubilee every 3rd year in which there are no sicknesses and no deaths'.[22] In fact, if the propaganda message were to be driven home firmly, it was unfortunately necessary that wounding comparisons must be made; and Duncan himself was not above claiming, in 1860, one year after he had made his complaint, that Liverpool's mortality was less than Manchester's, although in that case there was not yet a Medical Officer of Health to feel injured. It was, in a sense, a competitive game of juggling the death rates which each town played, drawing whatever favourable comparisons could be made with other places, or with its own recent record, or by demonstrating local improvements in certain areas within the city; but whatever criteria were employed, Liverpool was at the very bottom of the table for most years between 1840 and 1900. The danger from this poor showing was that the achievement of the first M.O.H. at Liverpool might be regarded as an act not of civic initiative or conscience, but simply a measure of the town's plight and the desperation felt as the vagrant sheds filled with 5,000 immigrants per week in the summer months. Some were transient workers, some long-term immigrants, described rather as 'poverty-stricken refugees' by Duncan. Yet, Liverpool depended heavily upon casual workers, and as the Parkes Sanderson Report to the Corporation pointed out in 1871, 'It is not possible to alter this without surrendering the commercial supremacy of Liverpool'.[23]

Liverpool headed the list drawn up by David Chadwick in 1854 (cited earlier) with 4,600 preventable deaths. Yet if one looks in more detail at the Registrar's figures, upon which David Chadwick based his table, it is clear that the best attainable death rate he postulated was not 17 per thousand but approximately 22; a little less for Manchester and Birmingham, a little more for Liverpool, but varying over no more than half a point.[24] By comparison the general levels in England and Wales in the same year, 1854, were 28.16 per thousand in all town districts, 20.26 per thousand in the rural registration districts, and 23.54 for the country as a whole. David Chadwick also gave similar figures for Salford, Manchester's immediate and coterminous neighbour. The population there in 1851 was 87,523, the total deaths in the year 1854, 2,655 giving a rate of 30.33 per thousand. On the assumption that this could be reduced to about 21 per thousand, 810 lives could have been saved there, valued, by his rough rule of thumb of £60 each, at £48,600.

These figures are worked out on exactly the same basis as those quoted for Manchester, Birmingham and Liverpool in Table 1. However, since David Chadwick was also Borough Treasurer for Salford, with full local knowledge, he was able to complete tentatively the other half of the equation for that town in a way he could not do for Birmingham, Liverpool and Manchester. According to the Salford District Surveyor, the Corporation, over the years 1844 to 1854, had paved and sewered 156 streets (14 miles) and 88 courts and passages, at an average annual expenditure of £5,785. This could be compared, David Chadwick argued, with the £48,600 valuation on the annual possible saving of lives and work-time which the complete improvement of Salford's mortality and morbidity figures could achieve.[25] The scope for a much larger (even an eightfold larger) investment in public health measures, and the justification for it, appeared to be self-evident.

David Chadwick's statistics were clearly too optimistic. They simply assumed that increased Corporation sanitary expenditure would produce automatically and with minimum delay the reduction of 10 per thousand annual death toll in the great Midland and Northern cities repeatedly claimed as feasible, or would at any rate contribute in substantial measure towards a positive and marked improvement. Such overstatements of the case, though they might provide welcome arguments for the already convinced sanitarians, were not likely to win over new support in other quarters, particularly from those who would be required to foot the bill.

Accordingly, when Edwin Chadwick returned to Manchester in 1883, to avoid any suggestion that he was 'neglecting people in the place of my nativity' he presented modified calculations which made a conscious effort to understate the possible social savings. Taking the unnecessary cost of funerals at £5 each on the 10 persons who could be saved annually out of every 1,000 living, and adding an estimate for the direct charge of treating sickness (£200), and for wages lost through sickness (£100), produced a total monetary cost of £350 per thousand inhabitants per year. If one added to this the mean average value of the loss of future earnings per person amongst the 10 per thousand unnecessary deaths, a total cost of £1,350 per thousand inhabitants could be arrived at; but to avoid weakening his argument Chadwick was prepared to leave it at the £350 loss on funerals, plus the direct cost and labour lost through sickness. The calculations continue:

TABLE 2

Possible Social Savings from Sanitary Improvements

Per thousand persons		*Per person per annum*
£350		7/-
Per thousand houses		*Per house per annum*
£1,750		35/-
For 50,000 houses	=	*Interest to service loan of*
£87,500		£1,750,000 at 5%

In other words, if one assigned the potential savings from improved mortality to each house, like a rating charge, on the common assumption that five was the average number of occupants, then a medium-sized town of a quarter of a million inhabitants (50,000 houses) could justify the immediate raising of a loan of £1,750,000, the interest charges upon which would be, so to speak, 'serviced' by the annual social saving. Such a capital sum would be more than enough to carry out all the works recommended by the General Board of Health in Manchester.[26] Better still, Edwin Chadwick asserted, the operations could be carried out by a specially formed Company, and not by the Corporation, which he accused of wasting £1 million on 'a palatial and decorative building for a Town Hall' rather than spending the money on the drainage of 'the houses of the most heavily death-rated wage classes':

> I consider that it would be safer to get the work done by a responsible contracting company with a staff of specialists, whose services would only be required for the occasion to complete the work; leaving it afterwards to be worked by the local authority, as Mr Brassey completed his railways and left them to be worked by the companies. I did get up a large company for the purpose, of which the late Sir Rowland Hill, who took a special interest in the subject was one of the Directors, together with Mr John Moss of Liverpool, Mr James Morrison, Sir James

Matheson, and the chief capitalist millionaires of the country, with whom also were Mr Jones Lloyd and the Barings. But, unfortunately, it was delayed to the time when all others were absorbed in railway speculations, and for other reasons, including the need of legislative authority, I could not press it forward. But plans and estimates were got out for Manchester.[27]

Chadwick was referring to his abortive General Towns Improvement Company, which collapsed during the railway mania of 1846. For capital expenditure of £750,000 spring water would be provided, rather than the Corporation's 'peaty washings'. Flush water closets for 60,000 houses would be supplied for £220,000 and self-cleaning sewers for a further £270,000. The total cost would be 3d per head per week (13/- per year); and for an extra halfpenny per week new street-sweeping water machines (as in Paris) could be supplied and operated.[28] The costing was dubious, the idea of spring water technically unconvincing, and undated estimates (presumably early 1846) by the General Towns Improvement Company's engineers Thomas Hawkesley and James Smith of Deanston, for a less ambitious scheme in Leicester, revealed another drawback. There the estimated cost of 2d per house varied from a minimum of 1d levy on the houses with an annual value of less than £5, 2d for houses valued at £5 to £10, 3d for those at £10 to £20. After that the rate rose very rapidly to 1/- and upwards. But the housing stock in each category below £20 annual value was in the proportion of 58%, 23%, 11% for each respectively. Any default upon these would have sent the levies on the remaining 7% of housing stock, valued at over £20, to unacceptably high levels. The distribution of houses in each category was no more favourable in Manchester. The houses which had the greatest need of improvement were able to make the smallest contribution towards it.[29]

Nevertheless Chadwick was sufficiently convinced himself that the joint-stock principle had not had a fair trial, or sufficiently obstinate about it, to return to its advocacy in 1883:

> The principles of sanitary science are now so far assured that data might be supplied almost to justify such a company as the one projected to undertake for a reasonable percentage to contract for the attainment of results; and with full powers, chiefly by the complete works I have described, to reduce the present average death rates by 10 in a 1,000.[30]

One might feel that by introducing commercial considerations Chadwick could be thought to have marred the impartiality of his case justifying social savings. On the other hand it did indicate a willingness on his part to put private capital and private methods of stocktaking and accounting to the test. But this willingness was not shared by any substantial group of speculators after the collapse of the General Towns Improvement Company. Either they moved on from the basic tasks of sanitary engineering to the opportunities offered in providing urban transport, and (by the 1880s) electricity; or they shifted the scene of their investment in utilities from British cities to those overseas. Evidently Chadwick's assessment of private contractors' willingness to finance as well as to execute the great works of mid-Victorian civil engineering was mistaken, or perhaps distorted by his obsession with amateurism in local government. Yet it did result in a steady re-assertion of the need to monitor progress in public health:

> In private business there is a regular stock-taking at shorter intervals to ascertain progress and make the changes requisite to ensure it. In the public business here there appears to have been none thought of, and it has yet to be provided for in view of sanitation. If stock had been taken here of sanitary progress, what must have been the result of its being ascertained that all this loss of money, from excess of sickness and of funerals, had been going on year after year, besides the annual loss of productive force?
>
> In private business, the question of responsibility, and accountability for such loss of money, would arise; but in the public service there is for the most part no pay, and where there is no pay there is, practically, no responsibility. I have never known an instance of any serious pecuniary liability being enforced for large public waste. For injuries to children, by cruelty or neglect, the law imposes responsibilities on the parent, which are frequently enforced. But for the wholesale injuries done by neglect or maladministration by the so-called self-government to the whole of the children of a town, no real responsibility at present attaches to the authorities for the most deadly defaults. Attention is only roused to single cases occurring with passion and violence, with maiming and bloodshed. But preventable deaths, without these conditions, pass unheeded by thousands.[31]

By 1883, however, in spite of Chadwick's *apologia* for private enterprise, the task of saving these lives was clearly defined as the concern and responsibility of local government. The increasing scale of the undertakings of the 1860s and 1870s ensured that even those utilities which had hitherto been supplied by private, competitive industry were municipalised in most major cities except the Metropolis. It fell increasingly to local councils, with a little prodding from the Health Committee of the Privy Council and the Local Government Board, to devise the increasingly ambitious measures to bring pure water and efficient sewage disposal; and the cost was borne by a system of local rates which accepted the principle that the services should be supplied by need, that in normal times water should not be metered, and that the operations would be loss-making. Behind all these costs still lay the argument that they would be more than offset by wide social benefits.

William Farr, in the 39th Annual Report to the Registrar General, went further than anyone, even Chadwick, in the attempt to provide a quantitative justification of public health expenditure. In his view it was not merely of visible local advantage but of measurable national benefit on a scale greater than most observers recognised. The annual 'overplus' of deaths generally in England, in the decade 1861-1870, he estimated as 115,833 people. 'The hope of saving any number of these 115,833 lives annually by hygienic measures is enough to fire the ambition of every good man who believes in human progress.'[32] Using calculations based upon the net value of agricultural labourers, Farr continues as follows:

TABLE 3

Mean gross value of agricultural labourer's wages	=	£349
Less average cost of subsistence at £199	=	£150
Extended to whole population including females	=	£110
x U.K. Population of 33,090,009	=	£3,640 m
+ Estimate of value of earnings, fees and salaries as per Tax Schedules B, D and E at £1,610 m	=	£5,250 m

This figure of £5,250 million, Farr asserted, was 'an approximation of the value which is inherent in the *people*, and may fairly be added to the capital in land, houses, cattle, stock and other investments'; for which he accepted Robert Giffen's estimate of £8,500 million. The value of all other assets, indeed, could be said to derive from the value inherent in the U.K. population

> as a productive money-earning race . . . The increase of the value of house property is directly due to the increased numbers and earnings of the inhabitants. The railways yield no profit where there is no population. The profits of quarries, mines, ironworks (Schedule D), and other concerns are mainly due to the skill and industry of the masters and men who work them.[33]

Of this skill and industry Farr, like Chadwick, had a high opinion. Chadwick, generalising from his experiences travelling in Europe, judged that the British workman was 50% more effective than his European counterparts. Farr's calculations led him to the conclusion that, during the forty years the Registrar General's office had existed (1837-1877), 7,619,759 people had been added to the population, who 'valued, as land is valued, by the annual yield of net profit, constitute an addition of £1,212 million to the wealth of the nation'. From this evaluation it was but one step to place a further value upon the hypothetical savings which the extension of the average useful working life could yield. 'Every improvement in health recorded makes it clearer and clearer that the gloom of sickness and premature death flies away before sanitary measures.'[34] The result on human happiness could not be calculated, but 'when the qualified health officers whom the Universities are offering to examine are in suitable positions under enlightened local authorities all over the country', they with 'their medical brethren' should be able, Farr predicted, to add at least a fifth part to the worth of a living and labouring population. 'Upon this estimate £1,050 millions will be added to the economic value of the population of the kingdom.'

The global figures for returns to investment in health measures which Chadwick and Farr propounded were elaborated still further by John Tatham, who took over the decennial Census supplements from Farr and Ogle. They were also discussed widely abroad. The rest of Europe, Chadwick claimed, looked to Britain as the first country faced with the urban consequences of rapid industrial growth; and Farr's calculations were used in America to argue that at $770 (£154) per human life a sanitary investment of $583m (£116m) over the period 1875 to 1890 had produced a return of $650m (£130m). By implication health investment, as the American sanitarian George Whipple wrote in 1908, 'will pay not only in the satisfaction of having clean and health-ful cities to live in, not only in the joy of having relieved the suffering and saved the dying, but it will pay in hard cash'.[35]

This was really the point: that these arguments, extending over half a century, served to reinforce the role of compassion and charity in the treat-ment of urban health by calculations of national economic interest. It did not particularly matter whether these calculations of the worth of human life were accurate, but whether they were thought to be accurate enough to warrant action.

In fact it is very difficult to prove, except in the most general terms, that there were quantifiable results directly ensuing from measures of public health. To begin with, there is the matter of timing. Inevitably there will be a delay before civic expenditure, even on the most massive and (to many) unwelcome scale, can be said to achieve results which are demonstrable. The returns upon most other large-scale investments in infrastructure are not expected to be forthcoming immediately, and there is no reason why it should be otherwise in public health investment. The length of time before improved water supplies could be achieved was at least ten years; and even after that the build-up of the increased supply was usually staggered over several further decades. The improvement of waste disposal systems similarly was, even after the tech-nology had been agreed upon, a slow process. In each case, moreover, the targets for improved provision were not constant but moving. The population of the five major cities doubled between 1840 and 1870, and almost redoubled by 1910. Under these circumstances there is a great deal of force behind the argument that the holding of a *constant* urban death rate in itself represented a considerable achievement. Of course such a result is unspectacular, even dis-appointing, compared with the positive drop in mortality which all the sani-tarians and Medical Officers of Health sought so assiduously. It has also troubled later writers upon the subject. Royston Lambert, one of the most perceptive, at the end of his classic study of Sir John Simon, found himself forced to conclude that

> the sanitarians of mid-Victorian days sorrowfully learnt to acknowledge that their efforts would have but a slow long-term impact upon disease and death . . . To argue from the behaviour of the crude *general* death rates for 1848-76, as is so often the case, that nothing much was being done in the way of sanitary reform in that period, is thus to misinterpret statistics, the history of science, and the efforts of the heroic epoch of health reform.[36]

The general death-rate may have remained 'disappointingly stable', in Lambert's words, but it must be set against a rise in the urban population both absolutely and relatively in Britain's population. He concludes, in his summary of Sir John Simon's achievement:

> The stable death-rates thus conceal a considerable victory for, by holding in check the powerful forces against health which swiftly growing population and rapid urban agglomera-

tion naturally generated, the sanitary pioneers could congratulate themselves upon a valuable, if negative achievement.[37]

One can only endorse and perhaps expand this judgment, adding that the 'mortification' (Lambert's word) which Simon felt at the lack of positive results for London was nothing compared with the disappointment which accompanied the efforts of the Medical Officers of Health's efforts in the great provincial cities. After all, although the crude death rate in London, 'to the immense distress and bafflement of the sanitarians', did not fall during Simon's period of office and that of his successor Dr Henry Letheby, the general levels in the Metropolis, at the 24 to 25 per thousand range, compared favourably with most in Europe and America (26 to 28 in Berlin, Paris, Vienna and New York: 30 in Rome, 40 in St. Petersburg).[38] The struggle in the Midland and Northern industrial cities was equally unremitting and statistically unrewarding, but took place from levels which were consistently 10% to 60% higher than those in London.

Boundary extensions, and corrections made to the figures returned by registration districts, make it extremely difficult to produce a long-run series of death-rate figures for the major cities which are comparable; and the competitive urge to quote figures for single good years, in order to represent to the public a progressive view of public health measures and their results, further distorts the picture. 'The Registration districts,' William Cowper complained in 1859, 'are not set out with a view to provide vital statistics, but simply follow the subdivisions required for Poor Law relief.'[39] It was a complaint echoed by many others concerned with local government and the taking of the census. To meet the more blatant distortions, corrected figures were produced for each registration district, at first locally, on the initiative of health officers, but by the decade of the 1880s incorporated into the national census supplements. These revised figures attempted to make allowance for any unusual concentration of deaths which a district might suffer if it contained a cluster of hospitals, asylums and other institutions, for it was to these places that many from adjacent areas came, or were sent, to die. Such retrospective corrections reduced the death rate in No. 386 Registration District, Birmingham, from 23.0 in the 1880s to 20.3; in No. 453 Registration District, Liverpool, from 33.1 to 30.7.[40] Usually the correction improved the city's official crude death rate but not always. Manchester, for example, relied to an unusual extent upon hospitals and institutions outside No. 466 Registration District, and in the same decade of the 1880s its death rate of 26.9 would actually have risen to 29.3 on correction. Where the corrected rates were actually worse, they tended to remain tucked away in the Registrar's reports, and not to find their way into local currency.

A second major distortion of which contemporary statisticians became aware was concerned with the differing age structures, and sometimes the balance between the sexes, in different cities, and in the twenty-nine different

Registration Districts in Greater London. The greater life expectation of women (one to three years more than men) obviously implied that an area with an unusual proportion of men might be expected to show somewhat higher death rates than 'normal'. The significance of differing age distribution was more complex, however, giving rise to what seemed to many to be a statistical paradox; and a heated disagreement developed over this issue between William Farr and William Letheby. Letheby, in his Presidential address to the Metropolitan Health Officers' Association, attacked the system adopted by the Registrar General (Major Graham) on Farr's advice. Since a high birth-rate was a token of prosperity ('the invariable concomitant' in Letheby's words), and since young children were much more vulnerable, then it could be argued that 'an increase in mortality is often a sign of prosperity'.[41] It was an ingenious argument, and one which shows the lengths of jesuitical reasoning to which Health Officers were prepared to go in the search for justification of unrewarding annual results. It was, in Noel Humphreys' words, 'so satisfactory to the sanitary authorities of urban districts having both high birth and death rates that it was long before its fallacy was recognised'.[42] But, as Farr showed, it was based upon a fundamental misconception. A high birth-rate in fact implies an unusually high proportion of young adults of the child-bearing range in a population, and consequently an unduly small proportion of elderly persons. The structural balance of the general age groupings of such a population should produce favourable crude death-rate figures. 'The fallacy involved in the assumption that high birth-rates cause high death-rates appears still to have lingering attractions for some medical officers of health, anxious to account for excessive mortality in urban districts,' wrote Noel Humphreys of the Registrar General's office in 1885, 'but it has never been authoritatively put forward since the discomfiture of Dr Letheby's attack.'[43] When Dr John Tatham took over the decennial supplements for the 1890s, the correction factors recommended by Farr and Humphreys were generally incorporated. 'In order that the death rate in a series of decennia may be fairly comparable it is necessary to compute them on a population of standard constitution to age as well as to sex.'[44] The result was on the whole unfavourable to urban returns:

TABLE 4

1891-1900

	Death rate as recorded	*Adjust for deaths in institutions*	*Death rate if standard balance in population*
Birmingham	24.1	23.8	25.4
Liverpool	33.2	29.5	35.4
Manchester	26.4	28.5	28.3
London	18.2	*	20.1

(* Given for each district)

So even if the two major rectifications of the available statistics were made, to reduce local protests at misrepresentations, it did not do much for the basic figures. Indeed, it made them worse rather than better. It will also be noted that even the simple 'Death rate as recorded' column is often higher in the Registrar General's retrospective surveys than the annual figures quoted at the time by contemporaries. The reason for this was quite simply that the Census was carried out decennially, and the complete returns were not available until the second or even third year of each decade. It was for this reason that the Supplements by Farr, Ogle and Tatham were presented in 1864, 1875, 1884-5, 1895 and 1905. All urban death-rate figures arrived at locally between each decennial census, from the second or third year of each decade to the same year of the next, had to be based upon a somewhat unreal correlation between the *actual recorded* numbers of deaths and (linear) projections of population for each district which were based upon the assumption that the rate of growth observed in the previous decade would continue. This was often seriously inaccurate, especially as the old inner areas, which featured largely in the census registration districts, began to show rates of population growth which levelled out, or even entered positive decline. Once again the result was that when a corrective allowance was made retrospectively to relate the actual deaths to the actual rate of population increase in central registration districts the rate worsened, and the year-to-year claims in the previous decade were shown to be based upon false assumptions. This is probably the main reason for the 'serious discrepancy' noted by Royston Lambert in Dr Letheby's Report of 1872-3.[45] In this twenty-five year retrospect, figures are quoted which are far less favourable than the annual death-rates reported previously by Letheby which, as Royston Lambert suggests, were 'but yearly approximations'. However, these annual death-rate statistics were presumably given credence at the time they were published; and the pressures upon local health officers and sanitarians to pounce upon any figures which could offer hope and encouragement in the unremitting struggle to improve public health explain their ready acceptance. The decennial retrospects by the Registrar General's Office, however, show that the struggle was even more arduous and unrewarding than contemporaries had known, or admitted:

TABLE 5

Annual average death rates per thousand living

	1840s	1850s	1860s	1870s	1880s	1890s
London	25	24	24	22.4	20.7	18.2
Birmingham	26	27	27	25.8	23.0	24.1
Liverpool	36	33	39	33.6	33.1	33.2
Manchester	33	31	33	32.9	26.9	26.4

It must be conceded that these figures are very disappointing, so much so that Farr and the later authors of the retrospective national supplements, though free of any concern with local patriotism, or professional interest in casting a favourable light on sanitary efforts, were almost as greatly exercised as the civic Medical Officers of Health to draw up a list of explanations for such poor results. The list was extensive, and the items arranged in changing emphasis as new interpretations were stressed.

'Hygienic topography' was frequently stressed as the prime criterion. Was the area of the registration district low-lying, uneven and poorly drained, or was it of favourable elevation? On these considerations Liverpool's health record could partly be excused, it was argued, and conversely Birmingham berated for not achieving a greater improvement in standards of health.[46] Apart from these basic environmental factors, the temporary local influence which even changes in the weather might have upon public health were examined, thoroughly but inconclusively. Meteorological tables were kept over a twelve-year period of temperature, humidity, rainfall, and even (as a result of the obsession with impure air) 'the mean weekly amount of horizontal movement of the air measured by Robinson's anemometer'; but the only conclusion reached was the rather obvious one that excessive heat or cold injure health, both directly and also indirectly, 'in the former case by giving rise to diarrhoea, in the latter to diseases of the respiratory organs'.[47]

In addition to these approaches, elaborate attempts were made on several occasions by Drs Ogle and Tatham to correlate district death and morbidity rates with occupations and professions. However, although they produced interesting evidence of wide-ranging differentials in health, much of it was obvious — publicans suffered heavily from alcoholism, innkeepers and physicians from the infectious zymotic diseases, butchers from contagion spread by decaying animal matter, plumbers and gilders from metal poisoning and so on.[48] Moreover the value of such evidence as an independent criterion was reduced by the income and class differentials implicit in the occupational structure.

Another issue which was bound to arise in contemporary studies of the causation of urban mortality was the very difficult question of how much allowance should be made for the effects of private, as opposed to public cleanliness, and for the effects of diet. Here there are grave obstacles to quantification, which did not however prevent William Farr from assigning the arbitrary figure of 2 per thousand to effects of dietary deficiency upon the crude death-rate.[49] It is no more than a guess, but even an intuitive assessment from such a source deserves record and consideration; and the steady improvement in overall health in the closing decades of the nineteenth century does coincide not merely with improved medical knowledge but with the cheapening and the increased variety and improved availability of food in city markets from abroad, as well as from the British countryside. On the question of personal cleanliness, all that can be said here is that this also was subject to a campaign of missionary intensity. Cleanliness took a place next to ventilation and temperance as the main prophylactic measures enjoined by the sanitary associations of the 1860s and 1870s.

Perhaps the only proper way to understand the mortality figures is to study closely the effect of each of the major avoidable diseases upon the body itself at different ages and stages of development, and a great deal of such information was collected by Medical Officers of Health and Government statisticians. Much of it is annual routine, and its cumulative bulk is almost overwhelming. But the material collated so tirelessly is of significance in two different ways. Amongst the youngest age groups classified, 0-1 and 0-5 years of age, the effects of all the various factors — diet, personal cleanliness, parents' employment, environment, social class, civic sanitary and medical measures — are greatly magnified, so that babies and children came, in Dr Greenhow's words, to 'form the most sensitive test of sanitary circumstance'.[50] In the second place, the reasons for children's deaths take us to the fringe of the area between strictly economic and predominantly social explanations of causation and responsibility. The study of these vulnerable age groups, and of local densities (the most consistent criterion adopted by the Registrar General's Office), is of considerable interest, and although space precludes their treatment here, it has been undertaken elsewhere.[51]

In conclusion, perhaps the best single explanation for the disappointing revised figures for adult mortality, and the even more disappointing figure of children's mortality in the great nineteenth century cities, is to set them against the background of remorseless growth in total numbers and the increasing density. Each of the major cities approximately doubled in size, and halved the space per person, over the testing decades from the 1840s to 1880s:[52]

TABLE 6

Acres per person/Death rates

	1841-50	1851-60	1861-70	1871-80
London	.04/25	.03/24	.02/24	.02/22.4
Birmingham	.02/26	.01/27	.01/27	.01/25.8
Liverpool	.01/36	.01/33	.01/39	.01/33.6
Manchester	.06/33	.05/31	.05/33	.01/32.9

Over these years the approximate total numbers, allowing for boundary changes, roughly doubled from 2.2 million to 4.7 million in London's case, .2 to .56 in Birmingham's, .3 to .627 in Liverpool's, and .25 to .50 in Manchester's, and this increasing pressure of population in the inner registration districts of the great cities should be set against the steady death-rate figures. To hold the toll of urban life relatively constant whilst density increased was arguably an achievement in itself; unspectacular perhaps compared with the dramatic downward curve on the graph, delayed until the last two decades of the nineteenth century for adults, the first decade of the twentieth for children, but an achievement which was none the less real during the difficult middle years of the century.

M

NOTES

1. 'Voices became strident. Reasoned consideration of evidence was drowned in a torrent of passionate speeches. Gesticulations became so aggressive that they were menacing. The collegiality achieved through years of work on common problems was ruptured as we turned away from each other in anger.' This was Robert Fogel's recollection of the atmosphere at the 1967 annual conference of the American Economic History Association where the attempts to quantify slaves' value for work and breeding were first aired publicly. R. W. Fogel and S. L. Engerman, *Time on the Cross* (1974), II, 17. Yet Fogel and Engerman were only engaging in 'the adroit use of professional skills in a cool detached manner, as in an operating theatre'. Something of the same detachment — scientific to some, inhumane to others — can be seen in Edwin Chadwick's treatment of a child's value in terms of 'the actual contract price of raising an orphan child in a well administered public institution . . . economically he may be viewed as an amount of available productive power'. *Journal of the Statistical Society*, vol. XXV (1862), 505.

2. Edwin Chadwick, *Report on the Sanitary Condition of the Labouring Population of Great Britain* (1842), M. W. Flinn ed. (1965).

3. P.P., 1842, XIX, 90.

4. P.P., 1875, XVIII, p. xiv.

5. P.P., 1842, XIX, 85-9. The three papers accompanying this Report were the earliest official submissions to the Registrar General, and through him to both Houses of Parliament, in which population theories were checked against factual evidence by William Farr. 'Dr Price, at the close of the last century excited alarm by a forcibly drawn picture of the depopulation of the kingdom; and no sooner had the census demonstrated that Dr Price's fears of depopulation were groundless, than the "increase of population by geometrical progression", enunciated in the theory of Mr Malthus, turned the gloomy forebodings of speculators in quite an opposite direction.' *Ibid.*, 85-6.

6. P.P., 1868-9, XVI, 210.

7. P.P., 1875, XVIII, p. xvii.

8. Henry Letheby, *On the Estimation of Sanitary Condition of Communities and the comparative Salubrity of Towns* (1874), 20-1.

9. *Journal of the Statistical Society*, vol. XXV (1862), 502.

10. Rashi Fein, 'On measuring economic benefits of health programmes', in Gordon McLachlan and Thomas McKeown, eds., *Medical History and Medical Care* (1971), 183.

11. Southwood Smith in *Fourth Annual Report of the Poor Law Commissioners*, 1838, quoted in Francis Sheppard, *London 1808-1870: The Infernal Wen* (1971), 251. Smith was prompted to this observation by his estimates of the amount spent on relieving the poor stricken by fever in Bethnal Green and Whitechapel.

12. David Chadwick, *A Lecture at the Mechanics' Institute, March 26th, 1855*. Manchester Reference Library, H251/17/4235, 10.

13. William Farr (ed. Noel Humphreys), *Vital Statistics* (1885), 229.

14. David Chadwick, *loc. cit.*, 16. Some friendly Societies worked on the assumption that 2.6 people were 'constantly sick' for each death.

15. *Journal of the Statistical Society*, XVI (1853), 41-44, Tables A and C. The net value of future income over maintenance fell to £1at the age of 70, and thereafter was negative. 'These values may be compared with the former cost of slaves in Rome, in the United States, and in the West Indies.' Professional men may have been relieved to note that their value was reached about 15 years later than the average citizen, and that 'in the highest orders of the church, law and politics, where experience and great weight of character are requisite, the life still increases in value at higher ages'. P.P., 1875, XVIII(11), p. xlii.

16. P.P., 1875, XVIII, p. ix.

17. P.P., 1859, XII, 174-6. The tables also introduce an extremely unfavourable comparison for the year 1857 between Liverpool and the 63 'Healthy Districts': viz. deaths 12,895, or 6,418 more than the 'healthy rate'.

18. Edward Headlam Greenhow, 'Papers relating to the sanitary state of the people of England', General Board of Health, P.P., 1857-8, XXIII, 273-4.

19. James Morrison, 'A few remarks on the High Rate of Mortality in Glasgow' (1874), in British Library, *Miscellaneous Tracts, 1849-82*, CT 321 (12).

20. P.P., 1862, XVII, p. xxi, quoting Charles Kingsley's *Miscellanies: Great Cities.*

21. W. M. Frazer, *Duncan of Liverpool* (1947), 100-1.

22. *Journal of the Statistical Society*, XXV (1862), 507.

23. E. A. Parkes and J. Burdon Sanderson, *Report to the Corporation of Liverpool, June 1871*, part 2, 51. B.L. CT 324 (5).

24. Manchester 21.87, Birmingham 21.9, Liverpool 22.38.

25. David Chadwick, *loc. cit.*, 12 *et seq.*

26. Edwin Chadwick, *On Imperfect Self-Government and its Results in Manchester* (1883), 9.

27. *Op. cit.*, 5. There are also references to this company in S. E. Finer, *The Life and Times of Sir Edwin Chadwick* (1952), 241. A. Redford and I. R. Russell, *History of Local Government in Manchester* (1939-40), II, 141.

28. Edwin Chadwick, *On Imperfent Self-Government*, 6. According to Sir Joseph Whitworth who invented one and demonstrated it in New York, the local authorities turned it down not because it did not work but because 'it had no votes'. *Ibid.*, 26.

29. *Idem.*, British Library, Chadwick Collection, CT 531 (3), 32-5.

30. *Idem.*, *On Imperfect Self-Government*, 7.

31. *Ibid.*, 11.

32. William Farr, *Vital Statistics* (1885), 60.

33. *Ibid.*, 61.

34. *Ibid.*, 64.

35. Rashi Fein, *op. cit.*, 188. An earlier American observer, Lemuel Shattuck, carried out calculations similar to Farr's and Chadwick's, for the State of Massachusetts in 1850. 6,000 avoidable deaths, or 108,000 years of productive labour at $50 per year = $5,400,000. This plus an additional $2,100,000 for the support of widows, and for time lost through sickness, could have been saved by expenditure on sanitation. *Ibid.*, 186.

36. Royston Lambert, *Sir John Simon 1816-1904 and English Social Administration* (1963), 597.

37. *Ibid.*, 602.

38. P.P., 1881, XXVII, 118.

39. W. Cowper, *Address on Public Health, 1859*, British Library CT 333 (6), 7. Cowper was also discerning enough to identify a further improvement in the vital statistics. 'We want a register of illnesses that do not terminate fatally.' The zymotically 'wounded' should be counted as well as the dead.

40. P.P., 1905, XVIII, 136, 159, 167.

41. *Journal of the Statistical Society*, XLVI (1883), 189.

42. *Ibid.*, Noel A. Humphreys, 'The recent decline in the English death-rate, and its effect upon the duration of life.'

43. *Idem.*, *Vital Statistics* (1885), 112.

44. P.P., 1905, XVIII, p. viii.

45. Royston Lambert, *op. cit.*, 213.

46. P.P., 1875, XVIII (11), p. xliii *et seq.*

47. William Farr, *Vital Statistics* (1885), 411 *et seq.* Also P.P., 1862, XVII, pp. xxxiii-v.

48. *Ibid.*, 396, or for a fuller treatment at the turn of the century see John Tatham, *Letter to the Registrar General on the Mortality in certain Occupations* (1908), p. v *et seq.*

49. William Farr, *Vital Statistics* (1885), 141.

50. P.P., 1857-8, XXIII, 300.

51. Chapter 2, *Victorian Cities: Problems and Solutions*, forthcoming.

52. P.P., 1884-5, XVII, 434 *et seq.* Unfortunately the figures for Glasgow are not comparable. The sharp drop in acreage per head in Manchester reflects the detachment of the Union of Prestwich from Manchester and its creation as a separate registration district on October 1st, 1874.

9. Urban Economic Morphology in Nineteenth-Century Glasgow*

W. Forsyth

THE central role of the industrial city in the evolution of British economic society has long been recognised. But to the urban historian it has presented a considerable analytical challenge. Its patterns and processes are complex, and especially before 1914, they were fast-changing. The scale and heterogeneity of its activities therefore require a macroscopic approach which needs not only a general analytical framework but also a means of standardising a wealth of often inconsistent data. The difficulties of such a large-scale analysis were recognised in the 1960s by Oscar Handlin and Sydney Checkland, amongst others. The Handlin solution was urban biography:

> we need fewer studies of the city in history than of the history of cities . . . focussing upon *a* city specifically in all its uniqueness.[1]

Writing in 1964 Sydney Checkland argued for a more rigorous approach in which the city was not only 'an organism of constantly changing related parts' but also a component in a regional or national system of cities.[2] Handlin's approach has been the one favoured by British urban historians, since it can be tailored to the particular characteristics of the individual city and allows scope for impressionistic narrative. Checkland's scheme, with its stress on comparative analysis, requires a more generalised, quantitative approach. This study is a contribution to the latter view. It attempts systematically to examine the changing patterns of economic activity throughout the nineteenth century in one city: Glasgow; and it develops some simple statistical and mapping techniques which make the resulting configurations comparable with other centres.

The nineteenth century was Glasgow's golden age. Between 1800 and 1900 it rose to its peak of economic and industrial power. By the Glasgow Exhibition of 1901 — the biggest and most ostentatious display of industrial self-confidence since the Great Exhibition — the city had become centre of the Clydesdale industrial region, commercial hub of Scotland, claimant to the title of Second City of the Empire and one of the world's greatest workshops. Over the century, as Table 1 shows, its population grew tenfold from 75,000 to 740,000, and its built-up area rose from four to 47 square kilometres.

* This study has benefited greatly from the comments and suggestions of Peter Payne, to whom I owe many thanks.

TABLE 1

The Growth of Glasgow, 1775-1900

	Population ('000)	Area (sq. km.)	
		Administrative	Built-up
1775	38	7.2	1.3
1800	75	7.5	3.5
1825	167	7.5	6.8
1850	323	20.5	17.3
1875	481	24.4	27.0
1900	739	51.4	47.3

Sources: The population data were calculated from the *New Statistical Account of Scotland,* Vol. 6, *Lanark* (Edinburgh, 1845), 129f; *The Third Statistical Account of Scotland, Glasgow,* Edited by J. Cunnison & J. B. S. Gilfillan (Glasgow, 1958), 800. The administrative data are from Cunnison, J. & Gilfillan, J. B. S., eds., *op. cit.,* 788f, whilst the built-up area data are based on original measurements.

Its fame, success and growth rested on several things. It was well sited. It occupied a classic, north-bank site: extensible to the west but not overlarge, and penetrated by navigable water. Moreover it was favourably situated for commerce and contacts with the Americas, the British west coast, the Scottish east coast, and the Lanarkshire mineral deposits. Beyond this locational good fortune was a complex and expanding network of economic and social activity patterns. These ceaselessly combined, divided and mutated to produce the sum of urban activity on which the city's success rested. In particular they responded to the influences of population change and technical innovation, especially those embodied in different forms of transport.

How is the urban historian to measure the speed, scale and spatial extent of these changes in metropolitan activity? For Glasgow three major sources are available: the local employment data in the official census, a sequence of large-scale maps and plans going back to 1773, and an annual series of city directories[3] starting in the late eighteenth century. Each source has shortcomings. The census data allow industrial specialisation to be measured, but they are rudimentary before 1841[4] and give no usable spatial information. The maps record the distribution of the large economic structures: mills, shipyards, engineering works, public buildings and the like. But their scales and the quality of their information vary; and they perforce omit such important but spatially insignificant activities as professional services and textile finishing. The directories provide greater detail but are also imperfect. Not all commercial activities are recorded; the lack of regular street numbering in the early decades of the nineteenth century prevents the precise location of activity, and the loose and widespread use of certain job descriptions, e.g. 'merchant', makes classification difficult. Moreover no source gives much direct information on residential function. Nonetheless, by using the employment information and by cross-checking the directory and map data, a comprehensive and consistent picture of other functional activity and change can be constructed. Following Sydney Checkland's suggestion,[5] this has been standardised into a series of 25 yearly 'snapshots' beginning in 1800.

Glasgow's growth can be discerned in the growth of its built-up area, the changing structure of its employment and in the constantly changing locational interaction of its commercial, industrial and residential activities. Between 1775 and 1800 the city's built-up area nearly trebled whilst its population doubled. This growth was dominantly eastwards where a booming cotton industry was fast expanding on greenfield sites in the industrial villages of Calton, Mile-end and Bridgeton. Rapid growth was also occurring elsewhere, in the industrial, weaving and engineering suburbs of Anderston in the west, and Hutchesontown in the south, both of them with access to the Clyde; and in the north where the Forth and Clyde and Monkland Canals delivered grain, timber and coal for the brewing, distilling, milling, sawmilling and chemical industries at Port Dundas. Northwest of the old core, round the town cross, a residential west end began to emerge as the commercial élite exchanged the cramped tenements of the old city for more desirable ones on newly feued land south of George Square.[6]

By 1825 the city's built-up area and its population had again doubled and its westward migration had begun. A clear division of spatial function had appeared, and distinct industrial, commercial and residential areas can be recognised. Existing industrial areas grew. But, like commerce and residence, industry also advanced westwards and northwards to new sites. The eastern edge of the city changed little despite the continuing development of cotton production. Northwest of Glasgow Cross residential expansion was underway as the civic élite moved from the desirable tenements of the 1790s and 1800s to the space and terraced respectability of a second west end on Blythswood Hill. But they moved only their homes. Their counting houses remained in the discarded residences of the earlier west end. Eastwards lay an area of obsolescent structures, low amenity, and jumbled activities which still retained remnants of its former centrality: the town Green, the Cross, the Exchange and the University. Into these cast-off buildings crowded warehouses, workshops and a growing stream of rural immigrants.

Expansion was most dynamic around 1850. Since 1825 the city's population had again doubled and was increasing by some 7,000 a year. And the growth of the built-up area was the largest of any of the time periods. Moreover the first major changes occurred in the city's political area. By 1850 the new parliamentary burgh was, at 20 square kilometres, treble the area of the old royalty in 1800. The built-up area continued its dominantly westward growth along the Clyde and the northern canals. But this hid an array of other changes. Much of the physical increase was due to the filling up of space in the industrial areas. Residential expansion was primarily in the west, where elegant terraces and circuses were being built for the high income groups. By 1850 the commercial and cultural élite, together with their solicitors, accountants and bankers, were living near the River Kelvin, 2-4 kilometres from the old core. In the old city little residential building had occurred for years. Yet this was the area which had long attracted immigrants. With heavy and uncontrolled immigration in the 1840s — the city's population rose by 70,000 in the decade — an old housing problem degenerated into an acute social crisis. By 1851 nearly 13 per cent of the city's people were paupers.[7] Grossly overcrowded and ravaged by epidemic diseases, the immigrant and the poor inhabited an x-shaped zone of decaying structures centred on Glasgow Cross:

> In the very centre of the city was an accumulated mass of squalid wretchedness which was probably unequalled in any other town in the British Dominions . . . (The alleys and other quarters) are filled by a population of many thousands of miserable creatures. The houses in which they live are altogether unfit for human beings, and every apartment is filled with a promiscuous crowd of men, women and children in a state of filth and misery.[8]

One axis stretched for two kilometres eastwards from the business centre; the other northwards from Gorbals, south of the Clyde, to the cathedral.

Between these areas of patrician comfort and proletarian blight lay Glasgow's commercial core, whilst around them was the horseshoe of industrial sections which had appeared between 1775 and 1825. In them change was extensive. New industries had appeared. In Anderston, shipbuilding and marine engineering eclipsed the textile sector. And from Hutchesontown to Tradeston textile bleaching and finishing, shipbuilding and engineering all grew. For the riverside activities, the improvement of the harbour and the Clyde navigation was a major influence. Between 1825 and 1850 quayage quadrupled to one kilometre whilst the river's depth increased to 4.4 metres. But both they and the industries in the northern centres of St. Rollox and Port Dundas were also being affected by a new and most powerful influence on the city's subsequent growth: the railway.

Until 1850 Glasgow's growth was subject mainly to centripetal forces. The railway and later the tramway changed that. They reduced transport and time costs, increased the worker's mobility, the periphery's access to the centre and the city's links to the British market. By 1875 centrifugal forces were of increasing importance. The built-up area and population continued growing, but at half the rate of previous periods. And, after 1871, the city centre began to lose population, though this was due primarily to urban redevelopment,[9] not to improved transport.

The third quarter of the century brought the suburban age to Glasgow. High-quality residential developments continued in the west. But they were now supplemented by new ones in other directions, beyond the horseshoe of the industrial areas which encircled the old city to the north, east and south. Contemporaries remarked on the mushroom growths which

> have sprung up within the last two or three years all round Glasgow.[10]

In addition to the villas of Pollokshields and the superior tenements in Crosshill and Dennistoun, there was residential expansion in a clutch of remote centres, especially in the shipbuilding and engineering areas on the lower Clyde.

By 1875 Glasgow's economic morphology was mature and stable. A full complement of functional areas existed. There was a sizeable central commercial and administrative area surrounded by the industrial horseshoe. Westwards, along the Clyde, was a ribbon of quays, shipyards and engineering works. And within and beyond these districts were distinct residential areas: the slums of the city centre, the cramped workers' tenements on the edge of the core and among the factories of the industrial neighbourhoods, and the superior tenements, terraces and villas.

Although urban activity grew substantially in the last quarter of the century, the city's functional distributions altered in relatively minor ways. By 1900 Glasgow was a world metropolis. It had a powerful economy based on commerce and a range of heavy industries. Its built-up area and political extent covered about 50 square kilometres; but in fact it was only the largest node in an industrial, Clydeside conurbation stretching almost unbroken for over 30 kilometres. It was also the focus of an extensive local and long-distance transport network which was fundamental to the city's undoubted prosperity. Much had changed since 1800; but, as will be argued presently, much remained remarkably the same.

The employment data

Only two census years — 1851 and 1901 — provide both adequate data and a close coincidence with the snapshot years. However, they provide important benchmarks in the city's economic evolution. Using C. H. Lee's 27 employment categories,[11] Glasgow's industrial structure can be analysed by calculating sectoral location quotients.[12] The results are shown in Table 2.

They show a city with an almost complete range of economic activities, but with a representation twice the national average in five sectors in 1851 (insurance, banking and finance; printing and publishing; mechanical engineering; textiles; chemicals) and in three engineering categories in 1901 (shipbuilding and marine engineering; instrument engineering; mechanical engineering). The under-representation of shipbuilding and marine engineering in 1851, and of coal and metallurgy at both dates is easily explained. These activities, although associated with Glasgow's economic rise, lay outside the city's political limits in the surrounding counties of Renfrew, Dumbarton and Lanark.

However, the sectors of highest specialisation were not significant employers. When the level of specialisation (i.e. the location quotient) is

TABLE 2

The Structure of Employment in Glasgow & Lanarkshire in 1851 & 1901

| | | Glasgow Employment '000 | | Location Quotients | | | |
| | | | | Glasgow | | Lanarkshire | |
Cat.	Sector	1851	1901	1851	1901	1851	1901
1.	Ag., For., Fish (S)	2.30	1.32	0.07	0.04	0.28	0.21
2.	Mining, Quarr. (S)	2.86	3.69	0.46	0.17	2.12	1.61
3.	Food, Drink, Tob. (S)	9.90	29.24	1.52	1.41	1.09	1.20
4.	Coal, Petrol Prods. (S)	—	—	—	—	—	—
5.	Chemicals (E)	1.61	4.13	2.12	1.42	1.49	0.92
6.	Metal Manufg. (E)	3.46	10.28	0.73	0.84	1.73	2.26
7.	Mech. Engrg. (E)	3.00	34.79	2.41	3.62	1.93	2.03
8.	Instrum. Engrg. (E)	0.38	3.02	1.05	3.75	0.57	0.95
9.	Elect. Engrg. (E)	—	—	—	—	—	1.25
10.	Shipbldg., Mar. Engrg. (E)	0.47	3.04	0.92	11.27	0.88	2.83
11.	Vehicles (S)	0.40	2.28	0.52	0.82	0.42	0.68
12.	Other Metals (S/E)	1.08	5.07	0.69	0.91	0.67	0.94
13.	Textiles (E)	46.98	27.56	2.23	0.92	1.98	0.75
14.	Leather, Fur (S)	0.87	3.07	0.86	1.22	0.60	0.86
15.	Clothing, Footw. (S)	10.82	34.71	0.74	1.29	0.97	1.05
16.	Bricks, Pott., Glass. (S)	2.06	4.12	1.31	0.98	1.05	0.89
17.	Timber., Furn. (S)	3.62	11.85	1.18	1.81	0.94	1.35
18.	Paper, Printg., Pubg. (S/E)	3.43	13.08	2.86	1.82	1.31	1.29
19.	Other Manufg. (E)	0.40	1.05	1.31	0.72	0.82	0.97
20.	Construction (S)	9.42	25.60	1.15	0.91	0.98	0.94
21.	Gas, Water, Elect. (S)	0.21	3.16	1.74	1.85	1.50	1.32
22.	Transp., Commns. (E/S)	10.54	42.26	1.53	1.43	1.13	1.16
23.	Distribution (S)	1.76	4.26	1.28	1.28	1.22	1.05
24.	Ins., Bkg., Fin. (S)	0.34	1.93	3.72	0.77	0.79	0.81
25.	Prof. Sci. Servs. (S)	3.91	9.76	0.91	0.70	0.67	0.75
26.	Miscell. Servs. (S)	19.37	34.93	0.86	0.61	0.71	0.57
27.	Pub. Admin., Defence (S)	1.97	4.71	0.88	0.54	0.62	0.47
	Not classified	11.17	43.19	1.46	1.60	1.06	1.39
	Total Employment	149.33	332.35				
	Total Population	329.10	622.37				

Sources: Lee, C. H., *British Regional Employment Statistics, 1841-1971* (1979); *Irish Universities Press*, British Parliamentary Papers Population Ser. 9: *1851 Census*, 1017-1021 (Dublin, 1970); HMSO, *Eleventh Decennial Census of the Population of Scotland 1901* Vol. 3, 325-336 (Edinburgh, 1903).

I am indebted to Clive Lee for allowing me to use his unpublished manuscript data for Lanarkshire.

E — basic, export sector; S — non basic, service sector; E/S — sector with dual role. In this case employment has been divided equally and arbitrarily between the basic and non basic sectors: see text.

weighted by the numbers employed, a significantly different pattern results, as Table 3 shows.

TABLE 3

The Top Five Industrial Sectors in Glasgow, 1851 and 1901

1851			1901	
Rank	LQ	LQ x Employment	LQ	LQ x Employment
1.	(24) Ins., Bkg., Fin.	(13) Textiles	(10) Shipbldg., Mar. Engrg.	(7) Mech. Engrg.
2.	(18) Pap., Printg., Pubg.	(26) Misc. Serv.	(8) Instrm. Engrg.	(22) Trspt., Commns.
3.	(7) Mech. Engrg.	(22) Trspt., Commns.	(7) Mech. Engrg.	(15) Clothg., Footw.
4.	(13) Textiles	(3) Food, Drink, Tob.	(21) Gas, Water, Elect.	(3) Food, Drink, Tob.
5.	(5) Chemicals	(20) Construction	(18) Pap., Printg., Pubg.	(10) Shipbldg., Mar. Engrg.

(1) = Sector number in Table 2.

Source: Table 2.

It clearly indicates the prime importance for the city's economy of textiles in 1850, and engineering in 1900. Their exports to the rest of Britain and abroad provided much of the city's income; and on them the city's reputation was based. But Tables 2 and 3 also reveal the importance of services in the city's economy. Not only does tertiary sector (categories 21-27) employment rise to exceed that in the main industrial sectors (categories 5-13, 16) by 1901, but also the preponderance of jobs in the non basic[13] sectors (i.e. those serving the basic industries, the city and its immediate hinterland) increases too. In 1851, 28 per cent of the classified occupations in the city were in the tertiary sector as against 43 per cent in the main industrial sectors. By 1901 the respective proportions were 35 per cent and 33 per cent. Moreover, if the sectors in Table 2 are divided into basic (export) and non basic (service) groups, the importance of the local economy for Glasgow's employment is clear. Although a crude measure which underestimates the importance of the basic sectors, hence the urban multiplier, this method highlights the much greater impact of the local economy's needs on employment than is usually admitted. In 1851 over 50 per cent of Glasgow's workers were already in jobs *serving* the city's 'export' sectors. By 1901 the figure was nearer 60 per cent. Glasgow's output was un-doubtedly dominated by the value added by its characteristic manufacturing industries; but in employment terms at least it was a service city with a high, internally generated demand.

Table 2 also shows that the city's employment structure remained stable as the local economy grew. This is confirmed by further analysis of the data. A Spearman rank correlation test reveals that there was a negligible shift in the

rank size of the industrial categories between 1851 and 1901.[13] Moreover
stability increased as the local job market diversified. This is implied by the
Lorenz curves[14] in Figure 1 and is confirmed by their Gini coefficients[15] (Table
4).

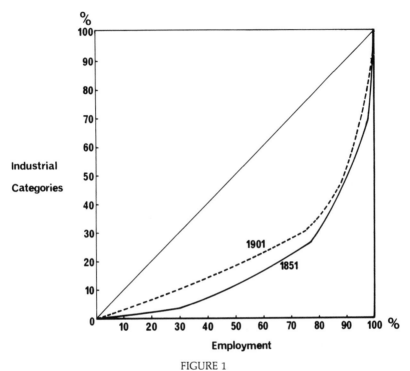

FIGURE 1

Lorenz Distribution of Employment in Glasgow 1851 and 1901

TABLE 4

The Diversification of Employment in Glasgow, Lanarkshire and Great Britain in 1851 and 1901

	Gini Coefficients	
	1851	1901
Glasgow	0.6383	0.5285
Lanarkshire	0.6315	0.5054
Great Britain	0.6355	0.5233

Sources: See Table 2.

The falling values between 1851 and 1901 indicate an increased dispersion of
jobs among the different industrial categories at both local and national levels.
But the figures also reveal that the dispersions in Glasgow and Lanarkshire

almost coincide with the national one. In employment terms, therefore, the dispersion of Glasgow's jobs shows little of the imbalance expected in an industrial city.

The spatial data

Employment figures reveal much about the sectoral distribution of economic activity in Glasgow, but little about its distribution in space. Here the urban plan and city directory are invaluable. By combining the accuracy of the former with the detail of the latter, a set of dot distribution maps was constructed for each 'snapshot' year. Although it ignores the size of individual establishments, the method yields a more comprehensive picture than the plans alone, in particular of the distribution of central area activity. The largest-scale plan used in this study, Fleming's 1:2400 map of 1807, locates about 110 commercial, industrial and social activity sites. The 1800 directory allowed post-1800 additions to be deleted and over 600 sites to be established. The 1900 directory also quadrupled the number of locations plotted on the 1:2500 Ordnance Survey plan of 1895. To standardise the resulting 7000 observations into some computable form, the data were placed and mapped in industrial orders, using the Standard Industrial Classification.[16] They were then further aggregated into two broad categories: central area activities and industry, including processing.[17]

The next task was to make the distributions comparable over time and independent of the shortcomings of the data sources, especially of the locational inaccuracy of the directories for the two earliest periods. This was done by superimposing a standard 100-metre grid on the central area data, and a 500-metre grid on the industrial distributions.[18] The result was a series of standard spatial units which lent themselves to statistical manipulation. By permitting tolerances of ± 50 metres for central area and ± 100 metres for industrial locations, they also largely eliminated the imprecision of the early data.

(a) *The built-up area*

In addition to analysing the distributions of urban activity, the grids permit some examination of the growth of the built-up area within which that activity occurs. Figure 2 shows the expansion of the built-up area between 1775 and 1900. For simplicity those grid squares where urban land use exceeded 50 per cent of the area were treated as fully occupied. Those where such occupation was below 50 per cent were regarded as wholly rural. The figure clearly shows a strong initial expansion eastwards between 1775 and 1800 and its subsequent translation into the sustained westward and northward movement described earlier.

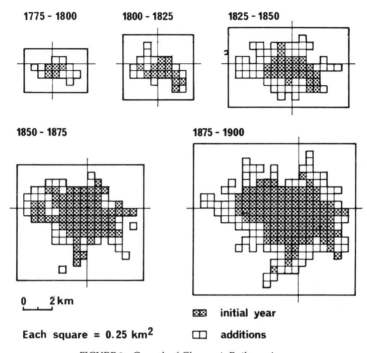

FIGURE 2. Growth of Glasgow's Built-up Area

Each diagram can also be used to determine the mean centre[19] of the built-up area: i.e. the position round which the physical structures cluster and a spatial analogue of the arithmetic mean of descriptive statistics. The changing location of the mean centre over the 125 years from 1775 is illustrated in Figure 3. Here too the pronounced eastward expansion of the city in the last quarter of the eighteenth century is clear. Between 1775 and 1800 the mean centre shifted 350 m. from a point east of Stockwell Street to one near St. Andrew's Square, then one of the city's choicest residential areas. By 1825 it had returned to Stockwell Street and by 1900 it was in the Anderston area, 1.4 kilometres west of its location a century earlier.

(b) *The central economic area*

The functional heart of Glasgow was its central business and administrative area. This was the focus of vehicular and pedestrian traffic, the area of greatest accessibility, the locus of most commercial activity and the area of the highest land values. It was also the focus for most of the city's services and for its cultural and political life. Most economic activities sought such a central location. However, relatively few could afford the accompanying high land

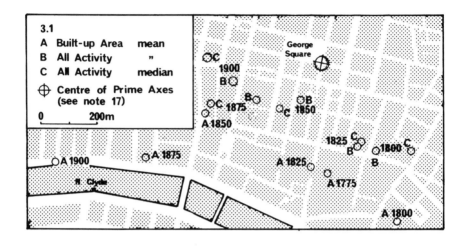

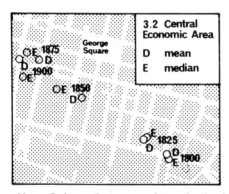

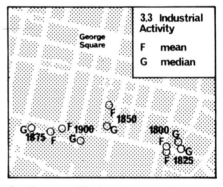

Note: Ordnance Survey co-ordinates for the above distributions will be found in Appendix 2.

FIGURE 3. Location of Mean and Median Centres 1775-1900

rents. Thus the economic core was occupied by particular activities: legal, financial and other specialist services which needed access to the city and regional markets; wholesaling; some retailing, printing and publishing, and certain small-scale industries like clothing which needed direct access to the largest possible number of clients.

Several factors also determined the composition and shifting location of the central economic area. Three factors in particular determined its location: the layout of the main routes, its ability to acquire prestige sites near the homes of the commercial élite, and its reaction to poles of repulsion centring on slums, tanneries, slaughterhouses and the like. For the individual firm there were three complementary determinants: agglomeration economies, the availability of suitable premises, and the firm's ability to generate an income per square metre of floor space sufficient to justify the high price of such centrality.

Until 1800 all activities crowded indiscriminately into the courtyards and alleyways round Glasgow Cross. But as the city grew, changes in land rents produced a continual shifting and sorting of activities. Inspired by Edinburgh's New Town and the terraced town houses of Georgian London, the wealthier citizens by 1800 had begun to separate themselves from the poor and their homes from their places of business. By 1825 a distinct business and administrative core had emerged northwest of the Cross. And throughout the nineteenth century this core grew in area and migrated westwards until by 1900 its centre was some 0.7 kilometre from its site in 1800. Using more than 3300 locations based on map and directory data, the pattern of growth and change is summarised in Figure 4 and in Appendix 1.1. The steady westward migration of core functions is especially clear between 1800 and 1850, but thereafter the size of the core makes simple observation difficult. Some statistical manipulation of the data is required.

Calculation of the mean centre shows that the greatest movement of the core was between 1825 and 1875 and that in the last 25 years of the century the shift was under 100 m. But a more useful measure is the median centre, since it is a measure of the minimum aggregate distance of the observed functions from the centre of the array. It is therefore a theoretically optimum location for services. Unlike the mean centre, however, it is a variable point since it is determined by two perpendiculars which bisect the data distribution. In this study the median centre was determined by perpendiculars parallel to the prime axes of the grids. An alignment along the north-south axes of the Ordnance Survey grid would produce a slightly, but not significantly, different result. The obvious feature of the data, as it appears in Figure 3, is the closeness of the mean and median centres throughout the century although the whole core area shifted substantially over that time. No similarly close relationship exists between the mean centre of the core and that of the built-up area. As both centres moved west, their axes of movement diverged until, by 1900, the mean centres were over 800 m. apart. Given the different array of forces at work on the development of the core and of the city as a whole, this is not surprising.

Mean and median centre calculations record only the weighted locus of all the selected central functions. They do not record the degree of their concentration within the overall array. However, the data do allow several measures of concentration to be calculated. The most general is the standard distance.[20] The spatial equivalent of the standard deviation, this measures the degree to which individual blocks' values cluster round the mean centre. The results in Appendix 2 show that central functions became increasingly dispersed about the mean centre till 1850, by which time their standard distance was over 0.5 kilometres. Thereafter the dispersion about the mean centre remained almost constant till the end of the century. This result is evidence of a different sequence of forces operating in the core from those which were affecting the development of the built-up area. In the former, after 1850, centripetal replace

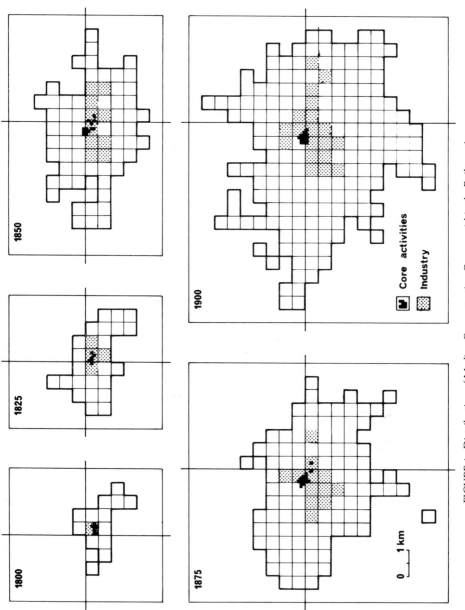

FIGURE 4. Distribution of Median Concentration Groups within the Built-up Area

centrifugal forces. In the latter the opposite is the case.

However, a more detailed analysis of the data can be made by plotting the cumulative percentage of establishments against the cumulative percentage of the blocks which they occupy. The resulting Lorenz distribution is shown in Figure 5.1. It reveals that core functions became concentrated on relatively fewer blocks, even though, as the standard distance data show, the actual dispersion of all such functions grew. In 1800 the recorded core activities were spread over 42 blocks; but half of these activities — the median concentration group[21] — were concentrated in only six. By 1850 this group concentrated on

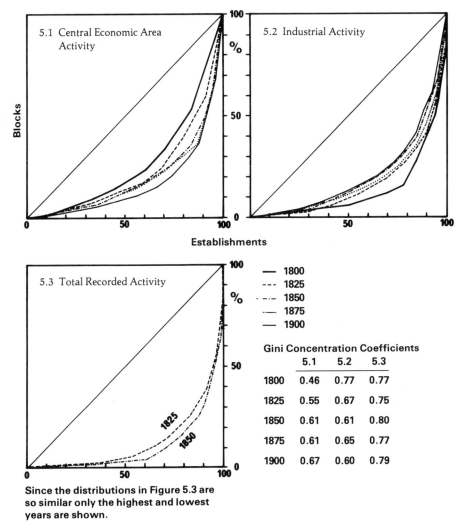

		Gini Concentration Coefficients		
		5.1	5.2	5.3
1800		0.46	0.77	0.77
1825		0.55	0.67	0.75
1850		0.61	0.61	0.80
1875		0.61	0.65	0.77
1900		0.67	0.60	0.79

Since the distributions in Figure 5.3 are so similar only the highest and lowest years are shown.

FIGURE 5. Lorenz Distribution of Economic Activity 1800-1900

13 of the 104 blocks containing core activities. In 1900 it was contained in 15 out of 167 blocks.

The Gini coefficients indicate the expected increase in the concentration of activity between 1800 and 1850. But there is an unexpected cessation over the next quarter-century. At 0.61 in 1875, the concentration index is the same as in 1850, as is the standard distance of 0.55 kilometres. This break in trend is further confirmed by the gains and losses of establishments as the cells of the median concentration group migrate westwards.

TABLE 5

Change in Establishments per Block: median concentration group

	Gains		Losses	
	No. of Blocks	Mean Gain	No. of Blocks	Mean Loss
1800-1825	6	13.0	5	3.4
1825-1850	14	21.7	3	13.0
1850-1875	10	19.1	10	13.5
1875-1900	14	28.5	8	8.1

Source: Appendix 1.2.

With as many blocks losing central area activities as gaining them, and with the difference between mean gains and losses falling appreciably, the rate of core expansion had clearly begun to slow. Several factors may explain this. First, the need to move declined. As urban redevelopment and improved public health measures made the old city environmentally less repulsive, the professional and business groups ceased so readily to retreat. So too did their offices, banks and clubs, and the Stock Exchange. Moreover they resisted displacement because, for a time, the newest residential developments were expensive and quite remote: so the zone of residential discard available for occupation by central area activities declined. Secondly, agglomeration economies and the growing volume of business generated a rising output per square metre of floor space, which justified their retention of central, high-rent sites. Thirdly, by 1875, core activities had begun to appear in peripheral sub-centres such as the burgh of Partick. They arose in response to central area congestion, to increased suburban activity, and to the lack of an extensive mass transit system. Not until the development of the tramway in the 1870s, the suburban railway and the city's underground loop in the 1880s and 1890s were the distance costs of Glasgow's increasing scale overcome. However, once transport technology did reduce the friction of distance, the advantages of centrality again outweighed those of access to peripheral clients and the process of concentration resumed, as the standard distance and Gini data for 1900 show.

This long-term movement westwards of the core was a response to several influences: to a zone of attraction in the west, poles of repulsion in the east, topographic barriers in the north and to the industrial pre-emption of riverside sites to the south. But the prime force was the shift of the commercial classes, led by the city's solicitors, accountants, insurance brokers and bankers. As they moved, their offices entered the zone of discard on the retreating eastern residential edge. This zone had advantages. It was still an area of high centrality since it was the focus of the urban road network before 1850 and, later, of the railways and tramways; its substantial structures were easily convertible; and it was accessible both to the professional élite who worked there and to their clients. This became the core proper with its retail shops, coffee houses, theatres, banks and civic institutions at ground level, and its complex of offices and small workshops in back courts and the upper storeys. On the area's eastern and southern flanks lay a zone of commercial discard and lower rents. This in turn was occupied by activities needing centrality, but less mobile and unable to generate the site income needed to obtain a more central location: printing, publishing, wholesaling, clothing and textile finishing.

The particular location of activities depended on several factors, notably the economic rent of suitable sites. As this rose, and as consumers moved beyond easy daily shopping distance, retailing dispersed, leaving specialised shops and, later, department stores in central localities. Wholesaling, however, remained central since its own market was city-wide and a site on the central fringes minimised aggregate costs. Small workshops engaged in the final stages of production also sought centrality. Their physicial inputs and batch sales were low; their products were usually complex, fragile, or required special packing; or they relied on individual consumer taste.

Inertia could also affect relocation. The Glasgow Exchange is a typical case. In 1800 its site at Glasgow Cross was only some 100 metres east of the core's median centre. But by 1825 it was twice as remote, in an increasingly un-savoury part of the city and too far from the homes and businesses of its members. Within a few years it had moved to Queen Street, a thriving com-mercial thoroughfare, and to a site 300 metres west of the median centre. By 1850 the continued migration of the core placed it only 70 metres from the point of maximum accessibility. But by 1875 its site was again increasingly in-convenient, too cramped for the scale of its business and too remote for the growing number of members who lived in the west end or even out of town. Shortly thereafter it moved again to its present site on Buchanan Street, under 200 metres from the median centre and within easy reach of the city's four rail-way stations, its subway and the tramway system.

(c) *Industry*

With industry it was a different story. Between 1800 and 1900 its com-position and extent changed substantially. The labour force rose from 67,000 to 330,000 and the proportions in metallurgy, engineering and services grew from 31 per cent of the labour force to 48 per cent in 1901. Moreover as industrial production grew it became more dispersed. In 1800, 47 per cent of recorded activity was contained within only one block. By 1850 the median concentration group occupied 10 blocks; and by 1900 18 blocks — a total area of 4.5 square kilometres. The standard distance results in Table 6 and the concentration indices in Figure 5.2 confirm the dispersal, though the latter index for 1875 reveals an anomalous rise.

Another feature of the city's industrial morphology also deserves mention: the stability of the locus of industrial activity. Over the century the mean centre of industrial activity shifted only 0.4 kilometres, a substantially smaller relocation than occurs in the core activities. Given the extensive changes in the mix of urban activities and in the influence of different locational forces, the result is unexpected. It is not due to any inner city bias in the directory data. When the map data alone were tested, the resulting mean and median centres differed little from those in Figure 3, whilst the standard distance was less than that of the whole sample.

How then are this dispersion and stability to be explained? The key to dispersion lies in the development of the city's transport system, particularly in relaxing the cost constraints which it imposed on industrial location. Until the late nineteenth century transport costs rose rapidly with distance. In the early decades this had resulted from technical limits to speed and carrier capacity in road, canal and river transport: in roads by the inherent characteristics of cart technology, in the canal by its obsolete, eighteenth century dimensions, and in

TABLE 6

The Standard Distance (km.) of Central Economic Area and Industrial Activity, 1800-1900

	Central Ec Area	Industry
1800	0.27	1.00
1825	0.35	1.14
1850	0.55	1.99
1875	0.55	2.08
1900	0.51	2.73

Source: Tables 4 and 5.

the Clyde by the restricted quayage and channel depth. In the middle decades of the century the advent of the railway reduced transport costs, especially those of intraurban traffic. It was only with the development of the tramway and suburban railway systems in the last quarter of the century that intraurban transport costs declined significantly as an element in industry's aggregate costs. The dispersion of industrial activity therefore is directly related to the fall in the cost constraints of transport. In 1800 and 1825 when these were great, industry was excessively concentrated. By 1850, river improvement, railway development, the social crisis of the inner city, and the expansion of economic activity all helped to reduce the earlier industrial overcrowding and to produce a dispersion of activities. Yet these same forces produced a reflux by 1875. Between 1850 and 1875 substantial improvements were made to the Clyde and the city's harbour, thereby confirming the profitability and access of central locations. Urban redevelopment, and the extensive intrusion of the railways into the urban fabric, displaced thousands of people and opened up new commercial sites near the city centre. Perhaps most important, access to peripheral, greenfield sites was restricted by the limited development of the intraurban railway network. By 1900 this constraint had again been relaxed. Industrial dispersion had resumed, reinforced by further improvement of the river and harbour,[22] the downstream expansion of shipbuilding and marine engineering and by the advent of transmissible electrical power.

Transport changes also explain why the locus of maximum accessibility for industrial activity changed so little in the nineteenth century. Cart traffic, horse omnibuses, and later the railways and tramways all sought to serve the area of greatest existing social and economic contact. In doing so they increasingly confirmed the superior accessibility of that area, in Glasgow's case the district south and east of George Square. For a range of industrial activities a central site was a rational, perhaps even the only, locational choice. Production costs were distance-related; but demand was usually independent of location. So a central site, whilst minimising the former, also maximised access to the latter. Several industries were dependent on speed, time, bespoke orders and rapid turnover of stock, so access to the transport termini — the harbour, Port Dundas, the railway stations and goods yards — was important.

Other factors also reinforced industry's preference for central location: inertia, an ignorance of true site costs, and the cost of relocation for heavily capitalised activities. Furthermore the presence of the largest, low-cost housing sector in the oldest parts of the city — round and to the south and east of Glasgow Cross — kept a large pool of labour in the centre. Despite transport improvements after 1875, time and cost limited commuting to richer workers with shorter hours, so central sites had more available labour, central activities lower labour costs and centrally based workers greater job opportunities and lower living and transport costs. With such substantive advantages, industrial activities also bid for central sites. These locations commanded rising land rents which, in turn, determined site allocation. Unsuccessful bidders moved outwards, opting not only for lower site rents and labour availability but also for higher transport costs and overheads such as the need sometimes to provide housing to attract workers.

Central access, however, was not the prime concern for all activities. Factors other than transport, land rent and labour supply also determined the site preference of many industries, especially the largest and most important. Location of customers and supplies, raw material needs, access to water, the threshold size of economic operation, zoning restrictions in the later century, and the pre-emption of sites for recreational, residential or other activities, all acted, jointly or separately, to affect the comparative costs and locational choices of the city's shipyards, engineering works, chemical plants, textile factories, grain mills, breweries, brickfields, woodyards and many other businesses. Of the possible sites, the optimum one for a given activity was that which minimised its mix of operating and transfer costs. But changing economic conditions throughout the century affected the optimality of any given site, as Lampard noted in 1955:

> From time to time the economic historian notices substantial changes or shifts in the location of activities, changes which often defy simple explanation in terms of comparative cost. Many short, medium and long-run influences determine these historical movements . . . But few of these currents work in the same direction simultaneously or with equal force.[23]

The three influences which may confidently be suggested as operating consistently to move the locus of industrial activity westwards were the increasing importance of maritime trade and industry for the Glasgow region, the presence and improvement of the Clyde navigation and the topography of the lower Clyde valley, which yielded more space downstream than upstream for industrial expansion.

(d) *Total activity*

When the sum of the activities recorded in the maps and directories is examined, the locational stability and compactness of economic life in Glasgow throughout its greatest age is clear. As Figure 3 indicates, the locus of activity, the mean centre, remained within the area of maximum accessibility throughout the nineteenth century, having by 1900 moved only 0.6 kilometres from its 1800 location.

Moreover, with declining industrial concentration offsetting the increase in core functions, the Gini index for all activities (see Figure 5.3) remains almost constant, at about 0.78, throughout the period. This high degree of concentration is confirmed by the distribution of the median concentration group of the data. In 1800 half of all recorded activity was in an area of just 0.25 kilometres. By 1900 the corresponding figure was 1 square kilometre, 2 per cent of the built-up area.

The distributions which have been examined in this study are the spatial expression of the flux of human economic and social interactions which occurred in nineteenth-century Glasgow. These interactions produced functionally differentiated areas which reflected different activities, different densities of physical and demographic structure, and the different circulation systems which served them. This study has shown that the key factors in Glasgow's changing economic morphology were the interrelated ones of accessibility and site availability. Accessibility had a profound effect on site rents and hence influenced urban structure and regulated the city's growth. When transport was poor, before 1850, or when there was a lull in improvement, access was constrained by high costs. Urban activities were therefore compacted round points of lowest transfer costs. When transport, hence accessibility, improved, especially after 1875, activities dispersed into specialised neighbourhoods. The series of 'snapshots' in this study therefore charts the progress of Glasgow's activities in overcoming the disadvantages of distance. Throughout the period there was a constant contention between income, access, space and distance. As one set of transfer problems was resolved, Glasgow's economic and physical size grew, throwing up another array of difficulties. The problem of distance produced three main responses: bouts of transport innovation, changes in the relationship between home and work, and the emergence of peripheral subcentres.

The availability of suitable sites at an economic rent also fundamentally affected the distribution of activity. Once an active property market emerged in the early part of the century, the rent-paying ability of different activities led to a redistribution of functions. In the high-access, high-rent central area, prime sites on the upper reaches of the rent gradient were occupied by activities able to economise on space yet able to generate high incomes from it. On the less accessible lower slopes of the curve were activities and house seekers whose rent-paying ability was less. However, the capacity to afford the market price of space and access was not the only locational determinant of function. It identified suitably endowed candidates. But the attractions of a site also depended on its linkages to and association with other activities. These externalities were a major factor producing the compact zones of interrelated enterprise which characterised both the manufacturing and service sectors of the Glaswegian economy.

Although the nature of the data prohibited a similarly detailed study of residential distributions, the historical record indicates that they too were deeply affected by externalities, land rent and the opportunity cost of accessibility.[24] These forces replicated in Glasgow one of the paradoxes of urban development: that the well-off occupy cheap, peripheral sites whilst the poor dwell on expensive, central land. The social élite and the professional groups, with a growing preference for space and social exclusiveness — and with the income necessary to satisfy these tastes — substituted land for access. To them site costs outweighed transport costs in their family budgets. Moreover the distinction of such areas as Kelvinside and Pollokshields attracted those who sought, by a kind of social externality, a physical and locational confirmation of their own self-esteem. The wealthier thus bought amenity and status and absorbed the costs of commuting. The artisans traded the lesser amenity of Partick, Govan and, later, Dennistoun and Crosshill against transport according to the size and regularity of their incomes. The poor by contrast substituted access to the job market for amenity and absorbed the attendant costs: overcrowding, noise, pollution, crime and obsolete structures. The income-site paradox was resolved for them by the slum: 'the main contribution of the Victorian Age to architecture'.[25] As elsewhere in nineteenth-century Britain, the Glaswegian house construction sector provided homes primarily for the wealthy, who absorbed the depreciation costs before passing the property on to poorer citizens. But the market mechanism was imperfect. With so few wealthy people and so many poor, the supply of low-cost housing was inadequate, especially in a rapidly growing city. With high site costs it was impossible to provide new structures at rents to close the gap between demand at 1/- to 1/6d and supply at 2/- to 3/- per week, especially when the Glasgow tenement tradition was for a structure whose size — and cost — were four to eight times those of an English terraced house.[26] Neglect and subdivision therefore generated the required supply at the offered rent. The slum gave the poor cheap lodging, the tenant, through sub-lets, a substantial net income, and the landlord, who neglected maintenance and subdivided his property, a large net return.[27] Thus the overcrowded, one-room slum tenement was a rational response to the large and otherwise unrequitable demand for cheap, central housing, a fact unrecognised by contemporary commentators who ignored the contradictions in their demands for low rents *and* greater amenity.[28] They also failed to perceive that areas of overcrowding and cheap, decaying housing were caught in an externality trap. Property improvement would have yielded a greater net gain to other landlords. So the optimum strategy for each owner was net disinvestment in order not only to maximise his short-term net income but also to retrieve the largest possible proportion of residual value still present in the structure. Socially too the slum played an important role in urban development. It was the permanent residence for the submerged population: the destitute, idle, fugitive, outcast and the respectable poor. It was a transit camp for new arrivals, like the Highland and Irish immigrants of the first half of the nineteenth century. And it was a springboard for those on their way up: earlier immigrants, entrepreneurs, and slum landlords.

This study has tried to indicate several simple techniques by which general, as opposed to particular, problems of the large industrial cities may be tackled by the individual urban historian. None of them is particularly original, or overly complicated, and most of them will be familiar to geographers. But they do provide a consistent basis for comparative work on large urban complexes over long periods of time. And they offer one positive response to Sydney Checkland's sound but often overlooked advice that 'those who have seriously chosen the city as their subject, cannot avoid committing themselves to some degree at least to a more scientific history'.[29]

APPENDIX 1. Establishments per Grid Block

1.1: Central Economic Area Functions

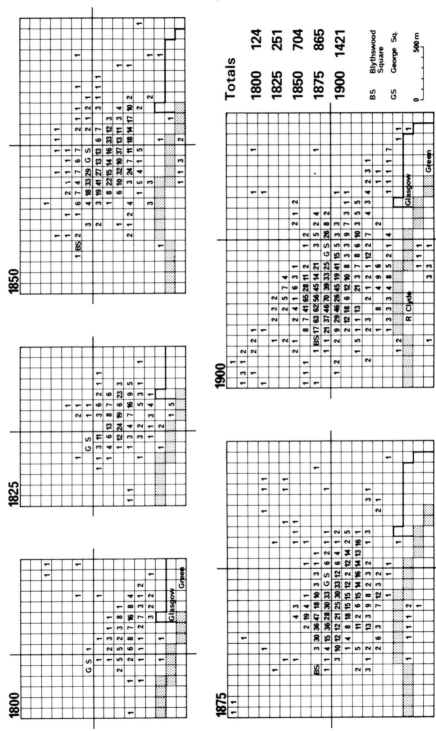

1.2: Industrial Functions

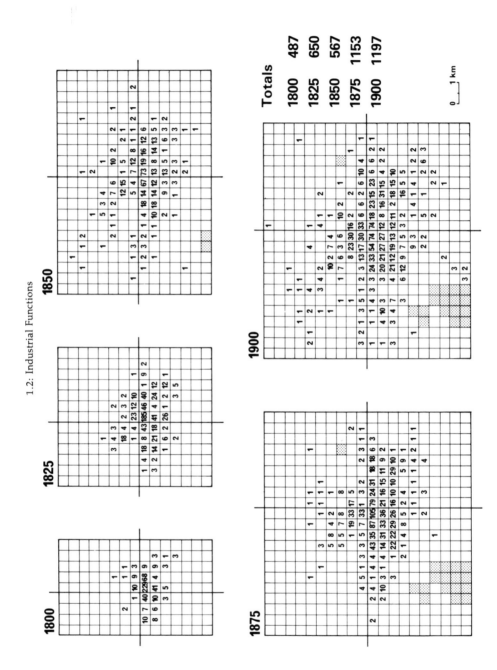

Totals	
1800	**487**
1825	**650**
1850	**567**
1875	**1153**
1900	**1197**

0 ___ 1 km

1.3: Total Recorded Activity

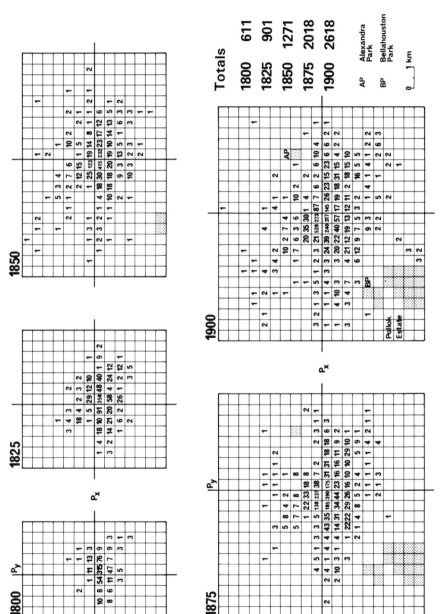

P$_x$, P$_y$: horizontal, vertical prime axes (see note 17)

APPENDIX 2

The Location of the Mean and Median Centres of Urban Activity, 1775-1900

Year	Mean Centre	Shift (km.)	Median Centre	Shift (km.)
		Built-up Area		
1775	5934 6488		—	—
		0.35		
1800	5961 6465		—	—
		0.42		
1825	5928 6491		—	—
		0.47		
1850	5886 6513		—	—
		0.29		
1875	5862 6497		—	—
		0.38		
1900	5824 6492		—	—
		Total Recorded Activity		
1800	5953 6496		5968 6497	
		0.08		0.23
1825	5945 6498		5945 6500	
		0.30		0.34
1850	5922 6518		5915 6516	
		0.16		0.26
1875	5906 6518		5889 6517	
		0.12		0.20
1900	5899 6528		5886 6537	
		Central Economic Area Activity		
1800	5950 6494		5951 6492	
		0.12		0.13
1825	5942 6503		5944 6503	
		0.28		0.43
1850	5918 6518		5906 6524	
		0.25		0.18
1875	5901 6536		5896 6539	
		0.08		0.10
1900	5893 6538		5894 6529	
		Industrial Activity		
1800	5952 6493		5957 6497	
		0.00		0.04
1825	5952 6493		5958 6493	
		0.30		0.31
1850	5930 6513		5929 6504	
		0.26		0.31
1875	5906 6502		5898 6504	
		0.04		0.21
1900	5910 6503		5918 6497	

The eight-digit reference is based on the Ordnance Survey 1:10560 Sheets NS 56 NE and NS 56 SE. It is accurate to within 10 metres.

NOTES

1. Oscar Handlin, 'The modern city as a field of historical study', in Oscar Handlin & John Burchard (eds.), *The Historian and the City* (M.I.T. Press, Harvard Univ. Press, 1963), 26.

2. Sydney G. Checkland, 'The British industrial city as history', *Urban Studs.*, 1,1 (May 1964), 34f.

3. The most complete collection of map and directory material is to be found in the Glasgow Room of Glasgow's Mitchell Library.

4. See Clive H. Lee, *British Regional Employment Statistics, 1841-1971* (Cambridge U.P., Cambridge, 1979), 3f.

5. Checkland, *op. cit.*, 37.

6. See John R. Kellett, 'Property speculators and the building of Glasgow, 1783-1830', *Scott. Jnl. Pol. Ec.,* 8,3 (1961), 211-232. Unlike the English freehold and leasehold forms of landholding, Scottish land was held in feu tenure: i.e. in perpetuity against the payment of an initial lump sum and continuing, fixed, annual payments to the landowner.

7. C. S. Loch, 'Poor relief in Scotland: its statistics and development, 1791 to 1891', *Jnl. Roy. Stat. Soc.,* 61 (1898), 315ff.

8. Captain H. Miller, Superintendent of Police, Poor Law Enquiry Commission for Scotland, Appendix 1, *Minutes of Evidence* Examinations, Glasgow, 12 April 1843 (H.M.S.O., Edinburgh, 1844), 323.

9. See Charles M. Allan, 'The genesis of British Urban redevelopment with special reference to Glasgow', *Ec. Hist. Rev.,* 18 (1965), 599-613.

10. House of Commons, Select Committee on Private Bills, Glasgow Corporation Tramways Bill, *Minutes of Evidence,* 8 May 1872, 59.

11. C. H. Lee, *op. cit.,* 18ff.

12. The location quotient measures the local representation of a function relative to its national occurrence. It may be calculated from the following formula:

$$LQ = \frac{LEs/LEt}{NEs/NEt}$$

where LEs = local employment by sector
NEs= national (i.e. British) employment by sector
LEt = total local employment
NEt= total national employment

A value under 1.0 indicates that a particular activity is relatively under-represented locally; a value over 1.0, that it is relatively over-represented.

See Walter Isard *et al, Methods of Regional Analysis* (M.I.T. Press, Cambridge, Mass., 1960), 123-126, 251f.

13. For a discussion of basic and non basic sectors see Wilbur R. Thompson, 'Urban economic growth and development in a national scheme of cities', in Philip M. Hauser & Leo F. Schnore (eds.), *The Study of Urbanisation* (Wiley, New York, 1965), 431-490.

The test yielded a significant value of $r_s = 0.85$.

14. The Lorenz curve is a graphic representation of the evenness of spread of a distribution, in this study of different groups of activities over a series of grid cells. Along the horizontal axis the number of establishments per block is plotted as a cumulative percentage of all establishments, starting with the block with the largest number of observations and adding progressively smaller blocks. The vertical axis similarly cumulates the proportion of occupied blocks. Thus the vertical spacing of points is at regular intervals whilst the horizontal spacing decreases progressively. The fullness of the curve indicates the degree of inequality in the distribution.

15. The Gini coefficient or concentration ratio expresses the area between the diagonal and the Lorenz curve as a proportion of the total area beneath the diagonal.

16. Central Statistical Office, *Standard Industrial Classification,* rev. 1968 (H.M.S.O., London, 1978).

17. The functions representing industrial activity were those recorded in S.I.C. orders III-XIX, i.e. food processing, chemicals, metallurgy, engineering, textiles, clothing; bricks, glass etc; timber and furniture; paper, printing and publishing, and miscellaneous manufacturing. Central area activities were those falling under S.I.C. minimum list headings: 486, printing and publishing; 489, other printing; 860-862, insurance, banking and finance; 871, accountancy services; 873, legal services; 861/2, entertainment services, and 906, local government services. Wholesaling is excluded since, with the exception of the city's markets, it proved impossible to isolate for the whole period.

18. The grids were arbitrarily centred on a point at the south-eastern corner of the city's principal square, George Square. The horizontal prime axis was a line drawn along the centre of St. Vincent Street, the main east-west thoroughfare on the south side of the square. The vertical

prime axis was aligned along the centre of North Frederick Street, the eastern boundary of the square. An arbitrary zero co-ordinate for the 100 metre grid was located at O.S. reference NS 56 5764 6458 and for the 500 metre grid at NS 56 5142 6215. This alignment was more convenient than the usual north-south one used by the Ordnance Survey since it gave a clearer horizontal prime axis against which to measure many separate distributions.

19. In calculating the mean centre each block may be regarded as lying in two planes: in a set of horizontal tiers equivalent to a frequency distribution along a y axis; and in a set of vertical columns along an x axis. The result is two frequency profiles which can be weighed by their distance from an arbitrary base co-ordinate (see note 17) to produce two mean values, the co-ordinates ($\bar{x}_c$, $\bar{y}_c$) of the mean centre. These values can be calculated from the following equations:

$$\bar{x}_c = \frac{\Sigma(x_i P_i)}{\Sigma P_i} \qquad \bar{y}_c = \frac{\Sigma(y_i P_i)}{\Sigma P_i}$$

Where x_i and y_i are respectively the horizontal and vertical distances of the ith block from the base co-ordinate and P_i is the number of blocks at that distance.

For a more detailed explanation of this method see W. H. Theakstone & C. Harrison, *The Analysis of Geographical Data* (Heinemann, London, 1970), 56. For an application see John Rannells, *The Core of the City: A pilot study of changing land uses in central business districts* (Columbia U.P., New York, 1956).

20. The standard distance can be determined by the formula

$$SD = \sqrt{\frac{\Sigma[P_i(x_i \text{-} \bar{x}_i)^2] + \Sigma[P_i(y_i \text{-} \bar{y}_i)^2]}{\Sigma P_i}}$$

Where P_i is the number of observations in the ith block, x_i and y_i are the distances of the ith block from the mean centre ($\bar{x}_c$, $\bar{y}_c$) and $\bar{x}_i$ and $\bar{y}_i$ are the mean distances of the blocks from the mean centre, measured along axes parallel to the prime axes and centred on $\bar{x}_c$, $\bar{y}_c$.

21. A concentration group may be defined as that number of blocks which contain a particular proportion of establishments. Here, for simplicity, those blocks containing 50 per cent of establishments were chosen; but division by thirds, sixths or any other desired proportion is possible. For a discussion and application of the method see Rannells, *op. cit.,* 95-99.

22. See John F. Riddell, *Clyde Navigation. A History of the development and deepening of the River Clyde* (John Donald, Edinburgh, 1979).

23. E. E. Lampard, 'The history of cities in the economically advanced areas', *Ec. Dev. Cult. Change,* 3, (1955), 93.

24. These considerations were tacitly recognised by contemporaries; see Michael A. Simpson, 'The west end of Glasgow, 1830-1914', in Michael A. Simpson & T. H. Lloyd (eds), *Middle Class Housing in Britain* (David & Charles, Newton Abbot, 1977), 44-85; Michael A. Simpson, 'Urban transport and the development of Glasgow's west end, 1830-1914', *Jnl. Transp. Hist.,* new ser. 1,3 (February, 1972), 146-160.

25. Robert F. Jordan, *Victorian Architecture* (Penguin, Harmondsworth, 1966), 18.

26. Enid F. Gauldie, *Cruel Habitations. A history of working class housing 1780-1918* (Allen & Unwin, London, 1974), 179f.

27. Enid F. Gauldie, *op. cit.,* 159f. See also John R. Seeley, 'The Slum: its nature, use and users', *Jnl. Am. Inst. Planners,* 25,1 (February, 1959), 7-14. Reprinted in Larry S. Bourne (ed.), *Internal Structure of the City* (Oxford Univ. Pr., New York, 1971), 464-474.

28. See e.g. the report of the city's Medical Officer of Health, J. B. Russell, to the City Improvement Trust:

> The class of people of whom I have been speaking cling tenaciously to their old haunts . . . it is this desire, and the competition which it begets for houses of small size in the heart of the city which stimulates the process of making down houses.

Glasgow City Improvement Trust, *Minutes,* 29 December 1875.

29. Sydney G. Checkland, *loc. cit.,* 34f.

10. Urban Growth and Municipal Government: Glasgow in a Comparative Context, 1846-1914

Tom Hart

TWO images of Glasgow had arisen by 1914. One presented the city as an outstanding example of municipal enterprise while the other emphasised the gigantic housing and slum problem, a large municipal debt and a range of municipal services so wide as to cause inefficiency, if not downright corruption and vote-catching. The predominant view, however, favoured the former image. Leading councillors and officials were becoming active publicists of Glasgow's achievements by the late nineteenth century,[1] but this was more than a public relations exercise. Many ordinary Glaswegians were proud of their water supplies from Loch Katrine, the excellent tram system and the parks, art galleries and numerous other services which had been created. Outside observers lent support to such views and Glasgow received a growing procession of visitors from other British cities and from across the Atlantic.[2] From the 1880s, Americans had become more conscious of the defects in their own systems of urban government[3] and turned to Britain and continental Europe for solutions. Albert Shaw was one such visitor who wrote extensively on European practice and its lessons for the United States. In his book, *Municipal Government in Great Britain*, published in 1895, he devoted a complete chapter to Glasgow. At that time, Birmingham was popularly regarded as the best example of municipal enterprise but Shaw had no doubt that Glasgow's performance 'took first place among the communities of Great Britain' (p. 69). He concluded his Glasgow chapter by saying that the city 'has shown that a broad, bold and enlightened policy as regards all things pertaining to the health, comfort and advancement of the masses of the citizens may be compatible with sound economy and perfect solvency' (p. 144). Glasgow was far ahead of American practice and E. L. Godkin, editor of *Nation*, argued that Glasgow's experience showed how the masses could live comfortably in a great city.[4] Yet, set against such views, there were adverse comments on the potential inefficiencies of extended municipal involvements and on the immensity of the housing and social problems which remained despite over sixty years of municipal expansion.[5]

Such contrasting images raise important issues in the evaluation of urban growth and urban government. Glasgow was no obscure city on the edge of Britain; it was in this period a world-ranking city which attracted international attention and which seemed relevant to the mainstream of urban problems and opportunities in a western world experiencing unparalleled economic expansion. Tertius Chandler has estimated that the number of cities with more inhabitants than Glasgow fell from 79 in 1800 to 38 in 1825, 19 in 1850 and 13 in 1875.[6] Thereafter, Glasgow's relative position fell — at least 66 other cities were larger in 1970[7] but, as late as 1925, only 17 cities were larger. The city's economy was also much stronger than that of several cities with a larger population and, in terms of local income and wealth, Glasgow ranked at the top end of the tier of great regional centres, coming immediately below a handful of political and commercial capitals such as London, Paris, Berlin, Vienna, New York and, from the late nineteenth century, Chicago and Tokyo. The eminence of Glasgow's position bears emphasis since it is often forgotten by modern commentators pre-occupied with the city's contracting role in a national economy itself of much reduced international status.

Without any doubt, Glasgow's economy experienced strong growth between 1850 and 1914, but did this growth lead to an improvement, or a deterioration, in urban government? Did Glasgow's government offer an example to be followed or was 'success' superficial, hiding both continuing problems and specially favourable features of the local situation? To deal with these questions, it is necessary to outline the main features of municipal activity and to relate these to suitable criteria for the assessment of civic performance.

The Nature and Chronology of Municipal Initiatives

The Governmental Pattern. Glasgow's burghal government dates back to medieval times, but the late eighteenth and early nineteenth centuries saw significant changes arising from a combination of faster urban growth and a reluctance to grant additional powers of local taxation to non-representative and often corrupt burgh councils. New bodies were created with specific functions and specific rights to raise income for the exercise of such functions. From 1800, the Police Commissioners existed alongside the burgh councillors. The Statute Labour Trust dealt with city streets and, as the nineteenth century progressed, separately constituted boards were created to deal with matters such as poor relief, the development of the port and education. The reformed franchise of 1833, itself substantially widened later in the century, removed some of the justification for such fragmented administration but it was still felt that certain functions were better handled by specialist bodies than by an 'all-purpose' city council. Poor Relief was dealt with by the new Parochial Boards from 1845, while the creation of elected School Boards under the Education (Scotland) Act, 1872 removed education from the city council's responsibilities. Another important loss of initiative affected the river and the port. With the modification of the Harbour Trust in 1858, the city council ceased to have a majority representation on the Trust. These losses of initiative were more than counterbalanced by new areas of activity, and it is to these that attention is now turned.

1800 to 1840s: The Emergence of Police Powers. Four features dominate this period. These were the improvement of the river and port, the provision of poor relief, highway maintenance and the development of police regulations and taxation. Only the highway and police functions fell within the mainstream of civic responsibilities as they were to develop from mid-century, and they did not yet require large amounts of financing. The police powers included provision for additional local taxation and covered a wider sphere than the modern police function. Police powers of civic regulation were to be carried much further, in Glasgow and throughout Scotland, in a succession of Police Acts running into the twentieth century, but the power to make bye-laws (imposing costs on others) minimised the financial demands falling on the city. The capital cost of most new streets and related sewers and pavements was also a charge on frontagers. The city was involved only in subsequent maintenance, a relatively light burden. Pre-1846 local taxation was therefore confined to the moderate amounts needed to pay the police force (in its modern sense), to finance street lighting and street maintenance and to cover certain other administrative costs.

1846-60: The Municipalisation and Extension of Water Supplies. Between 1825 and 1850, the urban population doubled. This scale of growth, and the expectation of continuing growth, placed urban problems and opportunities in sharper focus. The need for city spending, as well as civic regulation, became more evident and the shift to a more modern pattern of local government took place between 1833 and 1846. The reformed franchise was introduced in 1833, a more comprehensive Police Act followed in 1843 and, in 1846, the boundaries of the city were extended from 3418 to 5791 acres. Police spending began to increase rapidly to cope with the criminality of a large city while, for the first time, the highways department became a significant borrower as it sought to strengthen the foundations of existing streets. Bridges were also widened and controversial decisions taken to purchase land at Kelvingrove (1852) and Queens Park (1857) for the laying out of high amenity public parks in areas ripe for middle class suburban expansion.

But the outstanding issue of the period was water supply. Repeated concern had been expressed about the inadequacies of the water companies, while public wells could not provide either the quantity or the quality of water required for domestic and sanitary purposes. Municipalisation had first been considered as early as 1834[8] (thirteen years before Manchester municipalised its supplies), and a special committee of the city council made a firm recommendation for municipalisation in 1845. Problems in negotiating with the existing companies, uncertainty about which new sources should be developed, and the high cost of combining a takeover of existing companies with the tapping of major new supplies, involved a decade of research, debate and litigation, but parliamentary powers were finally obtained in 1855. There-

P

after, construction work proceeded rapidly and no less a person than Queen Victoria inaugurated the new supplies from Loch Katrine on 14th October, 1859.

1861-69: The Sanitary Revolution.   Though the introduction of Katrine water kept the city death rate below what it would otherwise have been, the death rate still rose and more sophisticated policies began to be advocated to meet the sanitary and social problems of the city. The public health issue had been on the urban agenda since the 1830s but did not receive high priority until the 1860s. In part, this reflected increased national concern that urban death rates remained so high, but there were also special features in the Glasgow situation. John Ure, subsequently Lord Provost between 1880 and 1883, pioneered a new political approach as Chairman of the Committee on Nuisances (created in 1857). He was helped by medical opinion and the accumulating evidence of precise levels of mortality gained from the systematic registration of deaths which had been introduced in Scotland in 1854, almost twenty years later than the equivalent action in England.

Strong suspicions had also arisen that housing conditions were a serious factor in mortality. Scottish sanitary reformers had failed to secure a modification in the 1851 Census to shed more light on Scottish housing but, with the 1861 Census in the hands of the newly appointed Registrar-General for Scotland, specific questions were introduced on the number of rooms per dwelling.[9] These housing returns provided incontrovertible data that housing conditions were even worse than had been commonly thought, with 73.4% of the city population being found to be living in dwellings of only one or two rooms.

Public health regulations were strengthened in the Glasgow Police Act, 1862, but the most fundamental change was the linking of a political priority for health with the formation of a sanitary bureaucracy. Under the 1862 Act, the city committed itself to appoint a Medical Officer of Health (following the example of Liverpool) and an inspectorate with powers to cleanse and disinfect housing and to reduce overcrowding through restrictions on the number of people authorised to sleep in dwellings liable to be overcrowded. These measures were supplemented by the notification by doctors of infectious disease, improved standards for new housing, a corps of Sanitary Inspectors (1866) and the assumption by the city of direct responsibility for the cleansing of streets, common closes and backyard middens (contract cleansing was phased out between 1866 and 1868). More spectacularly, provision was made for the thorough clearance of the grossly overcrowded medieval city. Railway-financed demolitions to make way for the City Union Railway and the new St Enoch terminal station started this process in the late 1860s but the City Improvement Act, 1866, tackled the areas untouched by the railway works.[10] These schemes were far larger than Joseph Chamberlain's similar plans for Birmingham ten years later. The final stage in the sanitary revolution came when the change was made from a Medical Officer of Health with substantial outside interests to a full-time appointment. J. B. Russell took over from the part-time W. T. Gairdner, who had retained his appointment as Professor of Medicine at Glasgow University, in 1872.[11]

1870-90: The Rise of Municipal Trading. In this period, many of the results of the sanitary revolution became apparent.[12] Techniques were refined as knowledge improved, but public health was already an established initiative; it was municipal trading which provided the principal example of innovation. When water municipalisation had been proposed in 1845, a similar policy had been considered for gas but had been rejected as less urgent. By 1860, however, most councillors felt that the principle of unified public utilities under municipal ownership was preferable to wasteful competition or the alternative of imperfect control through the regulation of a monopoly company. Gas municipalisation was finally approved by the city council in 1867 and, after the failure of efforts to secure a negotiated agreement with the gas companies, Parliament granted compulsory takeover powers in 1869. Powers for a large new gasworks at Dawsholm were added in 1871.

The council wished to follow similar policies in relation to the development of tram services. By 1870, it was obvious that horse trams were about to be adopted on an extensive scale in British cities, and companies were competing for franchises to operate on public streets. Parliament was opposed to direct municipal operation but the city council gained power to construct the tram tracks, leasing them for twenty-three years to a unified company obliged to make a hefty annual payment to the city and to observe regulations on fares and quality of service.[13] Fares were not to exceed 1d per mile, with further concessions for workmen's travel. The first tram route opened in 1872 and, as the system extended, the adjustment of the lease led to prolonged recriminations between the city and the operating company. Parliamentary opposition to municipal operation had weakened by 1890 and, with the expiry of the lease, such operation was introduced in 1894.

Meantime, the opportunity had been taken to introduce an element of municipal trading in the water undertaking. Meter charging was introduced for supplies to industry and trade, and this source accounted for over half the income of the Water Department by the 1890s.[14] Both gas and water were supplied to an area much larger than the city as defined in 1846 but at charges higher than those levied within the city.

Another initiative was taken in the construction of civic offices. New buildings had been completed in 1874 but, even during their planning, they had been criticised as below the size and status appropriate for Glasgow's rising prestige and level of municipal activity.[15] More flamboyant City Chambers, costing £590,000, were completed on the east side of George Square in 1889. This project was influenced by the expectation that, sooner or later, Glasgow's boundaries would again be extended to cover the bulk of the urbanised area. Strenuous efforts were made to secure boundary extensions but, apart from small gains to the east in the later 1870s, the boundary remained static between 1870 and 1890. The growing suburbs to the south and west, including many middle-class areas, formed themselves into separate burghs. One consequence was that the city's population and rateable value showed very little increase in the 1880s (Table 1). Since this was also a period of relative economic depression, this provided an added incentive to municipal trading rather than towards activities involving increases in city taxes.

1891-1900: The Golden Years. The general improvement in business confidence and the large boundary extension finally secured by the City Extension Act, 1891 (though the populous shipbuilding burghs of Partick and Govan were still excluded) marked a new era of civic confidence. The municipalisation (1894), electrification (from 1898) and extension of the tram system is the best-known innovation, yet the period also saw the expansion of municipal work in all sectors developed since 1846 and in important new areas. These included electricity supply (1890), sewage purification (from 1894), high pressure water supplies for hydraulic equipment (1895), libraries (1899), telephones (1900), museums, art galleries, public halls, golf courses, tennis courts, bowling greens, refuse incinerators, alcoholic rehabilitation centres, food and drink inspection, female health visitors, tram construction and municipal housing. In place of an authority which had shown only one or two initiatives per decade, Glasgow now seemed to have a multi-purpose council so experienced and mature that new developments could be readily assimilated within the broad financial and bureaucratic base which had been created over earlier decades.

1900-1914: Clouded Horizons. Looking back from the high unemployment and depression which characterised inter-war Glasgow, conventional perceptions saw the 'golden years' of the 1890s as extending over the whole period to 1914. Indeed, the completion in 1906 of the move by Yarrows the shipbuilders from the Thames to the Clyde strengthened impressions of a shift in the economic balance towards the north.[16] Yet, among those most concerned to forecast Clydeside's future, the expectation that the regional economy could sustain its nineteenth-century rate of growth was beginning to weaken. On closer analysis the years from 1900 saw a definite waning in municipal confidence and, though no fundamental change in policy took place, the intense debate on housing and social conditions revealed growing unease at the rate of improvement. House construction fell sharply from its 1902 peak and was virtually at a standstill by 1910 despite high levels of over-crowding. Thousands of houses remained vacant and the conflict between housing need and the lack of effective demand for housing became more apparent.[17]

By 1912, the incorporation of Partick, Govan and other surrounding areas into the city had brought the total population to over one million but, though Glaswegians liked to think that this confirmed their claim to live in the second city of the Empire, Manchester and Birmingham actually had larger populations in their built-up areas (Table 6). They just happened to have been less successful than Glasgow in absorbing most of the urbanised zones on their fringes.

The Financial Background: 1846-1914

Prior to the 1840s, the financial needs of Glasgow's urban government were small, and more evenly spread, than the demands of regional and longer-distance transport. Using turnpike tolls to finance the loan charges arising from capital spending, the regional road system had been transformed since the mid-eighteenth century and substantial borrowing, secured on higher user charges, had also been undertaken to deepen the river Clyde and extend the harbour. Yet it was not until the 1840s that similar pressures developed in urban government. By then, transport still seemed to require even higher investment but there was also a new conviction that a desirable quality of urban services could no longer be obtained on the cheap. Attention turned to local taxation as a means of financing higher levels of ordinary spending and the loan charges from a quite new level of borrowing for municipal purposes.[18]

A clutch of financial demands matured in the 1840s and began the process of reshaping the nature of urban government. More finance was needed for transport, for civic improvement and for a long overdue uprating of provision for the poor. Amidst these demands, the role of city government was seen to lie in civic improvement. Though originally reluctant to lose their majority say in port policy, the city councillors began to see that the offloading of responsibility for the port could allow them to concentrate on civic improvement free of the possible financial burdens arising from heavy capital expenditure on the harbour.[19] On their side, the port users were happy — indeed anxious — to have a greater say in port policy. With port users (and railway companies) financing their own schemes, the city could give full attention to the essentials of urban improvement. Such logic also encouraged the separation of poor relief from other aspects of local taxation. The responsibility of the new Parochial Boards for the poor helped to ensure that the city council turned its attention to the more dynamic aspects of civic improvement.

This political structure, as it emerged in the 1840s and 1850s, reflected the predominant liberal philosophy that 'value for money' was most likely to be obtained by a direct linkage of financial decisions in identifiable sectors with electoral responsibility. By now, however, the city council was more confident of electoral support for increased expenditure on civic improvement. Taxes on the rental value of property produced the overwhelming majority of local taxation and, in an expanding city, such taxes yielded extra income even if the tax rate per £ of rental remained static. Yet costs were also rising and, as Table 1 shows, the ratepaying public was willing to support a higher level of taxation.

TABLE 1

Taxes imposed by City Council on Owners and Occupiers of Property

Financial Year	Tax Income (£ thousands)	Rateable Value (£ thousands)	Population (thousands)	Tax per £ of rental	Tax per head of population
1846/47	35	900	300	4p	12p
1850/51	70	1100	330	6.4p	21p
1860/61	170	1625	396	10.6p	42p
1870/71	270	2126	478	12.9p	56p
1880/81	380	3427	510	11.2p	75p
1890/91	400	3455	566	11.4p	71p
1900/01	769	4953	762	15.4p	101p
1910/11	1067	5961	784	17.8p	137p
1913/14	1402	7473	1050	18.7p	134p

Notes

This table *excludes* the additional local taxes imposed by Parochial and School Boards. Tax receipts are derived from the annual financial abstracts of the various components of the city administration between 1846/47 and 1880/81. These abstracts are held in the Strathclyde Regional Archives. Collation of all branches of city administration did not become standard practice until the 1870s, and reasonable standardisation of local authority accounts throughout Scotland was not achieved until the 1890s. The Annual Local Taxation (Scotland) Returns were published as House of Commons papers from 1880/81, and Glasgow figures from 1890/91 onwards are derived from these returns. Except for the estimated figure for 1846/47, population is derived from the Decennial Census and annual revisions by the Registrar-General and Medical Officer of Health. These figures relate to the legal city, not to the built-up area (which was considerably more extensive, especially in 1890/91 and 1910/11 since these were years immediately preceding major boundary extensions). Rateable values were obtained from the Appendix (p. 73) of J. D. Marwick, *The Water Supply of Glasgow,* and from *Municipal Glasgow: Its Evolution and Enterprises,* 1914, p. 316.

Actual rate poundages were higher than the rates stated for tax per £ of rental. This arose because of the toleration of arrears and because rate receipts were reduced by various special exemptions. Rates also varied for different parts of the city — e.g. the water rate north of the Clyde was higher than south of the Clyde until 1865 — and rate payments varied in accordance with the division of liability for rates between the owners and occupiers of property. In housing of a low rental value, provision was made for incorporation of a rate element in the weekly rent. Details of rate poundages are contained in the Local Taxation (Scotland) Returns from 1880/81 and data for Glasgow are carried back to 1855/6 in Sir David Richmond's *Notes on Municipal Work,* 1898-9, pp. 216-7.

It is evident that rate poundages rose sharply between 1846 and 1860. Sanitary spending contributed to a further rise in the 1860s but poundages fell slightly between 1870 and 1890. Increases again became apparent from the later 1890s. Turning to average tax payments per head of population, a large increase took place between 1846 and 1860, in the 1870s and from the 1890s to 1911. Total rate payments (including payments to Parochial and School Boards) increased even more rapidly in the first two of these periods because of the respective impact of increased spending on the poor (from 1845) and on education (from 1873). Taking account of the deflationary price trend to the 1890s and the slight inflation thereafter, the steepest rise in the purchasing power of local tax receipts took place between 1846 and 1860, but the increase in the 1870s[20] was also larger than between either 1890 and 1900 or 1900 and 1910. The absolute level of local taxation was, of course, largest by the early twentieth century.

There are no available indices of average incomes and prices in Glasgow with which these figures can be compared to yield precise conclusions on the real level and incidence of local taxation. Nevertheless, rate poundages and other evidence can be used to give some indication of the realities of taxation. The rateable values of property, though far from perfect,[21] can be used as a guide to the prosperity of the city within its prevailing boundaries. On this basis, local taxation was rising more rapidly than prosperity until around 1870 and again from the later 1890s.

In the 1870s there was a substantial increase in local taxation but rateable values rose more quickly and permitted a reduction in rate poundage. Actual perceptions of the rate burden were influenced by the year-to-year economic position, by the details of rate proposals and by the boundary situation. During an upturn in the trade cycle, there was little opposition to increased spending — especially if this gave benefits valued by the middle class. But several years of increased spending on projects of less certain value could create opposition even in good times. A ratepayers' revolt against the 6d rate imposed on occupiers in 1867 to finance City Improvements (mainly slum clearance) displaced Lord Provost Blackie and forced a 2d reduction in the rate.[22] In years of trade downturn, it was even more difficult to secure rate increases and, in the 1880s, such a downturn, associated with the failure to incorporate the adjacent and expanding middle-class suburbs, was a powerful disincentive to additional rateborne expenditure. With ambivalent economic prospects in the earlier 1850s, rising police expenditure in an immigrant-deluged city and additional assessments for registration and land valuation had produced similar problems, but a 25% government grant towards the cost of police pay and clothing,[23] a strengthening economy and the directly perceived benefits of municipal water supplies, allowed rates to be increased with remarkably little complaint between 1855 and 1865. A similar situation, helped by the 1891 boundary extension, arose in the 1890s but, by the 1900s, a weakening in economic prospects and renewed difficulties over boundaries meant that rising rate poundages became an increasingly controversial issue.

Table 2 indicates the level of rate receipts relative to 'other receipts' which were increasingly derived from the city's trading undertakings. Clyde Navigation Trust receipts have also been included to highlight the growing turnover of the city compared to that of the port. The Navigation Trust was much the heaviest borrower in 1846 with authorised borrowing in excess of £450,000 compared to a Police and Statute Labour debt of under £50,000.[24] By 1914, the net debt of the Trust had risen to £7.2 millions, but the city debt amounted to £17 millions.[25]

The increase in the city debt first became a major issue during the post-1877

TABLE 2

City and Port Income, 1846-1914 (£ thousands)

	Total City Income	From Rates	From other sources	Port Income
1846/47	80	35	45	55
1850/51	120	70	50	66
1860/61	270	170	100	101
1870/71	850	270	580	164
1880/81	1000	380	620	236
1890/91	1260	400	860	355
1900/01	2740	769	1971	443
1910/11	3768	1067	2701	566
1913/14	4589	1402	3187	630

Source: As for Table 1, with the addition of the *Statistical Returns of the Clyde Navigation Trust.*

economic depression. This killed off any immediate prospects of heavy investment in sewage purification and drew attention to the need for better management of city borrowings. Previously, each department had made its own arrangements for borrowing, but a centralised policy was introduced under the Glasgow Corporation Loans Act, 1883. Significant savings in borrowing costs arose from this reform and it was also associated with greater concern that sinking fund and depreciation policies should make adequate provision for the renewal of assets. Borrowing was more closely linked to economic prospects and this became even more evident with the ending of the low interest rates of the mid-1890s.[26] All borrowing was subject to careful scrutiny and Glasgow prided itself that, unlike several English local authorities, depreciation provisions were related to a realistic asset life. The city was determined not to burden future generations with an excessive debt. Though large, the city debt was backed by sound assets; it did not represent profligacy and, if anything, the city erred on the side of financial caution by the early years of the twentieth century.

City Health and Housing Statistics

The historical pattern of city death rates is shown in Table 3. The death rate worsened until the early 1870s but then fell rapidly to 1900, with a slower fall

TABLE 3

Deaths per 1000 of City Population

1855-64	30.1	1891-1900	21.5
1865-74	30.5	1901-5	19.0
1875-84	26.9	1906-10	17.5
1881-90	24.2	1911-15	17.0

Source: A. K. Chalmers, *The Health of Glasgow, 1818-1925* (1930), p. 59.

continuing to 1914. More detailed statistical breakdowns also became available, dividing the city by area and by cause of death. This allowed public health efforts to be concentrated where they would be most effective but, by 1900, poor housing, poverty and the engrained habits of a residuum of the population were regarded as the main obstacles to further improvement. There was particular disquiet over tuberculosis and infant mortality. Tuberculosis had fallen much more slowly than the other infectious diseases and improvement seemed to depend on better housing conditions. There was no straightforward medical cure. Infant mortality, though consistently lower than in either Liverpool or Manchester in the second half of the nineteenth century, remained high. Glasgow's margin of advantage over these large English cities narrowed and, after 1901, Glasgow's infant mortality was the highest of the large cities of Britain. In absolute terms, however, the largest improvements in Glasgow's figures were gained in the 1870s and between 1900 and 1914.[27]

By British and American standards, Glasgow continued to have an exceptionally high proportion of the population living in one-room or two-room tenement dwellings. Those so housed fell from 73.4% of the population in 1861 to 66.3% by 1911 (Table 4); but though the quality of housing also

TABLE 4

Number of People in Houses of Different Size (thousands)

	1861	1911
1 room	106 (34.1%)	104 (20.0%)
2 rooms	160 (39.3%)	367 (46.3%)
3 rooms	52 (12.6%)	160 (18.9%)
4 or more	56 (14.0%)	78 (14.8%)
Persons per 100 rooms	204	185

Source: *Census*, as quoted in J. Butt, 'Working Class Housing in Glasgow, 1851-1914', p. 81, in S. D. Chapman (ed.), *History of Working Class Housing*, Newton Abbott, 1971.

improved, the rate of advance was frustratingly slow for the sanitarians. Economic recession worsened housing conditions in the 1880s and, between 1901 and 1911, the number of people living more than two to a room rose from 54.7% to 55.7% of the population.[28] House building was strongly cyclical and, after the boom of the sixties and early seventies, new building fell sharply from 5746 houses a year in 1875 to 500 a year by 1878. Revival did not set in until the late 1880s, culminating in an average of 4200 new houses a year between 1896 and 1902. Building then slumped to under 300 houses a year by 1910, and severe overcrowding co-existed with large numbers of unoccupied houses.[29]

The Comparative Evaluation of Glasgow's Performance

There is no simple way of assessing the impact and efficiency of urban government. Governments, both local and national, operate above as well as within the market mechanism and, by having legal powers (including powers of taxation) not accorded to any individual or company, they cannot be evaluated on commercial lines.[30] Their aim is neither profitability in a competitive situation nor the maximising of monopoly profits. Instead, governments have to be assessed on how best they achieved a variety of objectives, always with some element of conflict, within a broad level of satisfaction to leading interest groups and a wider public. Defined in such terms, however, the aims of local government can become so subjective and so related to particular local conditions that the purpose of comparative assessment is defeated.

In the later nineteenth century, attempts were made to break this deadlock by evolving agreed criteria for comparison. The collection of statistical material multiplied and was supplemented by the impressions gained from transatlantic and cross-Channel trips. The economic explosion of the western world and rapid urban growth provided a common backcloth for statistical (both financial and medico/social) and political comparisons.[31] For the urban 'progressives', social science offered the prospect of objectivity.[32] Techniques of comparison were spelt out in greater detail and began to be seen as an essential element in the control of financial and regulatory programmes so that local authorities could make an optimum contribution to the local economy and civic improvement. More careful monitoring of policies and programmes would assist growth and stability in the local economy. 'Progressives' welcomed economic initiatives by local authorities provided that it could be shown that these would assist the private sector or replace it in areas where the market operated imperfectly.

Yet the 'progressives' came under attack for having fundamentally conservative and limited goals.[33] Their 'objective' criteria concealed subjective preferences favouring the middle class and, especially in America, the main aim of the late nineteenth-century drive against corruption and inefficiency often seemed to be strict control of the tax burden rather than a restructuring of spending and regulatory policies to give greater benefits to those most in need. Spending preferences favoured the priorities of the better-off by encouraging transit improvements and 'city beautiful' schemes rather than helping those most affected by poverty, poor housing and petty crime. In the United States, the strongest resistance to the 'progressives' came from the populists who continued a tradition which combined corruption with programmes which appeared to offer more benefits to the diverse ethnic groups, on below average incomes, in the core areas of the expanding cities. By 1914, aided by political trends and a widened franchise, there were elements of both populism and a more developed socialist ideology on the British and continental urban scene, yet the main rival to the 'progressive' was the 'social bureaucrat'. Social bureaucracy had two components: a medical and middle-class clique who supported bureaucracy as a means to implement more radical urban policies, and an enlarged band of local officials with specialist knowledge and a new professionalism. It was in evidence in North America as well as in Europe,[34] but social bureaucracy flourished earlier, and more strongly, in the European heartland, nurtured by a high density of population and by a paternalist/statistical tradition.

Though blurred in practice, these distinctions between 'progressive', 'social bureaucratic' and 'social populist' philosophies provide valuable baselines against which municipal policies can be evaluated. The other difficulty which any evaluation has to tackle is the problem that no two cities were ever identically placed to implement policy goals. Consideration must therefore be given to the extent to which Glasgow may have been more successful in implementing particular policies because it was more favourably placed than other cities to adopt, and implement, such policies.

'Progressivism', Populism and Social Bureaucracy in Glasgow

Progressive philosophy supported increases in municipal activity and spending where these gave substantial benefits, not otherwise available, to those making the heaviest contribution to local taxation. On this basis, how far did Glasgow's policy goals fit the 'progressive' model? Clearly, the initiatives to strengthen the police force and to improve the city streets were progressive. They maintained law and order while improving the transport system. The municipalisation of water, gas, tram and electricity services was also strongly influenced by the practical desire to retain effective control over the public streets and by the more theoretical view that direct operation of unified public utilities could yield savings and allow pricing to be adjusted to reflect municipal, not commercial, priorities. Monopoly profits came under direct public control and could be used to reduce charges while taking full advantage of the ability of further investment and economies of scale to lower operating costs per unit of output. Comparisons were constantly made with other authorities and, on a simple cost basis, Glasgow emerged very favourably. After municipalisation in 1894, tram fares were lowered and the quality of service improved yet, despite low fares, the trams still achieved a significant surplus which was transferred to the city's Common Good Fund.[35] Gas prices were reduced from 4/7 (23p) per 1000 cubic feet before municipalisation in 1869 to 2/6 (12½p) by 1893, 2/2 (11p) by 1900 and 1/8 to 2/- (depending on the type of customer) by 1910.[36] A large part of this reduction was due to a 32% fall in coal prices between 1869 and 1895, while average consumers also gained from a reduction in the discounts to large customers. Had private operation continued, price cuts would also have been possible due to cheaper coal and economies of scale similar to those pursued by the city council, but comparisons with private and municipal gas undertakings elsewhere indicated that Glasgow secured even larger gains. Only Newcastle (close to good sources of gas coal), Plymouth and Portsea had cheaper municipal gas in the 1890s, and their gas had a lower illuminating power than that of Glasgow.[37] In 1900, the water undertaking combined the second lowest water rate in Britain (5d (2p) in the £) with an excellent quality and quantity of supply. The industrial use of water in Glasgow was much higher than in any other city and, as a matter of policy, charges for metered water supplies were arranged to permit a lower water rate for domestic users.[38]

While the total city rate did rise sharply between 1845 and the 1860s (Table 1), a large part of this increase was, in the terminology of the time, 'remunerative'; it was related to the benefits of improved and expanded services.[39] For example, the levying of a 1/2d (6p) water rate in the 1850s made a large contribution to the rate increase but, against this, the benefits of an improved system were gained and consumers avoided the payments which would have been due to the water companies. The softer Katrine water also produced savings on soap and in other ways for domestic and industrial users.[40] In contrast, the increased rates in rural areas at this time were more heavily concentrated on 'unremunerative' relief of the poor.[41] Most of the increase in urban rates reflected 'progressive' thinking. Some freestanding burghs did have lower rates than Glasgow but, with lower populations, they had less need, and less desire, for the more elaborate services of a large city.[42] The fringe burghs around Glasgow also had rates below those of the city but their inhabitants were seen as temporarily avoiding their proper contribution to a city from which they drew large benefits. 'Progressivism' required a regular extension of the city boundaries so long as there was confidence that the overall policy of the city would be 'progressive'. It was the lack of this condition which made it more difficult to extend the boundaries of the more populist American cities.

From the 1870s, there were fewer instances (apart from education which was being separately rated by the Schools Boards from 1873) where additional rates appeared to give clear benefits to the middle class. The relative stability of the city rate between 1870 and 1895 can therefore be seen as evidence of continuing 'progressivism', with further expansion being concentrated on the municipal trading sector which offered better services and lower costs with little risk of burdening the rates. Much of the interest in public parks, public halls and civic buildings, sewage purification, the prohibition of advertisements on trams, the aesthetic design of wires and poles, street cleansing and the removal of public health eyesores also derived from the middle class desire for an 'improved' city. However, when the rate costs of a large scheme were high in relation to the benefits to principal ratepayers, projects were deferred. This is best illustrated by the long delay in tackling the cleansing of the Clyde. The capital cost of this project, first contemplated in the 1850s, rivalled that of Katrine water but the benefits were less, especially since no easy way could be found of recovering the organic matter in sewage and selling it to farmers. Not until the 1890s did the city feel that it could afford sewage purification and, even then, action was influenced by the prospect of costs being lowered through the integration of intercepting sewers with construction of the Argyle railway tunnel.[43]

Park costs were, however, much lower. Not only was there a direct gain in amenity but costs could be recouped by the sale of parts of the land acquired for high-amenity housing. The same thinking entered the strategy of the City Improvement Trust. There were originally high hopes that the cost of slum demolition could be recouped by the sale of the land for the higher value purposes of an expanding city centre. When these hopes did not materialise, Lord Provost Blackie was rejected by city voters. Such evidence suggests a strong 'progressive' element in Glasgow's policy goals. This element was also well entrenched by 1850, forty years earlier than the peak of American concern about urban corruption and the need for more efficient government.

Apart from the removal of obvious eyesores, public health has not been discussed, yet the impression is often given that improved water supplies and public health, backed (as in Glasgow's case) by increasingly powerful municipal support for temperance, represented another middle-class effort to protect their own health and security while simultaneously creating a more efficient labour force and reducing the need for spending on poor relief and on the police force. Public health spending was frequently justified on such 'progressive' grounds, yet it can be argued that Glasgow's public health programme owed more to social bureaucracy. 'Progressive' justification of public health was more typical of the reforming movement developing in the United States in the late nineteenth century.[44]

Despite urban growth, public health measures were only slowly adopted in the United States. Even as late as 1900, dislike of higher taxes and the effect of tough building regulations on private enterprise deterred action except in a few cities like New York where the total population, and its density, was so high as to compel attention to health issues. The serious strike of 1894 in Pullman, the model town just south of Chicago, highly commended as the world's healthiest community,[45] also weakened the position of the minority who saw public health and planning measures as an important element in social stability. Instead, industrial firms began to introduce improved facilities for their own workers as a more cost-effective method of sustaining loyalty.[46] Local government involvement was distrusted, yet 'progressivism' did emerge as a reaction to gross corruption and heavy burdens of city debt. Public health was included only to the extent that overall economic benefits could be convincingly demonstrated.[47] Water supplies and sewerage did begin to be improved more rapidly, and private enterprise in transit was seen as a means of aiding health by sustaining low residential densities and decongesting the few cities with European levels of overcrowding. But there was little interest in the specific measures needed to help those most in need, and the gap between the mortality rates of the rich and poor remained wide.

In contrast, west European health programmes — and those of Glasgow in particular — evolved earlier and concentrated on the areas of greatest need. By

1900, the involvement with public health was leading to sophisticated linkages between health, housing, social habits and poverty, with strong doubts emerging about the ability of the market mechanism and established local government policies to secure the desired level of improvement. More than fifty years earlier Chadwick and other sanitarians had indeed argued that much of the cost of sanitary measures could be recovered from reduced spending on the police and the poor and from the general gains to health and stability, but these views are best seen as part of the tactical campaign to secure approval for stronger public health measures. The initial concern owed more to the realisation, by a few, of just how bad conditions were within certain parts of cities in the midst of economic expansion and apparent prosperity. Concern had humanitarian and religious origins; it was not a simple derivative from 'progressive' thinking.[48] Using a mass of detailed knowledge as ammunition, key councillors and bureaucrats were able to build up the case of successive modifications of policy which aided a remarkable improvement in health standards. Some of this gain must be attributed to the general improvement in living standards but, far more than in the United States, public health measures secured incremental gains and a marked narrowing of the gap between the richer and poorer areas of cities (see Table 5).

In Glasgow, the geographical division of mortality data available from the 1860s directed attention to the areas of highest incidence and to appropriate remedial action. J. B. Russell, the city's medical officer between 1872 and 1899, made an immense contribution both as a statistician and as a man able to awaken middle-class opinion to the need for new goals.[49] Initially, Russell was able to show that the extensive slum clearances of the earlier 1870s had not created new areas of overcrowding and had helped to reduce the death rate, but he became increasingly concerned about two separate factors which aggravated the health problem. These were the slump in house building from the late 1870s, and Glasgow's commitment to the high-density urban tenement. As the death rate was reduced by a direct attack on infectious disease, further reductions depended on changing both the housing pattern and the attitudes of those prone to higher death rates. By the late nineteenth century, private trusts and the newly formed London County Council were building healthy high-density housing, but Russell was at pains to point out that the apparent healthiness of such dwellings reflected the ability to select 'good' tenants with reasonable wages in a city where general housing densities were half those of Glasgow. Tenement standards were improved, and the city itself built some model tenements from the late 1880s, but Russell's constant theme was to reduce densities even further. Faced with a reluctance to change housing styles, the second slump in private building from 1902, and fierce opposition to the extension of municipal housing, the medical officers had to recognise that major change on the housing front was not yet feasible. Yet improvements could be, and were, made in fever hospital provision and in the provision of welfare and maternity services. Such schemes could improve the health of those most in need at a fairly moderate cost and were supported by a deliberate revision of parks policy to provide parks and playgrounds in the poorer parts of the city. Emphasis began to shift from neatly laid out parks towards the supplementary provision of kickabout pitches and play equipment to promote healthy exercise.[50]

Glasgow and other European cities continued to have death rates above the American average, but the European performance in reducing urban death rates was impressive (Table 5). This included a conscious attack, based on detailed local knowledge and political backing, on the worst areas of the great cities. Action was felt to be essential even if it could not be easily justified on

TABLE 5

Comparative Death Rates per Thousand of Population

	1871	1880-4	1885-9	1896-1900	1905-9
Glasgow	30.5	26.0	23.0	20.0	17.5
Hamburg	41.7	25.0	26.0	17.0	
Munich	40.9	31.6	28.8	23.8	
Naples	39.0	34.1	28.6	26.0	
Massachusetts	18.8	19.7	19.5	18.7	16.4

Sources: Data, except for Massachusetts, are derived from A. K. Chalmers, *The Health of Glasgow, 1818-1925*, pp. 59 and 60. For Massachusetts, *Historical Statistics of the United States: Colonial Times to 1957*, US Census Bureau, 1960, p. 30.

'progressive' lines. America was almost fifty years behind Scotland, and seventy behind England, in assembling accurate data on deaths.[51] Most states did not have adequate data until the early twentieth century. Several cities and eastern states had acted earlier but, even where reasonable information is available (as in the case of the urbanised state of Massachusetts), it reveals a death rate reduction of only 13% between 1870 and 1905/9. This contrasts with a 43% reduction in Glasgow and even greater improvements in cities such as Hamburg. By 1910, Glasgow's crude death rate was almost as low as that of Massachusetts despite very much higher housing densities, a less favourable age structure and lower average incomes. This was the measure of the achievement of a social bureaucratic desire to improve health rather than of a narrower 'progressivism'.

Glasgow's public health measures were a considerable departure from such 'progressivism', and similar departures can be found in other aspects of municipal policy. Water and gas charges were consciously arranged to favour the average domestic user, not industrial users. Municipal staff were better treated than in most of private industry, while 'fair wages' clauses began to be added to the conditions applied to outside contractors. Poorer wards had more spent on them than they supplied in rate income and, though part of this can be seen as necessary spending — as on police supervision — to safeguard the interests of the better-off, there was also a genuine desire to ensure that the needs of all areas were taken into account. Such an ideal was not, of course, perfectly fulfilled and it was also constrained by what was considered to be a realistic level of local taxation. Nevertheless, local taxes were rising more rapidly than rateable values from the 1890s and included spending on social provision which was more systematic than in corresponding American cities. Though Glasgow did lag in providing public libraries, the general level and distribution of services also compared well with other British cities.

Populism, feared by 'progressives' and social bureaucrats alike because of the danger of unsuitable objectives and debased administration, was found in Glasgow in issues such as the defence of the Green (the city's original park beside the highly populated east end) and in the pressure for further reductions in tram fares (after much agitation, the ½d fare for a half-mile stage was extended to cover one mile in 1911). It was also beginning to affect housing, staffing and welfare policies by the early twentieth century but remained a weaker force than in the United States. The main challenge to the 'progressives' came from the social bureaucrats, but there was no clash of 'bosses' and 'progressive' reformers on the American pattern. In Glasgow, there was a consensus on the need to implement policies effectively. Councillors and the new bureaucracy took pride in achieving better results, and 'progressive' goals were subtly adjusted to reflect the social priorities forged by combining a Christian 'social gospel' with extensive statistical data and bureaucratic experience of the changing nature of problems. Glasgow in 1900 was a notable example of municipal efficiency associated with goals which went beyond the narrower horizons of the 'progressives'. A concern to improve the condition of the masses was already evident, and the adverse criticisms of the city reflected new standards of expectation rather than the view that the city's response had been weak compared to other municipalities.

Changing Perceptions of Glasgow: 1900-14

In the decade before 1914, euphoric assessments of Glasgow's municipal enterprise underwent significant modification. As in the 1880s, doubts arose about the level of local taxation and the scale of city debt in relation to the economic prospects of the region. The city was far from being on the edge of bankruptcy — it had an excellent financial standing — but there was a strong consciousness that this standing, and a reasonable level of rating, depended upon sound financial policies. Borrowing was carefully controlled to restrict the increase in the rate burden and, though the immediate depression was less severe than in the 1880s, doubts about the longer-term growth prospects were stronger. Financial prudence was a significant factor in phasing sewage purification plans over a ten-year period, while the major new gasworks at Provan was designed to be completed in stages. The first phase was completed in 1904 but subsequent spending was slowed down in view of deteriorating prospects. Worries about local coal supplies, slow progress on boundary extensions, the contraction of housebuilding from 1902 and a reduction of the growth rate in locomotive and ship construction made City Treasurers and their officials less confident about a continuation of nineteenth-century levels of growth.[52] Economic weakness also revealed itself in a rise in the number of households with rate arrears from 12,834 in the prosperous year 1895/6 to 35,671 by 1908/9.[53]

Sound finance became the watchword and there was concern that departmental plans for expansion might take precedence over a more integrated view of the total objectives of the city in the light of realistic financing policies. By 1908, the *Glasgow Herald* was reporting proposals for the appointment of a City Manager[54] and, four years earlier, Mabel Atkinson had picked out poor co-ordination as one of the main weaknesses of even the larger Scottish local authorities.[55] Confidence in municipal trading was waning with the failure to sustain earlier performances. Fears about the abuse of monopoly, and socialist tendencies, became more common as a wider franchise opened up the potential for destructive impacts on the economy as voters sought special favours from city councillors.[56] The tram strike of 1911, and the national increase in labour unrest, were a reminder that cosy assumptions about comparative efficiency and a tranquil labour force could be rudely interrupted with the passage of time.

There were signs of weakening of the earlier resolve of councillors not to become involved in the details of management. This had first arisen in the appointment of teachers by School Boards, but the managers of city departments also began to face constraints on their freedom of action.[57] Councillors had always wanted to do more than decide broad policy but they had remained relatively free of pressure to interfere with conditions of work, appointments and sackings. Because most councillors for working-class, as well as middle-class, wards were drawn from the business community, they did not live in lower income areas, and this discouraged local requests for jobs and favours. In addition, the vote was denied to the large numbers of slum dwellers in arrears with rate payments.[58] Nevertheless, such pressures were beginning to appear and caused concern to traditionally minded councillors and department managers. Speaking in 1900, A. Murray as City Treasurer was already worried about the decline in business expertise among councillors and the growing difficulties in resisting working-class pressures for higher municipal spending.[59] 'But I fear no methods, however well devised, will check undue expenditure and secure economy, so long as the Corporation itself is inclined to be extravagant. The evil seems inherent in the system of Ward representation, which encourages competition for Municipal advantages, and by means of log-rolling in the Council defeats the best efforts of those who study economy. It seems destined to go on until the ratepayers feel the pinch, and call a halt. The strong socialistic bias of the present day is also responsible for a large amount of extravagance. The doctrine is popular that the more

Q

public money you spend in the city the better for the working classes; and as they have the preponderating vote it is not so difficult to understand the attitude of their representatives towards questions of finance.' Despite these fears, management still retained considerable freedom of action, bolstered by the professionalism and career opportunities which had arisen within local government. Significantly, however, the dynamic manager of the Tramways Department, John Young, turned down a senior post offered by the London County Council and opted in 1904 for a top position in the organisation of the American entrepreneur Yerkes, who was developing his own plans for underground railways in London.[60]

On policy issues, managers were also less sure of council backing. For many years the Tramways Committee and the Tramways Manager, James Dalrymple, had opposed any extension of the ½d fare for distances of half a mile to a full mile. However, this became a leading issue in the 1911 council elections and the extension was subsequently forced through. In the event, the extra traffic generated prevented the serious loss of income that the manager had feared, but the financial surplus was eroded. Tramway policy was caught between the social bureaucratic pressure to use surpluses for a more rapid extension of the system, which would help decongest city housing, and an alliance of populist and economy-minded pressures for lower fares and strict control of extensions which, at least initially, had a light traffic in relation to their capital costs. In a sense, the early extension of the electric tramways to the newly gifted park at Rouken Glen (some two miles beyond the dense tenement areas) worked against further extensions because it demonstrated the extent to which many of the tram routes served 'villa folk'. Yet, while tramway extensions were being criticised, the city was also being attacked for its failure to make greater progress in tackling the appalling problems of housing, poverty and social degradation which continued to exist on a scale far greater than in most British and American cities.[61]

These internal doubts could not be concealed from outside observers, and were themselves influenced by changing general attitudes to municipal enterprise. From the socialist side, such enterprise was welcomed, yet this very welcome aroused doubts in the minds of the earlier supporters of municipalisation.[62] By the closing years of the nineteenth century, municipal trading was a lively political issue in Britain, and the final conclusions of the 1903 parliamentary commission on this topic, despite vigorous defences by Glasgow, were less than enthusiastic about further expansion unless audit provisions were improved.[63] Americans were also beginning to doubt whether the British example of municipal enterprise was as impressive as they had thought in the 1890s. When Glasgow's Tramway Manager was invited to Chicago in 1905 in the expectation that he would reinforce the campaign for tram municipalisation, he refused to give the expected endorsement, and an ensuing visit to Glasgow by representatives of the National Civic Federation confirmed a more lukewarm appraisal of municipal enterprise.[64] By this time, American opinion was also being influenced by emotional reactions against socialism and by a private sector reviving in confidence after the depression of the 1890s.

Almost ten years earlier, in 1898, the Massachusetts Commission on Transportation had attacked the then prevalent praise of Glasgow. It concluded that, if American cities had been as compact and densely populated as Glasgow, their tramway operating techniques would have given better results than those obtained in Glasgow. Far from being an example to follow, Glasgow had procrastinated over the decision to electrify, and American cities had done more for their housing and health problems by encouraging a rapid extension of electric lines into the green fields constituting future suburbs.[65] A similar theme was taken up by H. R. Meyer, Assistant Professor of Political Economy at the University of Chicago, in his 1906 volume on *Municipal Ownership in Great Britain.*[66] In contrast to Shaw, this was a scathing and vitriolic attack on municipal enterprise. Closer to home, Glasgow was also being attacked on quite the opposite grounds. Socialists criticised the city for insufficient enterprise,[67] and even the more objective deputation from Liverpool to study Glasgow housing in 1901 concluded that the city's policies did not place sufficient emphasis on helping those most in need.[68]

The Special Circumstances of Glasgow

Not only are these changing perspectives of the pre-1914 decade a useful corrective to exaggerated views of Glasgow's enterprise, they also raise the whole issue of the special position of Glasgow. Until the turn of the century, Glasgow had a very strong economic base and, even allowing for some years of relative depression as the trade cycle varied, it seemed reasonable to expect a strong growth trend. This underlying position was an incentive to municipal enterprise and efficiency. Growth eased the burden of capital charges and, by raising rental values, increased municipal income. Growth also meant improvements in average incomes and encouraged the middle class to support municipal initiatives which increased rate poundages but produced desired benefits. Higher incomes and rateable values meant that the burden of poor relief (despite the attraction of migrants) was much less onerous than in rural areas with low incomes, low rateable values and many paupers. So long as growth continued, there was no serious clash between moderate levels of altruistic social spending and 'remunerative' rate expenditure along 'progressive' lines. The liberal revulsion from corruption and waste, already well established by the 1840s, meant careful scrutiny of all spending, yet this allowed the concept of civic improvement to be widened to promote a 'social gospel' without creating alarm at the rate burden. Improved management of borrowing and day-to-day administration facilitated a widening of overall goals. Economic growth also meant that municipal trading ventures took place in a context which virtually guaranteed a reasonable performance with average levels of management. The novelty and challenge of these ventures — and of other new ventures such as public health — actually attracted a high quality of management which experienced minimal intervention from business-orientated councillors in the details of administration.

In such circumstances, Glasgow could hardly avoid successful initiatives in urban government between the 1840s and 1900. As Table 6 shows, the Glasgow urban region had a high growth throughout this period and it achieved the highest growth rate of all the principal British cities between 1850 and 1875 when the earlier textile specialism was replaced by even greater growth based on engineering and shipbuilding.

TABLE 6

Population of Principal British Cities (thousands)
(based on built-up areas, not on the more restrictive legal boundaries)

	1800	1825	1850	1875	1900	1925
Glasgow	85	173	346	635	1071	1396
Liverpool	76	170	422	650	940	1235
Manchester	81	155	412	590	1255	1725
Birmingham	72	122	294	480	1248	1700
London	861	1335	2320	4241	6480	7742

Percentage Change in Population

	1800-25	1825-50	1850-75	1875-1900	1900-25
Glasgow	104	100	84	69	30
Liverpool	124	148	54	45	31
Manchester	91	166	43	113	37
Birmingham	69	141	63	160	36
London	55	74	83	53	20

Source: T. Chandler and G. Fox, *3000 Years of Urban Growth,* 1974.

With Manchester achieving the highest growth rate between 1825 and 1850, and Birmingham taking over from Glasgow after 1875, it is evident that the strength of local economies had a close bearing on civic enterprise. Manchester, Glasgow and Birmingham followed each other as leaders in this field, and even after 1875, Glasgow's growth remained high enough to ensure an enhanced range of initiatives. The city was also assisted by its ability to absorb surrounding burghs. It had no equivalents on the scale of Manchester's Salford and Liverpool's Birkenhead to splinter municipal enterprise.

London, much larger in total size, did not lead in the 'enterprise stakes', partly because it lacked a strong governing body until the 1890s[69] but also because, as a well-established city and financial centre, it lacked the brashness of the new industrial regions and was culturally inclined to rely on traditional sources of finance and private enterprise. Similar factors affected most of the other political capitals, yet both Germany and the United States had industrial cities with growth rates comparable to, or greater than, those of Glasgow,

Liverpool, Manchester and Birmingham. Many of these cities did, indeed, exhibit high levels of civic enterprise, but the poorer performance of the cities in the United States is a reminder that economic growth was no more than a permissive factor in civic enterprise. Given a tradition combining corruption with a leaning towards self-help and private enterprise, the United States was not favourably disposed towards municipal enterprise. The sheer vastness of America, the speculative potential and the low densities of most cities also led to less demand for civic action than in the more crowded and authoritarian cities of Europe.

Conclusions

The prior political and cultural context was always relevant to the nature of civic enterprise, but no city could undertake initiatives on a grand and sustained scale unless it was part of a dynamic, regional economy. Enterprise depended upon regional growth and, though sometimes apparent in transport,[70] the causal linkage running in the opposite direction was much weaker. Most urban governments were not expected to make a strong contribution to the economy; their role was to respond to the local economy, to run selected services effectively and to keep local taxes at a reasonable level. Once an economy showed signs of weakening, the gloss could soon disappear from civic enterprise. This was all the more likely if economic weakening coincided with changed political attitudes and increased disquiet over social deficiencies.

In Glasgow's case, its earlier economic success, associated with the Scottish tradition of crowded living conditions, created housing and social problems on which greater action was being sought just at the time when the city economy was beginning to weaken. It is in these circumstances that an explanation of the conflicting images of Glasgow is to be found.

Until around 1900, 'progressive' and 'social bureaucratic' tendencies could co-exist in Glasgow. Local ratepayers could tolerate, and even encourage, a certain amount of social spending which could not be fully reconciled with a 'progressive' philosophy. Some tensions did appear in the moderate depression of the 1880s, but improved conditions in the 1890s favoured further enterprise. Across the Atlantic, the United States was economically depressed in the 1890s, and this drew attention both to the deficiencies of America and the successes of European urban government. From 1900, however, American trading prospects and living standards improved relative to those of Britain. Glasgow ceased to be able to provide examples of continuous improvement, and a slowing of economic advance focused attention on the intensity of social problems, on the defects of the rating system and on the reasons for gaps between the rich and poor.

The gap between desirable standards and ability to pay had already been recognised in rural areas.[71] Many such areas clearly lacked the resources to finance acceptable, and nationally desirable, levels of poor relief and education. The remedy of extra aid from central government had been adopted before 1900, but the same problem was now beginning to emerge in urban areas. Technology, as in electricity supply, was also favouring larger units, while substantial modification of trade cycles was beyond the power of even the greatest cities. All of these factors contributed to a shift of emphasis from local to national government. The changing roles of the private and public sectors were coming to be debated at national level, and judgments on civic performance were giving way to new views on how national government should operate to implement an amalgam of social and economic objectives.

Glasgow's civic government still deserves commendation for its nineteenth-century enterprise, but success owed much to the city's strong economy. From 1900 it was becoming impossible to satisfy 'progressives', social bureaucrats and populists within the city framework, and the conflicting images of Glasgow, which became more obvious between the late 1890s and 1914, reflected a relative weakening of the regional economy aggravated by the shift of emphasis in public policy and financing from local to national issues. The debate on the merits of public and private enterprise intensified, but it was a debate being conducted at a different level.

NOTES

1. Sir James Bell (Lord Provost, 1892-96) and J. Paton, *Glasgow: Its Municipal Organisation and Administration*, 1896. Sir David Richmond (Lord Provost, 1896-9), *Notes on Municipal Work, 1896-9*. Sir J. D. Marwick (Town Clerk, 1873-1903), *Glasgow: The Water Supply of the City and other Developments*, 1901. *Municipal Glasgow: Its Evolution and Enterprises* (with a foreword by Lord Provost D. M. Stevenson), Corporation of Glasgow, 1914. W. Smart (Professor of Political Economy, University of Glasgow), 'The Municipal Work and Finance of Glasgow', *Economic Jnl.*, 5, 1895, pp. 35-49. W. Smart, 'Glasgow and its Municipal Industries', *Qtrly. Jnl. Economics*, 9, 1894-5, pp. 188-94.

2. Such visits are extensively documented in B. Aspinwall, 'Glasgow Trams and American Politics', *Scottish Historical Review*, 56, 1977, pp. 64-84.

3. C. N. Glaab, A. T. Brown, *A History of Urban America*, 2nd Edition, 1976, ch. 9.

4. W. Smart, *loc. cit.*, 1894-5.

5. Aspinwall, *loc. cit.*, p. 78 quotes both Keir Hardie's view of the city as 'A secret pandemonium of immorality' and the *New York Times* (12th May, 1901) description of it as a city of 'prolific poverty and crushing toil'. See also note 68 and H. R. Meyer (sometime Assistant Professor of Political Economy in the University of Chicago), *Municipal Ownership in Great Britain*, 1906, esp. chs. 5 and 6. W. Smart, *The Housing Problem and the Municipality*, 1902. R. L. Bremner, *The Housing Problem in Glasgow*, 1902.

6. T. Chandler and G. Fox, *Three Thousand Years of Urban Growth*, 1974, pp. 323-35.

7. K. Davis, *World Urbanization, 1950-70*, 1969, p. 240.

8. Bell and Paton, *op. cit.*, p. 238.

9. *Census of Scotland*, 1861, Vol. 1, pp. xxvii-xxix.

10. C. M. Allan, 'The Genesis of British Urban Redevelopment with special reference to Glasgow', *Econ. Hist. Rev.*, 18, 1965, pp. 598-613.

11. Current work by Mrs Brenda White, postgraduate student in the Department of Economic History, University of Glasgow, has indicated that city councillors took the initiative in dismissing Gairdner and appointing his assistant, J. B. Russell, to the full-time post of Chief Medical Officer of Health.

12. J. B. Russell (Medical Officer of Health, 1872-99), *Public Health Administration in Glasgow*, 1905 (with a foreword by A. K. Chalmers, Medical Officer of Health, 1899-1925). A. K. Chalmers, *The Health of Glasgow, 1818-1925*, 1930.

13. C. A. Oakley, *The Last Tram*, 1962, p. 20.

14. Bell and Paton, *op. cit.*, p. 255.

15. Bell and Paton, *ibid.*, p. 85.

16. C. A. Oakley, *The Second City*, 1967 edition, p. 235.

17. A. K. Chalmers, *op. cit.*, pp. 57-8.

18. T. E. Robinson, CA (Registrar of Glasgow Corporation Stock), 'The History of Municipal Borrowing in Glasgow', 1912 (being a paper read to the fourth meeting of the Students' Society of the Institute of Municipal Treasurers and Accountants, Scottish Branch, 13 March, 1912).

19. M. Mustapha, 'The Development of Dock Facilities on the Clyde, 1840-1914', M.Litt. thesis, University of Glasgow, 1981.

20. In terms of the total rate burden, this included a School Board rate of 5d (2p) by 1879.

21. Rateable values present the difficulty of not being directly related to incomes, while property valuations could also be poorly related to actual values. The latter is a lesser difficulty, however, since the Lands Valuation (Scotland) Act, 1854 sought to standardise procedures for valuation and for the regular review of values.

22. Bell and Paton, *op. cit.*, p. 222.

23. This grant was introduced in 1857 and subsequently rose to 50% of the cost of police pay and clothing.

24. Strathclyde Regional Archives: *Statistical Returns of Clyde Navigation Trust* (T--CN6), *Municipal Accounts* (D-CC21) and *Police and Statute Labour Trust Accounts* (E3, 2 and 3).

25. Local Taxation (Scotland) Return, 1913-14, *House of Commons Paper 336*, Session 1914-16.

26. A. Murray CA (City Treasurer), 'The Glasgow Corporation: Finance, Bookkeeping and Balance Sheet', 1900 (paper read to Students' Society of Glasgow Chartered Accountants, 20 March, 1900). A Murray CA (City Treasurer), 'The Glasgow Corporation Accounts with special reference to Depreciation and Sinking Funds', 1903 (paper read to Economic Science Section of the Royal Philosophical Society of Glasgow, 4 March, 1903). A. Walker (City Assessor), *City Rating*, 1911. T. E. Robinson (City Registrar), 'Municipal Borrowing', 1912, *loc. cit.*

27. A. K. Chalmers, *op. cit.*, p. 190.

28. S. D. Chapman (ed.), *History of Working Class Housing*, 1971, p. 85.

29. A. K. Chalmers, *op. cit.*, pp. 57-8.

30. H. Finer, *Municipal Trading*, 1941, pp. 27-35.

31. A. Shaw, *Municipal Government in Great Britain*, 1895. A. Shaw, *Municipal Government in Continental Europe*, 1895. A. F. Weber, *The Growth of Cities in the Nineteenth Century: A Study in Statistics*, 1899. F. C. Howe, *The Modern City and its Problems*, 1915. H. R. Meyer, *Municipal Ownership in Great Britain*, 1906.

32. D. Ross, 'Professionalism and the Transformation of American Social Thought', *Journal of Economic History*, 38, 1978, pp. 494-9. T. L. Haskell, *The Emergence of Professional Social Science*, 1977.

33. C. N. Glaab and A. T. Brown, *op. cit.*, pp. 190, 202. F. Choay, *The Modern City: Planning in the Nineteenth Century*, p. 109. See also note 46.

34. D. Ross, *loc. cit.* Glaab and Brown, *op. cit.*, pp. 183-4 and 198-9.

35. C. A. Oakley, *The Last Tram*, p. 58.

36. Bell and Paton, *op. cit.*, pp. 267, 271 and 272. W. Smart, *loc. cit.*, pp. 47-8. *Municipal Glasgow: Its Evolution and Enterprises*, 1914, p. 123.

37. W. Smart, *ibid.*

38. J. Colquhoun (Convener of Finance Committee), 'Glasgow Corporation Finance', 1894, p. 15 (paper read at meeting of Glasgow Institute of Accountants Debating Society, 18 January, 1894).

39. Report by Goschen (President of the Poor Law Board) on 'The Progressive Increase in Local Taxation', *HC Paper 470, 1870* — reprinted as *HC Paper 201, 1893*. The 'remunerative'/unremunerative' distinction is also taken up in the Local Taxation (Scotland) Report (Skelton Report), C 7575, 1895.

40. Bell and Paton, *op. cit.*, p. 245.

41. The Goschen Report refers to the substantial increase in spending on poor relief to the late 1860s, and the Skelton Report illustrates the high level of Poor and Educational Rate Poundages in rural areas with low rateable values.

42. In 1892/3, several small and poor towns had total rates (including poor and education rates) over 6/- in the £. Glasgow's combined rate, for a much wider and better range of services, was 5/- but the medium-sized towns of Airdrie, Stirling and Kilmarnock had rates as low as 3/7, 3/2 and 3/-, while rates in the burghs around Glasgow were: Clydebank (3/6), Govan (3/7½), Partick (3/5), Pollokshaws (3/8) and Kinning Park (3/5) (Skelton Report).

43. Bell and Paton, *op. cit.*, pp. 140-41.

44. F. Meeker, "The Social Rate of Return on Investment in Public Health (in the United States), 1880-1910', *Journal of Economic History*, 34, 1974, pp. 392-421.

45. S. Buder, *Pullman*, 1967, p. 79, and Glaab and Brown, *op. cit.*, p. 238.

46. E. O. Berkowitz, K. McQuaid, 'Businessman and Bureaucrat: The Evolution of the American Social Welfare System, 1900-40', *Journal of Econ. Hist.*, 38, 1978, pp. 120-142.

47. See quote from Whipple, *Typhoid Fever*, 1908, in Meeker, *loc. cit.*, 1974, p. 419.

48. See postgraduate paper by Calum Brown, 'The Civic Gospel in Glasgow' (presented to Economic History Department Staff Seminar, University of Glasgow, 1978).

49. Russell's leading pamphlets and talks are reproduced in J. B. Russell, *Public Health Administration in Glasgow*, 1905.

50. Minutes of the Parks Committee show that J. B. Russell was active in pushing this approach — see 'Memorandum on Open Space for Cowcaddens' (Parks Committee Minutes, 6 July, 1892), and letter from Russell on Bunhouse Playground (Parks Committee Minutes, 14 February, 1875).

51. *Historical Statistics of the United States: Colonial Times to 1957*, US Census Bureau, 1960, pp. 17-21.

52. See note 26, especially the 1900 paper by A. Murray, pp. 22-25.

53. A. Walker, *City Rating*, 1911, p. 22.

54. *Glasgow Herald*, 6, 13, 18-20 May, 1908 (quoted in Aspinwall, *loc. cit.*, 1977, p. 83).

55. M. Atkinson, *Local Government in Scotland*, 1904, pp. 54-60 and p. 397.

56. J. R. Kellett, 'Municipal Socialism, Enterprise and Trading in the Victorian City', *Urban History Yearbook*, 1978, pp. 36-45.

57. M. Atkinson, *op. cit.*, pp. 389-90. A. Murray, *op. cit.* (1900), p. 24.

58. A. Shaw, *Municipal Government in Great Britain*, p. 77.

59. See note 57; also, Anon., *The Lord Provosts of Glasgow, 1833-1902* (this reveals the growing difficulty from the later nineteenth century in inducing leading city businessmen to accept the Lord Provostship).

60. C. A. Oakley, *The Last Tram*, p. 49.

61. See note 5.

62. See J. R. Kellett, *loc. cit.*, and Aspinwall, *loc. cit.*, p. 82.

63. Aspinwall, *ibid.*, p. 80, and Finer, *op. cit.*, pp. 58-60.

64. Aspinwall, *loc. cit.*, p. 82.

65. Aspinwall, *ibid.*, pp. 78-9.

66. See note 5.

67. Councillor Joseph Burgess, a founder member of the Independent Labour Party and of the West of Scotland Housing Reform Council (established in 1900) was arguing for working-class garden suburbs linked with tram improvements by 1902 (quoted in S. D. Chapman (ed.), *History*

of *Working Class Housing*, 1971, footnote 20, p. 88. See also the discussion in S. Damer, 'State, Class and Housing: Glasgow 1885-1919', in J. Melling (ed.), *Housing, Social Policy and the State*, 1980, pp. 75-91.

68. *City of Liverpool Report of Deputation of Housing Committee to Glasgow*, Liverpool, 1901.

69. Even in the 1890s, the LCC had to share power with the Metropolitan Boroughs. It lacked the range of powers of Glasgow, Liverpool, Manchester and Birmingham.

70. In developing regions, such as North America, civic enterprise could help determine where economic growth was actually located; in developed regions, civic enterprise could sometimes shift trade or help sustain it against competition, e.g. the cases of Hamburg, Amsterdam, Liverpool, and the Manchester Ship Canal.

71. Royal Commission on Local Taxation (Balfour Commission): *Final Report (Scotland), Cd. 1007*, 1902. J. P. Day, *Public Administration in the Highlands and Islands of Scotland*, 1918.

11. Urban Transport Problems in Historical Perspective*

Derek H. Aldcroft

TRANSPORT problems in the urban setting are often regarded as relatively recent in origin, a product primarily of the vast increase in personal mobility within cities in the twentieth century as a result of the advent of the motor car. In fact most of the urban transport problems so familiar to us in contemporary society have their counterpart in the past, and in some cases they were just as acute as those experienced today. This is true not only with respect to the internal problems associated with the management and operation of transport undertakings *per se,* for example, competition, pricing policies and profitability, but it also applies to the external effects stemming from their operation and activities. The most important of these are traffic congestion, pollution, social displacement and environmental intrusion — all very familiar to modern society but no less so to our ancestors. This study is concerned primarily with this second set of issues mainly in the context of nineteenth-century conditions.

Traffic Congestion

Traffic congestion in urban centres and market towns has a very long history indeed. It can be traced back at least to Roman times, though Julius Caesar may not have been the first ruler to take measures to regulate the flow of vehicles.[1] Somewhat later, we find early sixteenth-century planners in Paris issuing dire warnings of the paralysis likely to ensue from the growth in street traffic.[2] In this country, London has had a traffic problem for centuries and one that had already become acute and persistent by the eighteenth century, owing to the failure to grasp the opportunity after the Great Fire of 1666 of replanning the whole city and replacing the medieval lanes by a system of wide straight roads.[3] In the light of subsequent history this was to prove an expensive mistake.

It is doubtful, however, whether these early traffic problems were anywhere

* Part of the research for this study was completed during a visit to the University of Queensland in 1979. The author would like to thank the British Academy for their generosity in awarding an overseas travelling research scholarship for that purpose.

near as serious as those which arose in the nineteenth century, though it must be acknowledged that we have little means of measuring relative intensities. The reason is simple: during the nineteenth century there was a great increase in mobility in urban areas as a result of industrialisation, most of which involved the use of some sort of vehicle. This additional traffic was superimposed on a road and street system which, like the early twentieth-century road system at the time of the introduction of the motor vehicle, was not adequate to cope with it and which was improved only very slowly and in a piecemeal fashion. Ironically, it was the railways which were the cause of much of the additional street traffic. While the long-distance coaching trade soon faded into oblivion in the face of railway competition, the impact of the railway on urban traffic was the very reverse. No other form of activity generated so much urban street traffic as the railways, since the main city termini became the chief focal point for cab and omnibus traffic as well as the delivery and collection point for goods vehicles. Without such feeder services the railways could not of course have functioned properly, and it is significant that as soon as the city termini were opened, the volume of street traffic grew rapidly. In Glasgow, for example, the number of cab stands rose five-fold in the two decades following the opening of the passenger terminals, and more than half of these were located at or outside the stations. There was also a sharp increase in the number of horse omnibuses which by the 1870s were running every two and a half minutes through the main streets outside the railway termini.[4] The same process had taken place in London in the 1830s and 1840s when the number of hackney carriages doubled (1500 to over 3000), that of stage carriages by 50 per cent (800 to 1200), while the number of omnibuses increased from 620 to 1300.[5] In fact in every major city there was a marked increase in street traffic following the arrival of the railways.

Though by contemporary standards the absolute volume of traffic was still quite small, it did nevertheless create serious capacity problems in city areas for two main reasons. First, the main thoroughfares were both fewer and narrower than those of today and the sudden upsurge in traffic gave little time for real improvement. Second, the horse-drawn vehicle of the nineteenth century was bulky, slow and cumbersome, and not always easily controllable, so that it required a larger operating space than the modern motor vehicle. By the middle of the nineteenth century, therefore, the problem of traffic congestion was already acute in some towns, and in London it was approaching crisis proportions. One of the worst spots was London Bridge, where the number of vehicles crossing the Bridge rose from 13,000 to 20,000 in the 1850s, nearly half of which were omnibuses; the flow of vehicles at the morning and evening peaks was in the region of 1700 an hour, and at times omnibuses were held up for twenty minutes or more because of congestion. For many journeys within the Metropolis, it was becoming quicker to walk than use transport, and in one case it was reported to take longer to travel from London Bridge to Paddington than it did to journey from Brighton to the City.[6] The position was not quite so bad in the provincial cities, though parts of Glasgow, in particular Jamaica Street where railway traffic met conflicting streams of heavy harbour traffic, were said to be as choked as Cheapside or London Bridge.[7]

Several attempts were made to tackle the problem of urban traffic congestion during the course of the nineteenth century, but these were often as limited in scope and vision as those in the present age, while some of the ostensible solutions tended ultimately to have the opposite effect. Street improvement and road widening occurred in most cities during the latter half of the century but it was a very piecemeal and patchy affair and in no way was it commensurate with the growing traffic needs of the period. One of the main difficulties in this respect was the awkward lay-out and configuration of many city areas, which meant that to achieve any worthwhile improvement would have required the complete razing of buildings. A second solution, and one that was adopted in London, was to build new lines of communication, at least for passenger traffic, by putting railways underground. While the creation of the underground railway network in the latter half of the nineteenth century undoubtedly improved London's transport capability, it did not, except in the short-run following the opening of new lines, do much to ease traffic congestion at street level. In fact, if anything it eventually tended to create more traffic above ground. A third possible solution, and one adopted in many cities in the latter part of the period, was to build street railways or tramways for passenger travel. These provided a valuable addition to urban transport facilities, and they were more economical in the use of capacity since the cost of horsepower for a tram was only half that for a bus carrying the same number of passengers. However, horse tramways did little to solve the problem of urban congestion since, for one thing, they took up valuable road space, an important consideration given the capricious nature of the horse. Secondly, the tramway network was still quite small until after the mid 1880s and it was only in the early twentieth century, when mechanisation became extensive, by which time the horse era had reached its peak, that the full impact began to be felt.[8] In fact, in the last quarter of the nineteenth century the older horse technology had its final fling with a renewed upsurge in street traffic which further intensified the congested conditions in urban centres.

Thus traffic congestion in towns refused to go away, and by all accounts it probably got steadily worse in many urban areas during the second half of the nineteenth century. The inexorable growth in railway freight and passenger traffic inevitably entailed an ever-increasing network of feeder services to deal with the traffic at the major terminals in the city centres. The railways themselves owned large delivery fleets of horse-drawn vehicles, and in fact the bulk of the general merchandise hauled by the railways was collected and distributed in their own vans. Though there is no complete inventory of the volume of horse-drawn traffic in the nineteenth century, the fragmentary data available clearly point to a substantial growth in the latter part of the period. Thompson has estimated that the number of horses not on farms more than trebled between 1851 and 1901, from 535,000 to 1,766,000, which gives some indication, however indirect, of the growing horsepower required for transport purposes. In 1890 London alone required 300,000 living horsepower to move its wheeled traffic.[9] The number of commercial road vehicles in the whole of Great Britain is estimated to have increased from 161,000 to 702,000 during the same period, that of private carriages from 205,000 to 450,000, while, judging by the experience of London, there was also a considerable increase in taxi-cab and omnibus facilities. In the Metropolis the number of buses rose from 1300 in the early Victorian period to 3,700 in 1902 and the number of cabs from 2,500 to around 11,000 by the late nineteenth century.[10]

At the peak of the horse-drawn era around the turn of the century there were probably about half a million private carriages using the roads of Britain, up to 700,000 commercial vehicles of one sort or another and in the region of 150,000 public passenger vehicles or cabs.[11] While the total volume of vehicle traffic was still small in comparison with today's motor traffic, one has to bear in mind that the bulk of it was concentrated in urban areas in conditions which were far from conducive to ease of movement. Horse-drawn vehicles, moreover, because of their length, bulk and unpredictable nature of the traction power, required much more room for manoeuvre than motorised equivalents, and as a consequence their capacity for creating congestion in city streets was far greater. It is difficult to make precise or meaningful comparisons between the different types of vehicles, but rough calculations suggest that motor vehicles created one half or less congestion than comparable horse-drawn vehicles.[12]

It is not surprising to find therefore that most major cities were still experiencing severe congestion problems in the later nineteenth century, the worst conditions again being in London where wheeled traffic was 'dense beyond movement'.[13] Small wonder that the Royal Commission on London Traffic, reporting in 1906, should devote considerable attention to traffic movement within the Metropolis where the average number of journeys per head had more than doubled in the previous thirty years, while the speed of street traffic had declined by about 25 per cent. While the Royal Commission could readily demonstrate the magnitude of the problem and the inadequacies of the traffic system, it could do little to accelerate change in any direction in the face of the unwillingness of metropolitan and central governments to embark on costly solutions to relieve the problems, least of all in relation to street improvements in the inner ring of boroughs where the major traffic problems of the next generation were already in the process of forming.[14] Ironically in view of later events, it was at the very time when the horse-drawn age was drawing to a close that the motor vehicle was being heralded as a possible solution to traffic congestion and a source of relief from the pollution problems created by the horse. In retrospect, the hopes of Victorian city dwellers were not to be realised. The speed of urban travel in the horse era still compares favourably with that in the contemporary motor age.[15]

Pollution

As with congestion, the problem of pollution is by no means of recent origin. The nineteenth century is littered with examples of the polluting effects of industry and transport. The smoke of the coal-fired railways and the fumes of the London underground are two of the most obvious examples in the transport context. Street railways also came in for their share of criticism on this score. Indeed, one of the principal reasons for the failure of steam railways in the later nineteenth century was the strict anti-pollution requirements imposed by public authorities in many countries to control the smoke, sparks, cinder and noise associated with such vehicles. In Britain, for example, the Use of Mechanical Power on Tramways Act of 1879 imposed very severe conditions on steam tramway operators, so stringent in fact that it was found impossible to develop an economically viable system which could comply with them. Such measures were designed partly for safety purposes, including the need to avoid scaring horses, but they also had the further objective of preserving 'the amenities of the city from a smoke-belching, ear-splitting inconvenience'.[16]

The pollution arising from mechanical means of transport was of relatively small significance, however, compared with that created by horse traffic. The stench and filth arising from the use of horses in city streets was probably as obnoxious and detrimental to public health, if not more so, as anything created by the motor vehicle. Cities as far apart as London and Sydney suffered from the same hazards. Writing about nineteenth-century Australian cities, Blainey notes that 'So long as thousands of horses drew vehicles through city streets, mounds of manure lay on the roadways and gutters and in the laneway stables; horses were as detrimental to public health as the exhaust fumes which replaced them as the distinctive scent of cities. So long as a city mainly used horses its backyard gardens were fertilized with manure and its kitchen windows swarmed with flies'.[17] In fact the problem had become so acute generally by the end of the nineteenth century that sanitary engineers were even advocating the more widespread use of the motor car as a way of solving the question of city hygiene. In September 1898 the annual conference of Municipal Engineers meeting in Birmingham resolved that '. . . the introduction and use of efficient motor vehicles should be encouraged by county, municipal, urban and other authorities, in view of the fact that the extended use of such vehicles would contribute to the general improvement of the sanitary condition of our streets and towns, and this meeting recommends the Council of the Sanitary Institute to make known this opinion as widely as possible'.[18]

Whatever other disadvantages horse traction may have had, it was the pollution hazard which probably caused the most irritation. Unlike car exhaust fumes, which are barely visible and at least dissipate into the atmosphere, horse droppings are bulky and easily visible, they do not readily dissolve except in wet weather, when they then turn into liquid manure, and of course they are extremely smelly. One horse can produce several tons of droppings a year, and since at the peak of the horse era there were probably anything up to 1.5 million horses domiciled in the urban areas of Great Britain, it is not difficult to visualise the magnitude of the total discharge. Rough estimates suggest that whereas in the 1830s English towns had to cope with three million tons of droppings a year, by 1900 this had increased to no less than ten million tons.[19] Not all of this of course was deposited on the main thoroughfares — horses did on occasions oblige by waiting until stabled — while street cleaners and manure gatherers did their best to remove some of the dung. Not enough, however, to prevent stench and squalor on the streets, with few managing 'to avoid a thick coating of slime in winter and dust storms of what was no doubt valuable fertilizer in summer . . .'[20] In his colourful recollections of late Victorian London, H. B. Cresswell, the architect, drew particular attention to the mud, smell and noise created by horse traffic. The most assertive mark of the horse, he claimed, was the mud which 'despite the activities of numerous corps of red-jacketed boys who dodged among the wheels and hooves with pan and brush in service to iron bins at the pavement-edge, either flooded the streets with churnings of "pea-soup" that at times collected in pools over-brimming the kerbs, and at others covered the road-surface as with axle grease or bran-laden dust to the distraction of the wayfarer. In the first case, the swift-moving hansom or gig would fling sheets of such soup—where not intercepted by trousers or skirts—completely across the pavement, so that the frontages of the Strand throughout its length had an eighteen-inch plinth of mud-parge imposed upon it. The pea-soup condition was met by wheeled "mud-carts" each attended by two ladlers clothed as for Icelandic seas in thigh boots, oilskins collared to the chin, and sou'westers sealing in the back of the neck. Splash Ho! The foot passenger now gets the mud in his eye! The axle grease condition was met by horse-mechanized brushes and travellers in the small hours found fire-hoses washing away the residues . . .'[21]

Apart from the horse droppings, there was also the problem of dead horses to contend with. Many overworked or maltreated horses simply expired on duty, while those injured in serious accidents were often destroyed on the spot. While it might be fanciful to imagine that city streets were perpetually clogged with dead horses, they were by no means a rare sight and many lay too long for hygienic safety. In 1880 New York City removed 15,000 dead horses from its streets, while even as late as 1912 Chicago was disposing of nearly 10,000 carcasses.[22] Dead horseflesh not only added to the smell and general unpleasantness in urban streets but, as with dung heaps, it provided a favourite breeding ground for flies which then became infection-carrying agents. Many nineteenth-century plagues and intestinal disorders such as cholera, typhoid fever, dysentery and infant diarrhoea, were attributed to this source. In New York alone, it was estimated that 20,000 people died each year from 'maladies that fly in the dust' arising mainly from horse manure.[23] It is not surprising, therefore, that sanitary specialists became increasingly concerned about the health hazards of the horse and that by the turn of the century they were campaigning vigorously for its replacement by the motor vehicle.

If anything, therefore, the danger to health from the use of horses in cities, quite apart from the generally unpleasant conditions they created, was a more urgent problem than that of traffic congestion. Unfortunately there was no ready solution other than that of frequent cleansing, a task which was increasingly difficult to perform by day as the volume of traffic rose. Ultimately the solution lay with the demise of horse traffic and its replacement by motor vehicles which, despite their exhaust fumes, created less filth and stench than horses with their perpetual habit of leaving 'their fly-attracting calling cards everywhere'.[24]

Social Displacement

One of the principal features of modern transport projects is that they often tend to benefit the wealthier sections of the community at the expense of the poor. This is particularly true of large prestige projects, for example modern airports or Concorde, where development and operational costs are not fully cleared through the market. But it also applies to more mundane transport projects such as roads and urban transit facilities. This situation arises partly because in some cases the pricing system is non-existent, as in the case of road space, so that the user does not directly pay for all the costs incurred, or where the pricing system is operative it fails to reflect fully the costs involved. Alternatively, the benefits to be derived from particular projects tend to be valued more highly than the losses incurred by the poorer sections of society, since the difficulty of quantifying environmental, social and aesthetic factors in a manner suitable to form part of an input into cost-benefit analysis leads to over-reliance on 'economic' assessment as a means of selecting transport systems and individual schemes.[25]

Experience in America and elsewhere has shown that it is generally the richer sections of society who stand to gain most from new transport projects (whether public or private), while at the same time they incur the least costs. In many North American cities it is usually the disadvantaged minority groups who benefit least from new highway building or mass transit facilities, yet often they suffer the greatest environmental sacrifices because they are both the cheapest element to displace and the least capable politically of voicing their opposition to new schemes. Thus highway structures disrupt neighbourhoods, spoil surroundings and intrude on human activities of residents in the 'twilight' zones, whereas the section of the community enjoying the most from the on-systems benefits in the form of better roads suffer the least from the ensuing disruption. For example, the main beneficiaries of Sydney's urban radial freeways, the building of which led to social displacement of the poorer residents in the inner suburbs, are a small band of middle- and upper-class residents of the North Shore.[26] In some cases, notably modern mass transit facilities, the poorer sections of society actually subsidise the more affluent citizens. When the swift rail link in Chicago connecting the village of Skokie with downtown Chicago and subsidised by the Federal Government and the Chicago Transit Authority was opened in 1964, it served a ridership consisting of households 86 per cent of which owned one car and 33 per cent of which owned two cars or more, the proportions for the whole of the Chicago area being 72 and 15.3 per cent respectively.[27]

The chief nineteenth-century counterpart in this context was, of course, the railways. Though they were funded by private enterprise (at least in Britain) rather than the public purse and hence involved no direct subsidy from one section of the community to another, the railways nevertheless distributed their gains and losses very unevenly. Their ridership, at least initially, consisted of the better-off members of society, whereas their physical impact was felt most by the poor urban dwellers. The railways had a greater influence on the configuration of Victorian cities and towns than any other form of economic activity. Their role was both creative and destructive: they created new towns or fostered the growth of existing ones while at the same time they destroyed the inner fabric of some of the older cities.[28] While their land-use requirements were not as great as those of urban freeways and modern street systems in today's motorised cities, nevertheless they were sufficiently large to cause serious upheaval and social disruption in the major cities. Kellett has estimated that between 5 and 9 per cent of the central zone land area in London, Birmingham, Liverpool, Manchester and Glasgow was acquired for use by the railways.[29]

In the process of building the urban rail networks the railway companies virtually dissected some of Britain's major cities, resulting in severe social costs for those who were unfortunate enough to get in their way. For obvious reasons the railways took the line of least resistance when planning their routes and locations for terminals and sidings by concentrating on lower-class residential areas rather than on commercial and industrial sites. 'In Glasgow, as in other towns without exception, the areas which were invariably selected for demolition were populous working class districts. The thinly inhabited commercial or industrial areas were meticulously avoided . . .'[30] It was clearly easier and cheaper to displace the 'powerless and the poor' since they had neither the ability nor the resources to organise effective protest and their legal standing as tenants was in any case very limited, with at best a claim to derisory compensation for eviction. Moreover, as Dyos has pointed out, schemes involving the demolition of the poorest property in slum areas were unlikely to raise much local opposition from any quarter, 'for these wiped off more liabilities than assets'.[31] Where the ownership of low-valued residential property occupied by thousands of tenants was concentrated in the hands of one or two landlords, there were distinct advantages in negotiating deals with

R

the latter, with the addition at times of a little bribery and pressure, rather than trying to acquire access to sites owned by industrial and commercial interests. This policy may at times have resulted in a less than optimal route network layout but, as the Manchester, Sheffield & Lincolnshire Railway found when choosing a site for its central station in Manchester, it was preferable to becoming embroiled in lengthy and costly negotiations and litigation with powerful business groups.

Inevitably, therefore, the brunt of the social unheaval arising from urban railway building fell upon the working population. The numbers displaced ran into many thousands, though the official returns do not provide a reliable guide to the totals involved since it was obviously in the railway companies' interests to minimise the amount of social disruption caused by their activities. Estimates for Glasgow and London suggest that the numbers of residents displaced as a result of the demolition of property by the railways were probably in the region of 20,000 and 120,000 respectively, though even these figures may underestimate the true picture.[32] For the country as a whole the total may well be found to be in excess of 300,000 when the tally for all cities is complete.

Eviction was one thing, but where to go after one had been displaced was quite another matter. As most of those evicted were poor people, there was little prospect of their moving into more salubrious surroundings since they had neither the time nor the money to take advantage of such opportunities. In fact, distant lodgings would have proved a crippling hardship for those dependent on casual labour in the city centres — in London alone, for example, there were said to be 680,000 residents dependent on such work in the 1860s.[33] The working classes were therefore very reluctant to move far afield and hence their only refuge was to decant into the nearby twilight zones created by the railways, thereby exacerbating the problem of overcrowding in the adjacent districts of the inner city areas. As *The Times* observed in 1861: 'The poor are displaced but they are not removed. They are shovelled out of one side of the parish, only to render more overcrowded the stifling apartments in another part . . . But the dock and wharf labourer, the porter and the costermonger cannot remove. You may pull down their wretched houses: they must find others, and make their new dwellings more crowded and wretched than their old ones. The tailor, shoemaker and other workmen are in much the same position. It is a mockery to speak of the suburbs to them.'[34] In other words, eviction effectively meant a shift from bad to worse — higher rents and more crowded conditions. The railways made virtually no provision for rehousing those they displaced, at least not until very late on in the nineteenth century, and even then the new accommodation was usually too expensive for the dispossessed poor to take up.

Thus if the railways effectively removed at one go some of the worst slum-ridden areas in the centre of cities, they simply helped to create new slum zones in the overspill areas through which their lines passed. In fact, not only did overcrowding increase in the latter districts, but the prospect of subsequent improvement and residential replacement was minimal, given the poverty of the inhabitants. Furthermore, because of the configuration of the railway network, the residents in these zones were sometimes trapped within their confines, lacking ready access to amenities and communication with the centre. Thus in Agar Town and Somers Town in North London, in Manchester's Ancoats, Birmingham's Saltley, Glasgow's South Laurieston and Liverpool's South Scotland and Vauxhall wards, residents were huddled together in cramped and drab quarters hemmed in by industrial premises and the approach lines of the railway termini. Each one in its turn became a derelict slum area where residential betterment was almost wholly absent and from which the inhabitants had little chance of escape. Laurieston, for example, was reported to be like a walled city after the arrival of the railways, and it rapidly deteriorated into an overspill slum annexe of the Gorbals as thousands of tenants evicted by railway demolition elsewhere sought refuge in its precincts. A similar situation developed in the Ancoats district of Manchester which became squalid and desperately overcrowded and whose many inhabitants lacked easy and direct access to the amenities of the city centre.[35]

Environmental Intrusion

Writing in the early 1970s about the impact of the motor vehicle, W. R. Siddall argued that 'no form of transport before or since has brought about so much of a change in the landscape or had such a deleterious effect on the quality of our environment'.[36] It is doubtful whether people living a century or so earlier would have had much sympathy with this judgment since the railways, the tramways and horse transport had a remarkably strong impact on the urban landscape and the configuration of cities, while these modes of transport also left their mark on the environment in several distinctive ways. Some of these have already been discussed, and in this section we look briefly at the problems of noise and visual intrusion.

Since the second world war society has become increasingly conscious of the noise and environmental disturbance caused by modern forms of transport, notably the motor vehicle and the aircraft, though only limited attempts have been made to control noise emission and regulate the design of structures so as to minimise visual intrusion. But such environmental hazards were equally familiar to earlier generations, and from time to time efforts were made to control the activities which caused them. The volume of noise in city streets at the turn of the century was possibly greater than it is today: 'with the clop of horses' hooves and the crude sounds of early motor vehicles, it was a noisier world at the beginning of the century. The tram also added its quota of sound, whether it be the rumbles of its wheels, the ululations caused by flats on the wheels where, especially on wet days, the powerful brakes had made them slide, the scream of the electric braking itself, and the brushing of the trolley wheel on the wire . . .'[37] Horse transport was probably the worst offender. Heavy traffic on cobblestones or granite sets was 'not any such thing as a noise. It was an immensity of sound',[38] which virtually drowned conversation. In London and other towns straw was often laid on the streets to deaden the sound, especially in front of hospitals and houses where people lay sick. In some American towns more extreme measures were resorted to as early as the eighteenth century. In 1747 the Town Council of Boston prohibited traffic from using King Street in order to allow the deliberations of the General Court to proceed undisturbed, while in 1787 New York City passed an order forbidding trams and waggons with iron-shod wheels from using the streets.[39]

The Victorians may not have had a highly developed social conscience but they were by no means total philistines as far as environmental issues were concerned. In the early days of steam railways concern was frequently expressed about their detrimental effect on the environment, and for this reason stations and terminals in many European cities were not allowed into the centre but had to be located on the outskirts of towns. Steam tramways, as we have seen, suffered a worse fate since they could not meet the stringent environmental regulations imposed upon them. Subsequently, the mechanisation of urban transit in Europe was delayed by vehement opposition to the visual intrusion caused by the overhead wires and poles of electric tramways. This aesthetic response was most pronounced in those cities, for example Paris, Vienna, Berlin, Budapest and Dresden, with grand boulevards and historic squares, where the erection of such apparatus appeared especially offensive, though even Birmingham was being advised by some of its councillors in 1897 to reject the overhead wire system. Thus, to satisfy the more sensitive aesthetic taste of the Europeans, the American system had to be adapted in order to minimise the 'visual pollution'. This led to experiments with battery and conduit forms of traction, but these proved technically inferior to overhead cable operation. The most commonly accepted solution, therefore, was to design a more attractive overhead structure by improving the design of the poles and making the wires less obtrusive. Some of the big European cities produced very elegant and ornate designs.

Conclusion

The introductory statement to the OECD report on *Urban Transportation* points out that, while urban congestion is not a new phenomenon, it is only recently that obstacles to mobility have begun to present a pressing social problem; and for the simple reason that to the modern urban dweller mobility has become a crucial factor in the enjoyment of life so that any impairment of the ability to move freely becomes a serious constraint on the individual's capacity to partake of the social and economic advantages of the city.[40] Similarly, the pollution, noise and other environmental problems caused by modern transport have been an issue of growing concern in the last two decades. However, it is the attitude of society which has changed rather than the basic problems themselves. Contemporary society has become more conscious and intolerant of the side effects of increased mobility, whereas earlier generations, though disgruntled, were, because of their different and somewhat circumscribed life styles, more prepared to accept the problems as an inevitable consequence of economic progress. Nevertheless, as this study has sought to demonstrate, environmental problems associated with transport development in the past were probably no less serious than those of today. The failure to appreciate the historical perspective in this context may have led to an exaggeration of current anxieties about transport. The fact that the speed of travel within the central zones of cities is very little greater now than in the horse-drawn age may of course be regarded as a serious deterioration in standards relative to modern expectations about mobility; alternatively it can be invoked in support of a claim that conditions are at least no worse than they were in the nineteenth century. If this provides little consolation to those with a nostalgic yearning for the days of horse transport, they should at least take time to consider both the costs and the benefits of that mode of travel *vis-à-vis* those of motor transport.

NOTES

1. L. Mumford, *The City in History* (1961), pp. 211, 219.

2. S. Plowden, *Towns Against Traffic* (1972), p. 11.

3. H. J. Dyos and D. H. Aldcroft, *British Transport* (1969), p. 60.

4. J. R. Kellett, *The Impact of Railways on Victorian Cities* (1969), p. 315.

5. T. C. Barker and M. Robbins, *A History of London Transport.* Vol. I. *The Nineteenth Century* (1963), p. 64.

6. Kellett, *op. cit.*, pp. 312-23; Barker and Robbins, *op. cit.*, I, pp. 66, 139.

7. Kellett, *op. cit.*, p. 314.

8. Though in London tramway traffic by the mid-1890s was nearly as large as that by bus. However, horse buses were protected by legislation from tramway competition in the central area with the result that the flow of horse buses and cabs in this zone was very intense. See T. C. Barker, 'Towards an historical classification of urban transport development since the later eighteenth century', *Journal of Transport History*, 1 (September, 1980), pp. 83-84.

9. Which, Gordon estimated, if stood in single file, would reach along the bridle-ways from St Paul's to John-o'-Groats. W. J. Gordon, *The Horse World of London* (1893, reprinted 1971), p. 113.

10. F. M. L. Thompson, 'Nineteenth-Century Horse Sense', *Economic History Review*, 29 (February, 1976), pp. 65, 72, 80. Barker and Robbins, *op. cit.*, I, p. 245; II, pp. 12, 329.

11. F. M. L. Thompson, *Victorian England: the Horse-drawn Society* (1970. Inaugural Lecture, Bedford College, University of London), p. 12.

12. J. A. Tarr, 'Urban Pollution — many long years ago', *American Heritage* (1971), p. 66; *Select Committee on Transport (Metropolitan Area) 1919*, p. 376.

13. H. B. Cresswell, 'Seventy Years Back', *Architectural Review*, 124 (December, 1958), pp. 341-42.

14. Dyos and Aldcroft, *op. cit.*, pp. 230, 352.

15. J. M. Thompson, *Great Cities and their Traffic* (1977), p. 23.

16. J. P. McKay, *Tramways and Trolleys: The Rise of Urban Mass Transport in Europe* (1976), p. 30.

17. G. Blainey, *The Tyranny of Distance* (1966), p. 295.

18. Quoted in P. S. Bagwell, *The Transport Revolution from 1770* (1974), pp. 221-22.

19. Thompson, *Victorian England*, p. 10; in Milwaukee (USA) with a population of 350,000 (1907) and a horse population of 12,500 the daily average of manure produced was three-quarters of a pound per resident. Tarr, *loc. cit.*, p. 66.

20. C. F. Klapper, *Roads and Rails of London, 1900-1933* (1976), p. 12.

21. Cresswell, *loc. cit.*, pp. 341-42.

22. Tarr, *loc. cit.*, p. 68.

23. *Ibid.*, p. 69.

24. K. H. Schaeffer and E. Sclar, *Access for All: Transportation and Urban Growth* (1975), p. 37.

25. House of Commons Expenditure Committee, *Urban Transport Planning*, Vol. III, *Appendices and Index*. H.C. 57-III, 1972-73, pp. 580-85. Memorandum of the Royal Town Planning Institute.

26. A. Jakubowicz, 'What About the People? Social Considerations of Freeway Development', paper presented to a symposium: *Are Urban Freeways Really Necessary?* University of New South Wales, 21 August 1973.

27. R. A. Buel, *Dead End: The Automobile in Mass Transportation* (1972), p. 150.

28. Bagwell, *op. cit.*, pp. 132-33.

29. Kellett, *op. cit.*, p. 290. For the land-use needs of twentieth-century highways see D. H. Aldcroft, 'Twentieth-Century Transport Revolution', *Arts: the Journal of the Sydney University Arts Association*, 10 (1975), pp. 12-13.

30. Kellett, *op. cit.*, p. 292.

31. H. J. Dyos, 'Railways and Housing in Victorian London. II "Rustic Townsmen"', *Journal of Transport History*, 2 (November, 1955), p. 95.

32. See Kellett, *op. cit.*, pp. 326-30.

33. H. J. Dyos, 'Railways and Housing in Victorian London. I "Attila in London"', *Journal of Transport History*, 2 (May, 1955), p. 15.

34. *The Times*, 2 March, 1861, quoted in Kellett, *op. cit.*, p. 330.

35. Kellett, *op. cit.*, pp. 292, 341, 343.

36. W. R. Siddall, 'No Nook Secure: Transportation and Environmental Quality', *Comparative Studies in Society and History*, 16 (January, 1974), p. 11.

37. Klapper, *op. cit.*, p. 15.

38. Cresswell, *loc. cit.*, p. 341.

39. McKay, *op. cit.*, pp. 84-6.

40. OECD, *Future Directions for Research in Urban Transportation* (1969), p. 15.

12. Publications by S. G. Checkland: A Bibliography

Compiled by Olive Checkland

I Books:

1. *The Rise of Industrial Society in England, 1815-1885,* Longmans, London, 1964; St. Martins Press, New York, 1965. pp. 471.

2. *The Mines of Tharsis: Roman, French and British Enterprise in Spain,* Allen and Unwin, London, 1967. pp. 288.

3. *The Gladstones: a family biography, 1764-1851,* Cambridge University Press, 1971. pp. 448 (Scottish Arts Council Book Award).

4. *The Poor Law Report of 1834* (with E. O. A. Checkland, eds., with introduction), Pelican Classics, 1973.

5. *Scottish Banking, a history: 1695-1973,* Collins, 1975, pp. 785 (Saltire Society Prize).

6. *The Upas Tree. Glasgow, 1875-1975, a study in Growth and Contractions,* University of Glasgow Press, 1976. pp. 124. New and enlarged edition: *The Upas Tree and After, Glasgow 1875-1980,* 1981.

7. *British Public Policy 1776-1939. An Economic and Social Perspective,* Cambridge University Press (forthcoming).

II Contributions to books:

1. 'Toward a definition of urban history'. In H. J. Dyos, ed., *The Study of Urban History,* 1968.

2. Foreword, Eric Richards, *The Leviathan of Wealth. The Sutherland Fortune in the Industrial Revolution,* 1973.

3. 'A stockbroker's view of the City'. In M. C. Reed, *A History of James Capel & Co.,* 1975.

4. 'Adam Smith and the bankers'. In A. S. Skinner and T. Wilson, eds., *Essays on Adam Smith,* Oxford, 1975.

5. 'Cultural factors and British business men, 1815-1914'. In K. Nakagawa, ed., *Social Order and the Entrepreneur,* Tokyo, 1977.

6. 'British public policy'. In P. Mathias, ed., *Cambridge Economic History of Europe,* Vol. VIII (forthcoming).

7. 'The British City-Region as historical and political challenge'. In Sidney Pollard, ed., *Region and Industrialisation,* Göttingen, 1980.

8. 'Banking'. In David Daiches, ed., *A Companion to Scottish Culture* (Edward Arnold, 1981).

9. 'The urban history horoscope'. In Derek Fraser and David Reeder, eds., *The Pursuit of Urban History*, Edward Arnold (forthcoming, 1982).

10. 'Stages and the state'. In C. P. Kindleberger, ed., *The Long Run. Essays in Honour of W. W. Rostow* (forthcoming, 1982).

11. 'A nation of shopkeepers and the workshop of the world, 1780-1914'. In Robert Blake, ed., *The English World*, Thames and Hudson (forthcoming, 1982).

12. 'British Urban Health in general and in a single city'. In E. O. A. Checkland and M. M. Lamb, eds., *Health Care as Social History: the Glasgow case*, Aberdeen University Press (forthcoming, 1982).

III   Articles:

1. 'The Propagation of Ricardian economics in England', *Economica*. 1949.

2. 'The Birmingham economists'. *Economic History Review*. 1949.

3. 'The advent of academic economics in England'. *Manchester School*. 1951.

4. 'Economic opinion in England as Jevons found it'. *Manchester School*. 1951.

5. 'Economic attitudes in Liverpool, 1793-1807'. *Economic History Review*. 1952.

6. 'John Koster, anti-bullionist'. *Manchester School*. 1952.

7. 'David Ricardo'. *Economic History Review*. 1952.

8. 'The prescriptions of the classical economists'. *Economica*. 1953.

9. 'An English merchant house in China after 1842'. *Bulletin of the Business Historical Society*. 1953.

10. 'English provincial cities'. *Economic History Review*. 1953.

11. 'The Lancashire bill system and its Liverpool protagonists'. *Economica*. 1954.

12. 'John Gladstone as trader and planter'. *Economic History Review*. 1954.

13. 'Marshall and the wages-wealth paradox'. *Economic Journal*. 1957.

14. 'The mind of the City, 1870-1914'. *Oxford Economic Papers*. 1957.

15. 'America *versus* West Indian Traders in Liverpool, 1793-1815'. *Journal of Economic History*. 1958.

16. 'Two Scottish West Indian liquidations after 1793'. *Scottish Journal of Political Economy*. 1957.

17. 'Finance for the West Indies, 1780-1815'. *Economic History Review*. 1958.

18. 'Corn for South Lancashire and beyond'. *Business History*. 1959.

19. 'Theories of economic and social evolution: the Rostow challenge'. *Scottish Journal of Political Economy*. 1960.

20. 'Scottish economic history: recent work'. *Economica*. 1964.

21. 'The British industrial city as history: the Glasgow case'. *Urban Studies*. 1964.

22. 'The Economic evolution of the modern world'. *Business History Review*. 1966.

23. 'Adam Smith and the biographer'. *Scottish Journal of Political Economy*. 1967.

24. 'Banking history and economic development: seven systems'. *Scottish Journal of Political Economy*. 1968.

25. 'The historian as model builder'. *The Philosophical Journal*. 1969.

26. 'The making of Mr. Gladstone'. *Victorian Studies*. 1969.

27. 'Soviet History: three reviews'. *Soviet Studies*. 1970.

28. 'Housing Policy: the formative years' (with E. O. A. Checkland). *Town Planning Review*. 1975.

29. 'The entrepreneur and the social order'. *Business History*. 1975.

30. 'Adam Smith as an interpreter of society'. *New Society*. 1976.

31. 'The prophet and the clown'. *New Society*. 1976.

32. 'Urban History in the British Idiom'. *Urban History Review*. 1978.

33. 'The urban historian and the political will'. *Urban History Yearbook*. 1980.

34. 'The British new towns as politics'. *Town Planning Review*. 1981.

35. 'Innocence and Anxiety. Canada between the wars'. *Bulletin of Canadian Studies*. 1981.

36. 'Very long term history and people's history'. *History of European Ideas* (forthcoming, 1982).

IV Reviews:

The Annals of the American Academy of Political and Social Science, Business History, Economic History Review, Economica, Economic Journal, English Historical Review, Historical Journal, History, Journal of Economic History, Journal of Economic Literature, Journal of Modern History, Times Literary Supplement, Urban History Yearbook, Urban Studies, Victorian Studies.